The British
Tax System

THE BRITISH TAX SYSTEM

THIRD EDITION

BY

J. A. KAY

M. A. KING

OXFORD UNIVERSITY PRESS

1983

Oxford University Press, Walton Street, Oxford OX2 6DP

London Glasgow New York Toronto
Delhi Bombay Calcutta Madras Karachi
Kuala Lumpur Singapore Hong Kong Tokyo
Nairobi Dar es Salaam Cape Town
Melbourne Auckland

and associated companies in
Beirut Berlin Ibadan Mexico City Nicosia

Oxford is a trade mark of Oxford University Press

Published in the United States
by Oxford University Press, New York

British Library Cataloguing in Publication Data
Kay, J. A.
    The British tax system.—3rd ed.
    1. Taxation—Great Britain
    I. Title   II. King, M. A.
    336.2'00941   HJ2619
    ISBN 0-19-877207-6
    ISBN 0-19-877206-8 Pbk

Library of Congress Cataloging in Publication Data
Kay, J. A. (John Alexander)
    The British tax system.
    Bibliography: p.
    Includes index.
    1. Taxation—Great Britain. I. King, Mervyn A.
II. Title.
HJ2619.K39 1983   336.2'00941   83-4073
ISBN 0-19-877207-6
ISBN 0-19-877206-8 (pbk.)

Typeset by Joshua Associates, Oxford
and printed in Great Britain by
Billing & Sons Ltd., Worcester

Fantastic grow the evening gowns;
Agents of the Fisc pursue
Absconding tax-defaulters through
The sewers of provincial towns.

Caesar's double-bed is warm
As an unimportant clerk
Writes I DO NOT LIKE MY WORK
On a pink official form.

From W. H. Auden, 'The Fall of Rome'
(*Collected Shorter Poems*,
Faber & Faber, 1966)

PREFACE TO THE THIRD EDITION

FOR this edition we have almost wholly rewritten the chapters on Social Security and Taxation and on Local Taxation. We have made substantial alterations in other areas, such as the taxation of husband and wife, corporation tax and the 'black economy', where the debate has advanced since the second edition even if the tax system has not. Our principal discussion of the problems of tax administration is now to be found in Chapter 2. The most important change is a new chapter on taxation and inflation, which describes the changes which fifteen years of rapid inflation have brought about. The material contained in the book has been brought up to date as at 1 January 1983. We should like to thank Andrew Dilnot for his assistance in this.

PREFACE TO THE SECOND EDITION

IN this second edition we have brought the information contained in the book up to date as at 1 January 1980. Although we have modified our view on a number of minor points in the light of new developments or more mature consideration, nothing has occurred which would lead us to reappraise the fundamental elements of our analysis or our recommendations.

The most obvious change is that we have now devoted a chapter to the subject of tax administration. This is not because we overlooked the topic in writing our first edition, but in putting forward some new ideas we found an opportunity to tighten the exposition by bringing together material which was previously scattered over a number of different chapters.

We are grateful to many readers of the first edition for their encouragement and for their comments. We would especially like to thank the Inland Revenue for providing detailed comments; we have not been able to agree with all of them but we have taken them seriously. We are indebted to John Hills for research assistance, and to Nick Morris who prepared Fig. 15.1.

Since we wrote our first edition, tax has become an even more topical political issue. But we had two primary objectives in mind—to raise the level of political debate and to make the case for specific reforms—and we cannot claim yet to have had much success with either. There are two aspects of current discussion which are especially dispiriting. First, politicians appear to combine wholly unrealistic expectations of what tax reform can achieve with unwillingness to contemplate the new approaches which are required in order to secure the marginal gains which are actually attainable. It is possible that if Britain had a more sensible tax system instead of the present one— and that would require genuinely radical reform and not mere tinkering—that national income would be say five per cent higher than it is currently. That is enough to make tax reform an important subject, and it is a lot in comparison with what might be achieved by other explicit policy changes. But we can see no evidence to suggest that differences in tax policy could possibly account for more than a small fraction of the difference between income per head in Britain and that of other countries such as West Germany.

Second, too much demand for tax reform degenerates into self-interested agitation for a reduction in one's personal tax bill. It is trite to observe that structural improvements cannot lead to large reductions in tax payments for everyone. It follows that insistence that reforms be uniformly favourable to oneself—and hence at the expense of other people—is either a recipe for social conflict, or an obstacle to change of any kind. When managers benefiting from large reductions in the top marginal rates of income tax demand that their employer should nevertheless continue to pay for their private motoring, they make it inevitable that at some future date an opposing interest group will reinstate the high marginal rates of tax.

It is particularly distressing that there is no sign of planning for the unique opportunity for tax reform which the next five years offers. During this period, the budgetary position of the U.K. government will be transformed by a tidal wave of oil revenues from the North Sea. There is no more favourable background for changes in the structure of taxation than a revenue position which permits substantial tax reductions all round. It seems all too probable that we shall see nothing more forward looking than temporary reductions in the rates of existing taxes.

This said, it would be churlish to deny that the British tax system is now slightly better than it was when we first wrote. The reduction in the maximum rates of income tax to realistic levels is a substantial advance, and the shift from income tax to V.A.T. a marginal gain. The Inland Revenue is a little closer to installing a computer. There is still a long way to go.

PREFACE TO THE FIRST EDITION

WE should like to thank the many people who have directly or indirectly helped us to write this book. We could not have written it without the knowledge and experience we gained as members of the Meade Committee on the Structure and Reform of Direct Taxation between 1975 and 1977. We are indebted to all those who worked on that project and to the Institute for Fiscal Studies which made it possible. We know that they will not think it invidious if we express our special gratitude to James Meade, not only for what we learnt from him about taxation but also for the influence of his combination of unfailing personal sympathy and understanding and uncompromising intellectual rigour on both the content of our work and our approach to it. The impact which the contents of the Meade Report have had on our thinking is obvious: but the analysis and opinions expressed here are our own and do not represent the contents of the Meade Report nor the views of any of its other members. The reader who attributes our errors to the Meade Committee, or who believes that he will find here a substitute for reading that Report, is quite mistaken.

We are grateful to P. J. Thompson for research assistance. We have received help on particular problems from J. A. Beath, M. B. E. White, and representatives of the Inland Revenue, Central Statistical Office, and the Bundesministerium der Finanzen; also from the finance directors of a number of the companies cited in Table 13.1. An earlier version of the manuscript was read by A. B. Atkinson, J. S. Flemming, P. M. S. Hacker, R. W. Houghton, E. F. King, R. I. McKibbin, J. A. Mirrlees, J. K. Rutter, and S. M. Waldman, and without their comments there would have been many more obscurities and errors in our presentation. It is hardly necessary for us to say that not of all these organizations and individuals share the views we express; we hope that some of them do but we cannot commit any of them. We should also like to thank Miss B. Atkinson, Mrs. P. Hawtin, and Mrs. J. Saxby for organizing the preparation of the manuscript.

Since many of the properties of a tax system depend on the rates of taxes and benefits and the relations between them, a book like this would be incomprehensible if we did not use specific figures in our description and analysis. But it is rare for more than a few weeks to pass without some changes in these rates, and rare for more than a few months to pass without some structural changes. We have attempted to ensure that the information given here was correct on 1 January 1978.

CONTENTS

LIST OF FIGURES

LIST OF TABLES

INTRODUCTION

IN this book we seek to use economic analysis to examine the problems facing the British tax system. We try to do this in a practical way by looking at real day-to-day problems. We were ourselves surprised that economics was useful to us not only in analysing the economic effects of taxes, but also in thinking about administrative problems. The reason for this is that much of the muddle and complexity of the present system derives from the absence of any clear view as to what principles do or should underlie it.

This is not to suggest that economics provides all the answers. Public finance is one of the most rapidly developing branches of economic theory, but we found much traditional theory of little help in dealing with the everyday problems of the British tax system and it is instructive to consider why. Much of this material is concerned with evaluating the economic effects of taxes, and this is quite properly done by contrasting the characteristics of different theoretical taxes. But the ways in which actual taxes differ from these theoretical taxes are often of much greater economic significance than the ways in which theoretical taxes differ from each other. We pursue in this book the question of whether income or expenditure should be the major component of the tax base: the extent to which savings should or should not be taxed. It is conventional to think of this in terms of how aggregate savings respond to changes in taxes. But there is little evidence to suggest that aggregate savings are likely to be very sensitive to tax changes. What is more significant is that the ways in which people save are very sensitive indeed to the ways in which different savings media are taxed. The present tax system, in effect, exempts some forms of saving from tax but not others; and this, we think, has more marked economic effects than a structure in which all forms of savings are taxed or one in which none of them is taxed. We pursue this argument, and others like it, in more detail below; but we note at this stage that the loopholes and anomalies in the tax system can often be much more significant in their effects on behaviour than the taxes themselves. The economist who thinks that because the main U.K. personal direct tax is called an income tax it has the same characteristics as income taxes he encounters in public finance texts is likely to be seriously misled.

These observations are not in any way intended to question the need for any analysis of applied economic problems to be rooted firmly in economic theory: indeed it is because we are convinced of this that we offer, in Chapter 1, a crash course in some simple, but central, economic concepts. We would like to stress that we shall only make proposals for change if we believe them to be practicable. It is necessary to spell out what this means. The most usual definition equates the impracticable with the unfamiliar. This definition is convenient for those who find adaptation to new ideas difficult or disturbing, but it is not very useful for a discussion of the tax system. It is perfectly clear that there are many other systems of all kinds which differ from those at present in operation which would work, and it would be surprising if some of them would not work better than existing systems. Those who believe that being practical involves confining attention to minor modifications of the *status quo* are simply showing that their minds, or the minds of those to whom they are reporting, are closed.

A related error is to confuse a practical outlook with an obsession with detail. As an example, the Inland Revenue in its memorandum on local income tax to the Layfield Committee was apparently exercised by the problem of people who live in caravans. It would be foolish to deny that there is such a problem. It would also be foolish to deny that the problem is, like the number of people who live in caravans, small. It is very unlikely that anyone would say 'I would be in favour of a local income tax if only I could think of a way of dealing with people who live in caravans'. Given that this is so, it is pointless to discuss the matter further at this stage. Not only is it unnecessary to consider the difficulty in advance of making basic decisions about the structure of such a tax (such as whether to have one); it is positively undesirable to do so, since this kind of problem can be more sensibly tackled in the light of other, more important, decisions that would need to be taken first. The enumeration of endless lists of unimportant objections is a common administrative tactic for resisting change, and the man who seeks to deal with it by answering them is lost. Since most people are—rightly—uninterested in the minutiae of hypothetical tax systems, we shall not take our description of alternatives beyond the point at which we are confident that we, or a competent firm of management consultants, could fill in the remaining details. It is extremely unfortunate that the Inland Revenue has cried wolf so often on the impossibility of administering reforms—including several which were subsequently implemented—that its views on what is and what is not feasible can no longer be regarded as reliable.

All this said, it must be recognized that administrative feasibility is an important constraint on tax policy, and we have given it due weight in our discussion. We shall regard measures as practicable if we believe they can be operated reasonably cheaply and simply in a manner which corresponds to the underlying intention of the measure. Most things can be made to work, after a fashion, if we are prepared either to spend a good deal of effort on policing them or to accept many *ad hoc* expedients and anomalies in their operation. Practicability is therefore a matter of degree (so that it is not easy to make firm statements about it) and we judge something to be impracticable if it would cost too much in one or other of these directions; too much administrative burden or too extensive compromise with the original objective. It should be clear from this definition that it is not only not necessary for a measure to be part of the *status quo* for it to be practicable; it is not sufficient either. There are substantial parts of the British tax system which do not work satisfactorily and could not, without great difficulty and expense, be made to do so. We shall return to this point in various specific contexts.

We begin our discussion in Chapter 1 with a brief explanation of some basic economic concepts which we believe to be of fundamental importance to an understanding of the tax system. The style of this chapter is necessarily rather different from the rest of the book and we suggest that if it poses difficulty the reader should move on to Chapter 2, referring back to Chapter 1 when necessary. Table 1 shows the ways in which different taxes contribute to overall tax revenue. Income tax yields the most revenue and it is with this tax that we begin in Chapter 2, which describes the evolution of income tax and the main features of the tax as it operates today. We describe how income tax is administered and the topical subject of the black economy. The economic effects of taxes on earnings are analysed in Chapter 3, and in Chapter 4 we discuss the taxation of investment income and the tax treatment of savings. In Chapter 5 we examine the choice of the tax base and the possibility of a direct tax which is levied not on income but on personal expenditure. Chapter 6 explores how such a tax might operate.

Two of the most controversial of current issues are the interaction between taxation and social security benefits, and the role of indirect taxes. We discuss these issues in Chapters 7 and 8 respectively. Problems

TABLE 1

Sources of tax revenue

	1978–9 £ m.		1981–2 £ m.	
Taxes on personal income				
Income tax	18 791		28 504	
National insurance contributions	12 033		20 548	
Advance corporation tax	1422		2000	
	32 246	(63·2%)	51 052	(58.4%)
Taxes on company income				
Mainstream corporation tax	2496		2800	
Petroleum revenue tax	183		2380	
Supplementary petroleum duty	–		2050	
Special tax on bank deposits	–		355	
Development land tax	13		35	
	2692	(5·3%)	7620	(8·7%)
Taxes on transfers of capital				
Capital transfer tax	369		486	
Stamp duties	433		800	
Capital gains tax	353		· 540	
	1155	(2·3%)	1826	(2·1%)
Taxes on commodities				
Value added tax	4900		12 300	
Duties on oil and petrol	2460		4550	
tobacco	2445		3325	
alcoholic drink	2335		3000	
betting and gaming	345		500	
other items	10		20	
Car tax	380		525	
Vehicle licences	1113		1629	
Customs duties	740		920	
Agricultural levies	220		210	
	14 948	(29·3%)	26 979	(30·8%)
TOTAL	51 041		87 477	

Note: The classification of taxes in this table is not intended to reflect any economic judgements about the effective incidence of particular taxes.
Source: Financial statement and budget report, 1979–80 , 1982–3.

of rates, local authority finance, capital taxes, and the taxation of companies are dealt with in Chapters 9–12. The final three chapters discuss the tax system as a whole. In Chapter 13 we consider the way in which inflation has influenced the development of the tax system. Chapter 14 looks at the question of the distribution of the tax burden among different groups and individuals in society and at how progressive the tax system should be. We conclude the book with a description of some reforms which are worth pursuing and others which are not.

There are two aspects of the tax system about which we shall have little to say, its use to stabilize fluctuations in the economy and relations with other countries. Following the Keynesian revolution much attention was directed to the use of fiscal policy as a way of controlling fluctuations in aggregate demand. Stabilization policy based on marginal changes in Government expenditure and taxation was to be the means of eliminating the business cycle. Indeed Musgrave in his classic work on public finance (1959) explains that he began with the idea of producing a tract on 'compensatory finance' dealing with the question of how the public budget affected certain key macroeconomic variables such as the level of unemployment. But the gaps in the theory of public finance which he discovered, many of which still exist today, lay in the more traditional areas of the effect of taxes on income distribution and economic efficiency. In the end stabilization policy occupied less than one-third of his treatise. This trend has continued. In his latest book (Musgrave and Musgrave, 1976) only 100 out of 750 pages are devoted to fiscal stabilization.

Part of this decline in interest is due to the realization that macroeconomic policy is more complicated than the simple text-book Keynesian models led us to believe and that 'fine-tuning' of the economy is considerably more difficult than we might have hoped. This is because there is uncertainty as to what will happen to the economy in the future in the absence of any change in policy, and because there are long delays between when a decision is made to alter taxes and when the desired effect on spending or unemployment becomes apparent. First of all there is the inevitable delay in collecting statistics, so we may only have an adequate idea of what was happening to the economy some months or even a year ago. Even when the Government has looked at the statistics, deliberated, and then decided to, say, reduce taxes there are still more lags in the system. Individuals will take time to adjust their spending decisions and, at least initially, the impact will be felt on the level of stocks in shops. Producers will

probably wait before increasing their output rather than running down
stocks, and the extra output will be met by overtime working until
firms are convinced it is worth expanding their labour force on a more
permanent basis. These lags in conjunction with uncertainty about the
future make stabilization policy a hazardous business.

It has been seriously argued that the net effect of British Government policies has been to destabilize rather than to stabilize the
economy, and that they have in any case been motivated more by elec-
toral factors than by considerations of demand management ('the
political business cycle'). (See Worswick, 1971; Nordhaus, 1975.) We
shall not attempt to assess these views. For our purposes we may simply
note that it is unlikely that the choice of the *structure* of the tax
system will make these problems any easier. It is with the structure of
the system that we shall be concerned and to say that we shall not
answer every question is not to say that we shall not tackle the most
pressing.

Another issue about which we shall say little is the international
aspect of taxation. This may surprise some people who regard harmonization as one of the most important practical issues in the determination of tax policy. We do not share this view, but we consider
issues of tax harmonization in the E.E.C. where they arise in three
specific contexts—for corporation tax, value added tax, and the duties
on tobacco products. In each of these cases, we show that harmonization has been a purely cosmetic activity. We share the widespread desire
to break down barriers to trade and capital movements within Europe,
but these efforts at tax harmonization have contributed absolutely
nothing to this, and we do not expect much change in the foreseeable
future. In practice, it is clear that harmonization is always used as a
secondary argument—as a reason why we can, or cannot, do something
which is proposed, or opposed, on other grounds.

THE ECONOMICS OF TAXATION: SOME BASIC CONCEPTS

Tax incidence

ECONOMISTS have long been concerned with the question of who actually pays any particular tax: the *incidence* of the tax. At first sight, it may seem surprising that this is a problem. The house-owner who is required to write out a cheque in payment of rates to his local authority, or the employee who sees income tax deducted from his wages, knows very well who is paying the tax. But things are not really so simple. The tax on tobacco is paid by the trader who withdraws it from a bonded warehouse, at some intermediate stage of the process which turns tobacco leaves into cigarettes. But no one imagines that he really pays the tax, in the sense that he is personally worse off by the amount of the duty which he regularly pays over to the Customs and Excise. The tax is paid by those who ultimately smoke the cigarettes. There is no law which requires or even entitles the tobacco distributor to recover his liabilities from them—indeed in all probability he has no direct dealings with them and does not know who they are. He simply adjusts the terms on which he sells in order to reflect the tax which he is required to pay: so, in turn, do those who buy from him: and the final result is that the tax burden is passed on to the consumer.

We can therefore usefully distinguish the formal incidence of a tax from its effective incidence. The formal incidence falls on those who have the actual legal liability for paying the tax. The effective incidence identifies those who are, in the end, the people who are out of pocket as a result of the imposition of the tax. Naturally enough, it suits traders to encourage some confusion between the two. Suppliers will from time to time express regret that they are obliged to charge V.A.T. on a particular invoice. But the truth of the matter is that they are not obliged to charge V.A.T. at all: they are merely obliged to pay it, and in adding it to a bill they are seeking (as those who devised the tax intended they should) to pass that burden of payment on to someone else. The formal incidence of V.A.T. is on the supplier: the effective incidence (subject to some qualification) is on the purchaser.

Even where popular usage distinguishes the formal and effective incidence of tax, we tend to make 'all-or-nothing' assumptions about the incidence of a tax. Thus it is assumed that V.A.T. is essentially a tax on consumers, and there is no doubt that this is basically true. But it is not completely true. When a special discriminatory rate of V.A.T. was imposed on television sets and some other electrical goods in 1975, their price rose and purchasers of television sets suffered accordingly. But the demand for television sets fell: so did profit margins in the manufacture and distribution of television sets, and the profits of companies engaged in these activities were reduced: the earnings of those who worked in these industries were lower, and some of them lost their jobs. Thus the major part of the incidence of the tax was on consumers, but some of it fell on the owners of, and workers in, activities related to the supply of television sets.

Income tax is assumed to be paid by those who earn the income, and this is a good first approximation to the effective incidence of the tax. But it is only a first approximation. This is especially true at higher income levels: when the Board of Directors ponders on the appropriate differential between the Chief Executive and his deputy it is unlikely that they are entirely oblivious to the fact that much of it will be absorbed in tax, and if this induces them to make the pre-tax margin a little wider than they would have done in the absence of the tax, then the company is sharing some of the incidence of the tax with its employee. (It is also, as we shall suggest later, likely to encourage them to think of some more efficient way of paying him.) Nor are these problems confined to higher income levels. When a householder meets a tradesman who offers to work for £100 in cash or £120 by cheque he is faced with a useful reminder that on taxable transactions part of the effective incidence falls on the employer rather than the employee.

Although the general notion of incidence is an indispensable concept in the analysis of taxation, it is one which cannot easily be given a precise meaning. The reason is that it implicitly requires a counter-factual hypothesis: what would have happened if the tax had not been imposed? It is not sufficient to say 'there would have been no tax' since public expenditure would have had to be financed in some other way. So we must specify either what other tax would have been imposed, or which item of public expenditure would have been reduced, or how the Government would have met its borrowing requirements, and the answer to our incidence question will depend on the alternative assumption which we make. For this reason the issue is sometimes described as 'differential incidence' because we examine differences between alternative tax systems which raise the same revenue. Several different concepts of incidence can be found in the theoretical literature on public finance, each reflecting different counterfactual hypotheses; while, as we see in Chapter 14, empirical studies of tax incidence either make intolerably crude assumptions or become impossibly complicated.

Thus we noted above that a consequence of imposing a heavy tax on television sets was that some of those employed in their manufacture suffered reduced earnings, and others lost their jobs: had the same tax revenue been raised in some different way, other groups of workers would probably have suffered similar hardships. But without exploring these issues in detail—as a rigorous answer would require—we can say that a significant part of the incidence of this tax fell on those who were previously employed in making televisions.

What factors govern the incidence of any particular tax? We can set out two basic principles. First, the formal incidence of a tax is generally irrelevant to its effective incidence. It makes little practical difference to the incidence of the tobacco tax whether it is levied on importers, wholesalers, manufacturers, retailers, or individual smokers: and the sensible decision is to impose the legal liability at the point at which the tax can be collected most cheaply and conveniently. Second, the harder it is for someone to substitute other things for the taxed activity, the greater the proportion of the incidence of the tax which he will bear. V.A.T. is imposed on most goods: and since there is not very much (except leisure) that can be substituted for consumption in general most of the burden of V.A.T. falls on consumers. But if a specially heavy rate of V.A.T. is imposed on one or two items, as with television sets, the situation is rather different. Consumers can substitute other things for television sets, and if the price rises sufficiently they will tend to do so. Producers, on the other hand, are in the short term stuck with capacity for manufacturing television sets: and if the only way to sell them is to keep down the price and absorb part of the tax themselves then that is what they must do.

If the tax were more discriminatory still—if it were imposed on a single manufacturer of television sets in isolation, for example—then that manufacturer would have no alternative but to hold down his price, accept the resulting losses, and grin and bear it until in the long run he could try to move into a less adversely treated business. For most people, there is no alternative to work which is both attractive and feasible and that is why the major part of the incidence of the income tax falls on the employee. But there are alternatives to effort, to overtime, and to increased responsibility: and to the extent that these are important and valuable components of the package which a particular employer is buying that employer will have to pay the price, at least to some extent, by raising the gross wage which he pays to a level which takes some account of the burden of taxation on the employee.

The first principle—the irrelevance of formal incidence—is easy to understand in abstract, but has some wide-ranging implications. For instance, it suggests that it is a matter of no practical importance whether national insurance contributions are levied on employees or employers (see pp. 21–25 below). It is not too easy to determine what the effective incidence of such a tax is—though the argument above has suggested that it mostly falls on the employee—but whatever it is, it will be the same for both kinds of contribution. When wages come to be renegotiated, the employer's concern will be with gross labour costs, inclusive of any pay-roll taxes to which he may be subject: and that will determine the level of employment which he will provide at any particular wage and the offer he will be prepared to make to avoid industrial trouble. On the other side of the table, the employee's interest is in his take-home pay, net of any deductions imposed on him; and that should determine the amount or quality of work which he will provide at particular wage rates and the minimum he will accept in preference to incurring the costs of a strike or other action against the employer. None of these calculations is in any way affected by the proportions in which a given tax is divided between employers' and employees' contribution, and this will therefore not have a significant effect on the final outcome.

Of course, none of this denies that the nature of formal incidence may have significant short-term effects. If a shift from employees' to employers' contributions were to be made, then next week workers would be better off and firms worse off. But this is simply to say that adjustments may take time, and that the incidence of a tax may differ in the short and long run. In practice the restoration of net real wages to their initial level might come about as much through an uncompensated rise in prices as through a diminution in the rate of increase of money wages. But the proposition that effective incidence is independent of formal incidence in the long run is true generally. The invoice that says £60 + £9 V.A.T., or the pay-slip that says £60 less £15 deductions gives £45 net, may in the short run mean what they appear to say. However, it is erroneous to suppose that if these tax items were not there the price or the wage from which these computations start would necessarily remain unchanged, and likely that the price might be £64 or £66 and the wage £54 or £57.

Tax capitalization

The easiest way to see *tax capitalization* in operation is to start with a rather artificial example. Suppose there exists a range of bonds, each of which sells for £100 and yields 10 per cent in perpetuity: income tax on this yield is levied at 50%, so that the after-tax return on each bond is £5. Now suppose that the Government decides, for some reason, that among these bonds there is one particular one that should be tax exempt. As a result, this bond—let us call it bond X—now returns £10 per annum after tax as well as before it. Because of this, it is worth twice as much to any taxpayer, and so its price rises to £200. Now look ahead a few years. By this time, most of the holders of bond X will be people who have purchased it since the tax concession was given— people who have paid £200 for it. They are only earning 5% on their investment—which is the same as they could earn from other bonds— and are therefore no better off than if this concession had never been granted. In spite of this, however, they would suffer if the concession were withdrawn—if they intended to continue holding the bond, their after-tax income would be halved, while if they intended to sell the bond, they would discover that its capital value had halved. As a result of this, even people who are deriving and have derived no direct benefit from the concession would lose if it were repealed. The holders of such a bond might include some pension funds and charities, who do not pay tax and therefore gain nothing from the apparent concession (such groups would not find bond X especially attractive, but they might have other reasons for wishing to hold it). They too would suffer capital losses as the price of bond X fell if it became again subject to tax: although they obviously gain nothing from the concession, they would suffer by its withdrawal.

This is a simple case of a capitalized tax exemption. The only people who gain from it are those who hold the favoured asset at the date when the concession is introduced (and perhaps their descendants). In the example above, the fortunate holders of bond X on the critical day when the Chancellor made his announcement saw the capital value of their asset double. Subsequent to that, no one derives any benefit from the concession at all. Nevertheless, later holders of the bond would lose if the concession were discontinued: in effect, they have bought the right to it from the former holders, and would have the part of their savings which they have invested in this form eliminated. Indeed, they would probably lose rather more than would be generally recognized. Not only would they be worse off by virtue of the extra tax they would themselves have to pay, but they would additionally be worse off because the asset they hold would fetch much less on resale. In other words, tax capitalization is a trap. In such a situation, almost everyone could agree that it would be better if the concession had never been given in the first place. But once it has been given, it is inequitable to withdraw it, and such a course is likely to cause real hardship. Thus the apparent beneficiaries of the concession will feel insecure: although their gains from it are small, their potential losses are significant, their position is anomalous and hence vulnerable. But once a concession of this kind has been made, there is not very much that can reasonably be done except to resolve not to fall into this particular trap in future. There is no point in considering the possibility of phasing out capitalized tax concessions, or any other method of retrieving the position. The Chancellor who has made such a move is almost literally in the position of a man who has unwisely given his assets away. After the first flush of gratitude, the original recipients will have spread ownership far and wide, and there is no method, except theft, by which he can ever get them back.

Needless to say, there are numerous examples of capitalized taxes in the British tax structure. It seems useful to give two concrete examples here. One, and probably the most important, is the effect of tax concessions to owner-occupied housing. These are discussed in more detail below. For present purposes, we may simply accept that investment in housing is very favourably treated relative to investment in other kinds of asset. As a result, house prices are higher than they would otherwise be. This means that the interest and capital repayments being made by current house-buyers are substantially greater than they would be if there were no tax concessions, and hence the concessions are of little net assistance to them. Nevertheless, they would be seriously injured if, for example, relief on mortgage interest were reduced or withdrawn: not only would they find they had to pay more in tax every year but the anticipated capital gains on their houses would fail to materialize and might well be turned into capital losses. New purchasers are not gaining much from the present tax system, nor indeed has this ever been true: those who have gained have been those who have owned houses, over the thirty or forty years in which the favoured position of housing has been built up, who have seen substantial real appreciation in value of their assets. They have not benefited much either, since the gain one derives from living in the same house of ever-appreciating nominal value has very little practical utility.

This analysis is well illustrated by the effects of the withdrawal in 1974 of tax relief on mortgages in excess of £25,000. This change did not necessarily make it more difficult to buy expensive houses, since the loss of tax relief led to a fall in the price of such houses. The principal losers from the change were those who owned such houses in 1974. Moreover, people in this position lost whether they actually had large mortgages or not, since the fall in prices affected all property without reference to the personal tax position of the owner.

A second illustration of tax capitalization was provided at around the same time in the market for agricultural land. Under the pre-1974 estate duty, substantial reliefs were given for agricultural assets. Their nominal purpose was to assist working farmers. It is more likely that they damaged the interests of such farmers, since the capitalization of such concessions raised land prices to levels which were nonsensical in terms of any likely agricultural returns from the land and at which working farmers were squeezed out of the market by those avoiding estate duty. When the withdrawal of such concessions was proposed as part of the shift to capital transfer tax, land prices fell by a third or more. However, political pressures for the restoration of these reliefs were largely successful, and land prices have fully regained their earlier levels.

Tax and welfare

What are the costs of collecting tax revenue? Some costs are obvious. Any tax diverts resources from the taxpayer to the Government, and leaves him worse off by that amount. Of course, that is not the end of the story; these resources are presumably used to provide public services, which may be more or less valuable to him than the possibilities for private consumption which he loses. But there are bound to be administrative costs to tax collection, since it is necessary to provide inspectors to receive the revenues and gaols to receive those who do not pay them. There will also be 'compliance costs' for taxpayers, who will spend time and suffer distress completing tax returns, and who may employ advisers to help them fulfil their obligations and suggest how to minimize them. All of these latter activities represent the necessary costs of tax collection and are pure social loss, simple subtractions from the total of goods and services—private and public—available to the community.

There is a less obvious cost, which has been called the 'excess burden' of taxation. Suppose I earn £2 per hour, and my employer is willing to give me as much, or as little, work as I require at this rate. However, a 25% income tax reduces my take-home pay to £1·50 per hour, and given this I choose to work 40 hours per week, thus paying £20 in tax each week. For £1·50 I do not think it worth working any more than this, but if I were paid a little more I might. (Premium payments for overtime often succeed in inducing additional effort.) In fact for £2 per hour I would stay late on one or two evenings and put in an extra three or four hours' work a week. My employer would be better off—why else would he allow this overtime? I would be better off—why else would I stay? And if the £20 which I pay in income tax were levied, not as income tax, but as a weekly contribution to public revenue which I was obliged to pay regardless of how much work I did that week or whether I did any at all, then my net earnings from overtime would be £2 per hour and I would decide to do it.

But with an income tax, I turn this opportunity away. The problem results from the way the tax depends on how much I choose to work. These disincentive effects imply that the losses imposed by the tax are greater than the £20 which I have to pay—if I had the opportunity to do so, I would prefer to pay the £20 as a lump sum, and everyone would be better off. The idea that income taxes have undesirable disincentive effects is of course familiar, and the 'excess burden' concept is simply the economist's formal expression of it. But the idea is quite general, and commodity taxes impose losses of just the same kind. If a bottle of whisky costs £1 to make but, because of tax, sells for £6 then it is easy to imagine that I do not buy it because I am willing to pay only, say, £2. If I were able to buy it at that price, I would more than cover production costs, be able to contribute something (though less than the regular £5) to the Customs and Excise, and enjoy a warm inner glow myself. Because of the tax, none of these things happens. There is a disincentive effect here too—a disincentive to consume whisky—and this imposes an 'excess burden' or welfare loss of the same kind as disincentives to work.

It is very important to recognize that the magnitude of such effects depends on the impact of taxation at the margin—on the tax implications of a decision to work a little more or a little less, or to buy slightly more or less of a particular commodity—and not on the over-all or average burden of taxation. My reluctance to put in more effort to obtain higher earnings arises because the Revenue will take such a high proportion of these additional earnings. Thus there are two basic components to the welfare effects of a tax. There is an 'income effect', which reflects the reduction in the taxpayer's net income which occurs when part of it is compulsorily transferred to the Government, and which depends on the average rate of tax. There is also an 'excess burden', which reflects additional losses arising from the way in which the tax is levied. This depends on the marginal tax rate and the way in which behaviour responds to that marginal rate. The total loss is the sum of these two.

Tax and incentives

We have considered the question 'How do the disincentive effects of taxation on effort affect welfare?' We now look at a different but closely related question: 'What effect would an increase in taxation have on the amount of work you do?' Any individual considering his answer would probably feel the influence of two conflicting pressures. On the one hand, he would realize that the tax change would make him worse off. As a result, given his commitments and expectations about the style of life which he aims to enjoy, he would feel some pressure to do more work in order to earn sufficient to live up to these expectations. This effect (the *income effect* of the tax change, so called because it results from the fall in his real income) depends on the *average* rate of tax: on the total size of the burden imposed by the tax structure. On the other hand, he will also be conscious that the tax change reduces the amount of additional consumption which he can enjoy as a result of additional work, so that increased effort becomes less attractive relative to idleness or staying at home and redecorating the bedroom. This effect (the *substitution effect* of the tax, so called because it implies a substitution of leisure for work) depends on the *marginal* rate of tax—on the proportion of any additional earnings which are absorbed in tax. The net impact of such a tax change on the work done by any individual therefore depends on the balance of these two factors—one, tending to increase effort, which is related to the average rate of tax, the other, tending to reduce it, which depends on the marginal rate of tax.

We can illustrate this by returning to the example above. We were able to eliminate the excess burden in that case by transforming the 25% income tax which reduced gross earnings from £2 to £1·50 an hour into a fixed tax of £20 per week. This revision of the tax restored his overtime rate to £2 and persuaded him to do more work. In this way, we eliminated the substitution effect of the tax. We could now eliminate the income effect also by abolishing the tax of £20 per week. If we did, the worker would discover that he could achieve the same standard of living—which requires a net weekly income of £60—by working for 30 rather than 40 hours per week. It is very likely that he would in fact respond by reducing the amount of work he did, and this would tend to offset the increase which had resulted from the reduction in the marginal rate of tax. Thus the net effect of complete abolition of income tax on the amount of work he does may be small, and may even lead him to reduce it. This observation does not, however, upset our excess burden analysis at all. The gains we made from eliminating the excess burden—from encouraging him to do work which both he and his employer wanted—remain. Adding in the income effect—conferring on him an opportunity to take out increased income in the form of greater leisure—raises his welfare further. The disincentive effects of taxation, which discourage additional work effort or other kinds of economic activity, make society worse off; the offsetting incentive effects, which force people to greater effort to maintain living standards reduced by taxation, do not make anyone better off.

Care is therefore necessary in evaluating empirical evidence on the effect of taxation on incentives. In our normative analysis—where we asked how taxation affected welfare—there was an income effect and a substitution effect, and they both operated in the same direction. The income effect is the welfare loss which results from having to pay the tax—a loss which is offset by the benefits of public expenditure—and its size is determined by the average rate of tax paid. The substitution effect is the welfare loss which results from the disincentive effects of taxation at the margin and this depends only on the marginal rate of tax. This is a pure social loss, and there is no corresponding gain to anyone. The sum of these two components gives the total loss which any tax imposes on the individual who pays it.

In our positive analysis—where we asked how taxation affected the quantity of effort—we also identified an income effect and a substitution effect, but discovered that they generally worked in opposite directions. The income effect of taxation increases effort, the substitution effect reduces it, and the observed change in work effort is the net effect of the two. It follows that even if empirical studies show that tax has little effect on work effort, we cannot necessarily infer that incentive effects are not a matter for concern. Such an outcome might result from a small substitution effect, offset by a small income effect, in which case our inference would be justified; or from large income and substitution effects, in which case the effects on welfare would be correspondingly large. More sophisticated analyses are required to enable us to discriminate between these possibilities.

We have used as an expository device the possibility that a man might be subject to a tax of £20 per week rather than a 25% income tax on his earnings of £80. If such a tax were related to his earning potential rather than his earnings, it would take the form of a fixed weekly sum and would, as we have seen, have no disincentive effects at all. Economists have dreamt of such 'lump sum taxes' which eliminate the excess burden of taxation, but it is not easy to find taxes which have no disincentive effects. Nevertheless, they illustrate that it is possible to envisage a tax system where average rates are high but marginal rates are low. In practice, the easiest way to reduce marginal rates is to reduce average rates: but it is possible, by improving the structure, broadening the base, or altering the rate schedule, to achieve one without changing the other and hence to effect a more or less unequivocal improvement in the effects of the tax system on economic efficiency. We consider these effects and possibilities further in our discussion of particular taxes.

Neutrality

In discussing these issues, we shall use the concept of tax neutrality. A neutral tax system is one which seeks to raise revenue in ways which avoid the distortionary substitution effects we have described; it is designed to minimize as far as possible the impact of the tax structure on the economic behaviour of agents in the economy. This is a distinctly unfamiliar idea in the U.K., where it is widely thought that a major function of the tax system is to encourage good things and to discourage bad things. Even if one takes this view, there is much to be said for understanding the notion of neutrality and what a tax system which generally sought to achieve it would be like. Even if you know where you are going, it is generally valuable to know where you are starting out from, and if you are aiming to influence people in certain directions, it is useful to have an idea of what things would be like if you were not trying to do so. The neutral tax system, in effect, provides a bench-mark against which non-neutralities, intentional or otherwise, can be judged.

We have described one argument for neutrality—minimization of the excess burden of tax disincentives. But there is a more basic argument. The effects of taxation are generally not obvious, and are very often not what they seem. We will describe in subsequent chapters the ways in which behaviour and institutions have been moulded by the British tax system—and while there is room for argument about the desirability or undesirability of these effects, it is really very difficult to argue that many of them have ever been explicitly intended by anyone. The present state of the British tax system is the product of a series of un-systematic and *ad hoc* measures, many undertaken for excellent reasons —for administrative convenience or to encourage deserving groups and worthy activities—but whose over-all effect has been to deprive the system of any consistent rationale or coherent structure. We should be rather content if a tax system can achieve its basic functions of raising revenue and relieving inequalities of income and wealth without doing too much damage in the process. Clearly, this is a good deal less than an ideal tax system, but it is a good deal better than what we have at the moment. We now turn to some description and analysis of what that is.

THE U.K. INCOME TAX

INCOME tax was first introduced to Britain during the Napoleonic Wars, but it only became a permanent feature of the tax system in 1842. As part of Peel's economic reforms it was reintroduced to replace in large part the revenue previously derived from tariffs and from various archaic taxes. It was imposed at the single low rate of 7d. in the £ (3%) and, although this varied from time to time and ministry to ministry in the course of the nineteenth century, these essential elements never changed. The highest rates were reached during the Crimean War, when the tax threshold was an annual income of £100 and the rate 1s. 4d. (7%): but even at this time there were less than half a million taxpayers. Thus income tax was then an impost of no interest or relevance to the great majority of the population.

The numbers of taxpayers did not exceed a million until the early years of the twentieth century. In 1909 effective progressivity came to the income tax with Lloyd George's 'people's budget' in which he proposed a 'supertax' on incomes over £5,000 per annum (equivalent to over £100,000 at 1980 prices). This took the maximum rate to the unprecedented level of 1s. 8d. (8%). These proposals generated a constitutional crisis (the supertax was not the most bitterly resisted element, although it was the most quantitatively significant) and they were implemented only in association with a fundamental reform of the House of Lords. During the First World War enormously increased revenue requirements led to top rates of tax at over 50%. Although there were reductions thereafter, rates and revenue remained well in excess of pre-war levels while the supertax, renamed surtax, became a permanent and accepted feature.

Even then, however, liability to income tax was still confined to a small and affluent minority. Average wages in 1939 were around £180 per annum; there was no possible liability to tax for a married couple with earnings below £225 at that time, and there were less than four million taxpayers in a working population which exceeded 20 m. The decision that Second World War expenditure should be substantially financed from taxes changed this situation radically. Tax rates were increased and thresholds lowered at a time when money wages were rising rapidly. This brought about not only a quantitative change in the significance of income tax, but also a qualitative change in its method of operation. The number of taxpayers soon exceeded 12 m., so that that the majority of working people now came within the ambit of the tax. These included large numbers of households lacking significant capital resources and accustomed to budgeting on a weekly basis: so the only practical method of enforcing tax liabilities was by deduction from wages before they were received. The Inland Revenue concluded that this was impracticable, and published a White Paper (Cmd. 6348) explaining that view: simultaneously, however, it was instructed to devise a scheme for doing so. P.A.Y.E. (pay-as-you-earn) was introduced and has remained the principal means of collecting income tax since then. By 1960 essentially the whole of the working population was covered by income tax.

Some caution is required in interpreting historical information on the rate structure and tax thresholds, since from 1920 to 1973 there operated a system of 'earned income relief', by which in addition to the basic personal allowance (the tax threshold) a fraction of earned income (lately two-ninths) was deducted in the computation of taxable income. This means that in measuring their effect on earned income, the nominal tax rates which applied during this period should be reduced by two-ninths: the rate of 8s. 3d. which applied from 1965 to 1971 was in fact equivalent to 32% on earned income. It also means that the real value of tax thresholds was actually nine-sevenths of their nominal value, since they were credited in full against only seven-ninths of earned income. Thus the indicated tax threshold of £325 in 1970 is equivalent to an effective tax threshold on earnings of £418. This mumbo-jumbo was swept away in 1973, and at the same time the separately assessed and administered surtax was integrated into a single system of unified income tax. In consequence, the essentials of the current structure of U.K. income tax are relatively easy to explain, and to this we now turn.

The taxation of individuals

First we set out the position for a single individual, later considering explicitly the relationship between the tax treatment of individuals and households. Everyone is entitled to a 'personal allowance', a fixed amount of income which can be received free of tax. This allowance is £1,565 p.a. (1982–3). It is virtually inconceivable that any adult in full-time work could have earned less than this figure, and most long-term recipients of social security benefits would receive more than this. It therefore follows that anyone who does not pay income tax is likely to fall into one of four categories: (a) dependent on someone who is an income tax payer; (b) in receipt of considerable amounts of tax-exempt income (of which certain types of supplementary benefit or pension, and student grants are the most important examples); (c) having a very low income and living off capital (there cannot be many people in this category, since the capital would usually produce some income); (d) a pensioner (although the old age pension is taxable, a specially enhanced personal allowance for the elderly ensures that the national insurance pension is not in fact taxed in the hands of those with no other source of income).

All income in excess of this personal allowance is subject to tax is at the *basic rate* of 30%. When taxable income exceeds £12,800, higher rates apply, commencing at 40% and rising to 60% on taxable income above £31,500 (i.e. this rate applies when the total income of a single person exceeds £33,065). These rates are graphed against income in Fig. 2.1, as is the corresponding schedule of average rates of tax. The average rate of income tax rises continuously, but is always below the marginal rate of tax (it is easy to check that each of these characteristics implies the other).

In Fig. 2.2 we show the average and marginal tax rates implied by the tax schedules of the U.K., U.S.A., and West Germany. The diagrams illustrate the rates which apply to a single man with a given proportion of average earnings (which are much higher in the other two countries). The long basic rate band in Britian is unusual. In other countries, the starting rate is lower but it rises more or less continuously. Before 1979–80, the marginal rates on high incomes and the average rates charged on very high incomes were much higher in the U.K. than in these other countries. This is not now true, and the top marginal rate of tax on earned income of 60% is no longer out of line with 50% in the U.S.A. and 56% in West Germany.

This description ignores, however, the role of national insurance contributions. Before 1978 it was clear that these so-called contributions were simply another form of income taxation; the payment of additional contributions normally yielded no additional benefit. Since 1978 there have been differential rates of national insurance contribution. The

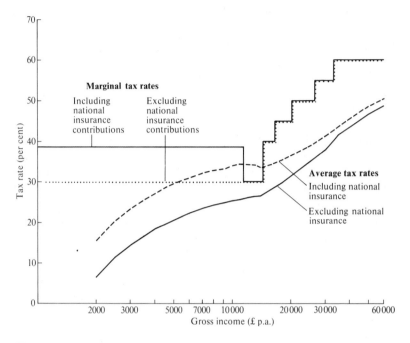

Fig. 2.1. Average and marginal rates of tax in the U.K.

standard rate is 8¾% on earnings up to £220 per week. Those who are
contracted out of the State Earnings Related Pension Scheme (SERPS),
discussed in Chapter 7, pay a lower rate of 6¼% on their earnings above
£29·50 (but still below £220). In consequence their state pension will
be reduced by an amount known as the guaranteed minimum pension
(GMP), but their employer must promise them an occupational pension
at least equivalent to this.

Perhaps the most logical way to describe this is to treat the contracted
out rates of contribution as a tax, with the additional contributions
payable by those who are not contracted out being treated as an investment which ultimately earns then the amount of their GMP. However,
the probability that many workers distinguish between the reasons for
the various different stoppages from their pay, far less the different
reasons behind one particular stoppage, is remote. On balance, therefore, we have concluded that the least misleading procedure is to treat
the whole of the national insurance contribution as a tax, since that is
how we believe most of those who pay it regard it.

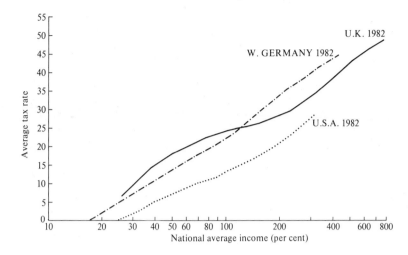

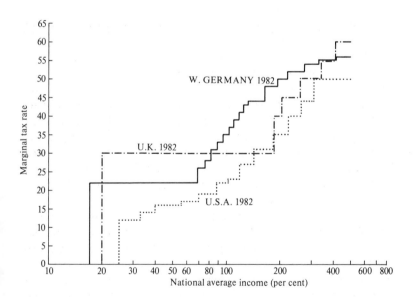

Fig. 2.2. Average and marginal rates of tax in different countries.
Sources: Inland Revenue, evidence to Treasury and Civil Service Com-
mittee, The Structure of Personal Income Taxation and
Income Support (1983)

Before we leave this issue, there is one further complication we should note. SERPS is unusual among occupational pension schemes in that there is at least some probability that extra payments yield extra benefits. In the vast majority of pension schemes—public or private—benefits are based on final salary and are therefore independent of contributions. In these cases, the contributions payable by an individual are simply a tax, albeit one paid to a pension fund rather than to the government. Since contributions to many pension schemes are 5 or 6% of salary, this addition to the effective marginal rate of tax is far from negligible.

In Fig. 2.1, we show how the income tax schedule is modified by the existence of national insurance contributions. With this schedule, there is actually a range in which the average rate of tax falls. Someone who earns £11,000 p.a. pays an average rate of tax of 34·5% and a marginal rate of 38·75%. Thereafter, the marginal rate falls to 30% and because it is below the average rate, the average rate falls, until at an income of £14,000 it is 33·8%. On higher incomes, the marginal rate of tax is 40% or more and so the average rate rises once more. It is surprising that the lowest average rate of tax should be paid by someone who is well within the top 5% of the income distribution.

Investment income is not liable to national insurance contributions. However it is subject to investment income surcharge, which is now payable at a rate of 15% on annual investment income over £6,250. The maximum rate of income tax payable in the U.K. in 1978-9 was therefore 98%, made up of a top marginal rate of 83% and a 15% surcharge; from 1979-80 it has been 75%. It is not easy to rationalize the combination of the two surcharges—one of which applies to all earned income *below* £11,440 and the other to all investment income *above* £6,250.

We have still understated the effective rate of income tax, since as we noted in Chapter 1 there is in the long run no substantive difference between employees' and employers' contributions. It would be incorrect, however, simply to add on the 12·2% paid by employers to the basic 38¾% tax rate, since the employer pays his fraction without this being a taxable benefit for the employee.[1]

Thus for every £100 paid in gross wages, the cost to the employer is £112·20 (£100 + £12·20 employer's contribution): the taxes payable on this total £50·95 (£12·20 + £8·75 in national insurance contributions

---

[1] 2% of the 12·2% is described as a 'surcharge', from which charities are exempt.

and £30 income tax), so that the effective tax rate is £50·95 ÷ £112·20 or 46%. It is worth pursuing this calculation a little further to see what the total tax burden on marginal income is likely to be. On spending the remaining £61·25 of the initial £112·20 our worker would have to pay consumption taxes. The size of these would of course depend on his consumption patterns, and if these were deemed sufficiently meritorious by the Government's expressed preferences (for books, bread, and British Rail) it would be possible (though boring) to pay no or even negative consumption taxes. But on a representative collection of commodities the average tax rate would be 17·9% (Dilnot and Morris, 1982) so that of the £61·25 some £11 would go in tax. This calculation raises the effective marginal tax rate to 55%: it still underestimates the true figure since there are several taxes (such as corporation tax and capital taxes) which have been left out of account, but it is clear that the figure exceeds 50% and that this is a minimum figure applicable to virtually everyone in the U.K.

Families and children

So far, we have described the system simply as it relates to a single individual. We should now consider how it is modified in its application to households. In general, the British tax system starts from the premiss that a wife is a dependant of her husband. Thus the husband is responsible for submitting a return of their joint income and is liable for their joint tax. Any income of the wife's is aggregated with his, and in recognition of these obligations he is given an addition (£880 in 1982-3) to his personal allowance. There are two modifications to this general principle. One is 'wife's earned income relief'. A working wife receives a personal allowance of her own, equal to the personal allowance of the single individual, and this is available against her earnings (but not her investment income). There is no consequential reduction in the additional personal allowance given to the husband. The second modification is the availability of an option for separate taxation of the earned income of the two partners. Investment income continues to be added to the income of the husband, who receives only the personal allowance of the single man. Since this option implies the loss of the increment to the married man's personal allowance, it is only advantageous to a couple who would otherwise pay substantial amounts of higher rate tax: i.e. if their joint income exceeds about £19,500. We consider further in Chapter 14 the appropriate treatment of the tax unit.

The household may also include children. Their dependent status was traditionally recognized by conceding an additional allowance to a taxpayer who was responsible for the maintenance of a child. These allowances interacted somewhat uneasily with the system of family allowances, a weekly cash payment made to the mother through the Post Office. In 1979, these two allowances were integrated into a single child benefit, now £5.85 per week, payable in the same manner as family allowances.

The head of a single-parent family receives the additional personal allowance of £880 payable to a married man, but with unimportant exceptions this is the only allowance for dependent children which is now provided via the tax system. A single-parent family also receives an additional child benefit of £3·30 a week for the first child.

Children are taxed on their own income, as separate individuals. Obviously few children have amounts of income which exceed the exemption limits. To prevent avoidance of too blatant a kind, the investment income of children is taxed as if it had been received by the parents if it is derived from money which the child has been given by the parents. For a brief period, all investment income of children was taxed in this way, but this provision has now been repealed.

The tax base

For earned income, the definition of the income which is potentially subject to tax poses no particular problems. For investment income, the tax base primarily relates to interest, dividends, and net rents received. Capital gains are not subject to income tax; thus the dividend received from a share is subject to income tax, but any profit made on selling the share is not. Until 1965 such capital gains were generally exempt from tax: since then there has been a distinct capital gains tax. From 1982 gains are calculated after deduction of an 'indexation allowance' designed to reflect part of the impact of recent inflation on the value of the asset. The first £5,000 of the remaining gain is tax free and the rest is charged to tax at 30%. The distinction between income and capital gains is blurred, and someone who generates capital gains in a regular way of business may be deemed a trader and find his profits subjected to income tax. Regularity is broadly a sufficient definition of trading, but not a necessary one: the classic case in English law is of a man who made a shrewd purchase of toilet-paper in Germany—once—and whom the Revenue successfully charged with income tax on the resulting profit (*Rutledge* v. *C.I.R.*, 1929).

The tax base is also modified by the existence of a number of minor allowances. In the U.S.A., where such allowances are much more extensive—taxpayers there can, for example, deduct the amount of their medical expenses and their losses from theft—they have become known as 'tax expenditures'. The implicit or explicit suggestion is that such exemptions require justification of much the same kind as is given to positive items of Government expenditure. Such allowances are available to the blind, for single-parent families, to those who need and use the services of a housekeeper. Apart from the basic single and married personal allowances, the items of most significance, in both the amount of the tax expenditure involved and the number of taxpayers affected, are the allowances for mortgage interest and pension contributions. Historically, tax relief was available on all interest payments: and since interest receipts are taxable the logical case for permitting interest payments to be deductible is quite persuasive. In recent years, however, this relief has been systematically restricted, and it is now generally confined to interest on loans of up to £25,000 whose purpose is stated to be for the purchase or improvement of the taxpayer's main residence.

An employee who contributes to a pension scheme approved by the Inland Revenue can deduct the whole of what he pays from his taxable income. Nor is he liable for tax on contributions which his employer makes on his behalf. Until 1979, partial tax relief was also available on individual payments of life insurance premiums. In 1979, this was replaced by a system by which a subsidy of 15% of the premiums on 'qualifying policies' is paid directly to insurance companies by the Inland Revenue. The practical effect of this procedure involves virtually no change, but the administrative mechanism is different.

How tax is collected

For the vast majority of taxpayers, all or virtually all their earnings are from employment and tax is deducted by their employers under P.A.Y.E. procedures. People in this category, with simple incomes and modest earnings, are normally required to make a return of income only every five years. When they first become potentially subject to tax, they will be asked to file a tax return. This is in general somewhat confusing, since the form appears to be principally concerned with their past income when in fact its actual purpose is to elicit their present circumstances with a view to establishing their future allowances. On the basis of this information the Revenue issues a 'notice of coding' to the taxpayer and to his employer. The notice of coding is a cryptic document, which concludes with a code number of the form 282H. The numerical part of this code is one-tenth of the taxpayer's total allowances for the year; the letter indicates marital status (H, higher, for married; L, lower for single persons or married women). But no action is required from the taxpayer: his employer will now deduct tax in the light of this coding using the tax tables with which he is supplied.

Before describing how these tables work, we should notice an important administrative difference between the ways in which the two taxes on earnings—income tax and national insurance contributions— are levied. Income tax is levied on a cumulative basis, so that the whole year's income is taken into account. So in computing liability, low earnings in one week will be offset against high earnings in the next and vice versa. National insurance contributions are charged non-cumulatively, so that liability in each week depends only on earnings in that week, and is not affected by the amounts which are earned in earlier or later weeks. This is why students, who may have earnings which exceed the exemption limits for only a small number of weeks in the year, pay national insurance contributions but do not usually pay income tax; and why people who start work midway through a tax year pay less in the first months of employment than they do subsequently. An unusual feature of the British tax system is that income tax is not only levied on a cumulative basis, but also collected on a cumulative basis. In other countries it is common to levy tax cumulatively, but to collect it non-cumulatively: tax is paid each week on the basis of earnings in that week and if an adjustment is necessary when the whole year's income is assessed (as is often the case for those with fluctuating earnings) this is done at the end of the year.

The British tax system, by contrast, tries to ensure that at each point in the tax year an appropriate proportion of the whole year's liability has been paid. A non-cumulative system credits the taxpayer each week with $\frac{1}{52}$ of his annual allowances. The cumulative system does this also: but if income in any week is less than the allowance for the week then the excess is credited against tax which has previously been paid in the year, and a tax refund becomes due. If all the tax previously paid has been refunded, or at the beginning of the tax year when little or no tax has been paid, these unused allowances cannot be credited against earlier tax payments and are carried forward to be offset against taxable income in future weeks. It is therefore necessary to maintain throughout the year for each taxpayer a record of the total tax he has paid so far and the total allowances ('free pay') for which he has already been given credit. If these procedures work well, they ensure that by the end of the year the taxpayer will have paid the right amount of tax and no significant adjustment to his liability will be required. The advantage of a system which reaches the right answer in this automatic way are obvious. So are the problems; each taxpayer must carry with him from week to week and employment to employment records of his tax position for the year so far, and this is an expensive administrative operation.

The system works less smoothly when an individual's allowances change during the year (perhaps a male taxpayer marries). He must then inform the Inland Revenue which will revise his coding. He receives an immediate refund which reflects the tax he has overpaid in each week of the tax year so far. This system cannot operate in reverse for someone whose allowances go down (because he gets divorced, for example); if it did the taxpayer might have no net income for several weeks as previously underpaid tax was recouped. Broadly, he will be credited with the tax he *should* have paid so far, and the deficiency collected by a reduction in his allowances in future tax years. Fortunately, allowances rise in practice much more often than they fall. An exception was when mortgage interest rates fell sharply in 1982 and tax allowances for many owner-occupiers were reduced correspondingly. Then the cumulative principle was in effect simply abandoned for many taxpayers in this position.

Earnings from employment are taxed under what is known as schedule E. Earnings from business are taxed under schedule D. (The authors' salaries are taxed on schedule E but any royalties from this book fall under schedule D.) These terms, which derive from the income tax legislation of 1803, are not referred to in the forms or guidance supplied to the taxpayer, but are of some practical importance to him. A much wider range of expenses can be deducted under schedule D than E: under D the test is broadly that the expenditure was incurred for the purpose of earning the income, while under E it is necessary to suggest that one would be dismissed if one did not spend the money in that way; and in the case of expenditure on travel to work even that is not sufficient justification. Schedule D earnings are subject to a surcharge, described as national insurance contributions, of a flat weekly sum (£3·75 in 1982-3) plus 6% of earnings between £3,450 and £11,000. The administrative procedures for collection are quite different. Tax under schedule D is paid in two lump sums—for the tax year 1982–3 these would be due on 1 January 1983 and 1 July 1983. Liability is calculated on a 'preceding year' basis: thus these assessments would be based on earnings in the year 1981–2. Since business accounts take time to compile there is some reason for this. The tax therefore appears to be paid a year in arrears, which sounds a rather favourable option. However, the system is in fact much more complicated and less advantageous to the self-employed than this would suggest. It is impossible to provide a brief and intelligible—or indeed lengthy and intelligible—description of the rules but a consequence is that in the early years of a business some components of income may be taxed two or even three times while others will not be taxed at all. This is obviously a licence for abuse.

The scope for abuse is much increased where partnership taxation is involved. The reason is that tax is in theory levied on the partnership rather than on the individual partners. Of course it is not really possible to do this in a system where there are personal allowances and progressive rates on individual income but the appearance is maintained by an elaborate apparatus which first disaggregates the calculation to the level of the individual partner and then adds up the answers. But a consequence is that the partnership may be deemed to have closed down and restarted when partners are added or leave (which in the case of a large partnership happens all the time). By a suitable choice of closing and restarting dates, a partnership with fluctuating profits—stockbrokers are particularly well placed—can arrange to pay tax twice on their poor years and not at all on their good years. A sample of partnership accounts examined by the Comptroller and Auditor-General showed that these partnerships had paid tax on 77% of the profits which they had actually earned in the period in question (Public Accounts Committee, 1977).

The principle of getting hold of the money before the taxpayer has a chance to spend it is applied as far as possible to investment income also. Most payers of interest (though not commercial banks or the National Savings Bank) are required to deduct and transmit to the Revenue the basic rate tax due before sending the balance to the lender. It is interesting to note that one security, War Loan, is exempt from this requirement and stands at a premium in consequence. This tax can be reclaimed by anyone not liable to tax: higher rate taxpayers will be assessed for an additional charge. The treatment of company dividends is more complicated (see pp. 175–8 below) but the effect is the same. A different arrangement is applied to building society interest. In return for a negotiated payment by the societies (the so-called composite rate) their interest is exempted from basic rate tax. No refund is available to those who are not liable to tax, who would therefore be well-advised to deposit their money elsewhere (but are often not well advised). Investment income is also taxed on a preceding year basis, though there are some minor differences between the methods used here and those for schedule D income.

Administrative problems

The administration of any tax system is an inevitable butt for criticism, but there are two characteristics of British tax administration which can be given objective description. Few people understand how it works, and it is very expensive. The first of these propositions is easily documented.

In the 1950s the Government Social Survey concluded that 'our evidence suggests that if productivity is related to income tax in any way it can only be related to misconceptions about the system. It cannot be related to the system because only 3 or 4% are sufficiently informed of the system' (Radcliffe Report, 1954, App. 1, para. 129). Brown (1968) also found almost total ignorance of the rates or operation of the tax structure; though Lewis (1978) indicates that the administrative changes of 1973 (the unified tax system) may have increased understanding. And in spite of the apparent advantages to him of a wholly automatic system of tax deduction, the bewildered British taxpayer is in contact with the Inland Revenue more frequently than his American counterpart (four times as often, according to the estimates of Barr et al., 1977). The American taxpayer must complete a return every year, but normally that is the only correspondence with the Internal Revenue Service which he has.

Why is British tax administration so complicated? It is easy to reply that this is because of the extensive demands made on it, and this is a continuing theme of annual Inland Revenue reports. But we do not agree that the system is so complex because it is so fair; indeed it is complexity which is a principal source of inequity. (The taxation of partnerships is a good example—the opportunities for abuse are entirely the product of an unnecessarily tortuous administrative mechanism). And in its central elements, the British tax system is actually rather simpler than that of most countries. The range of allowances available is very limited and the rate structure straightforward. It is peripheral elements which are the obstacle to understanding. Although the system of cumulative P.A.Y.E. has some advantages, it has the effect that the weekly deductions made from wages are computed on a basis which is not explained or in practice explicable to the average worker. The inter-action of cumulative income tax deductions with non-cumulative national insurance contributions computed on different principles aggravates this. The schedular system and the preceding year basis require professional tax expertise for adequate comprehension, and indeed description of them is to be found only in technical literature. The representative taxpayer rarely makes a tax return, and as a rule does not see any statement of how his liabilities have been computed. Filling in such a return is not a purposive activity: it does not enable the recipient to check how much tax he owes or is owed, or indeed to do anything except post the form back to the tax inspector, and it is therefore not surprising that this generates irritation rather than under-standing. It is extraordinary that the design of tax forms which do allow the respondent to check his liabilities is left to commercial organizations such as the magazine *Money Which.* The appearance of both the tax return and the accompanying instructions compare very unfavourably with similar documents in other countries (though there have been recent improvements). But it remains difficult to resist the conclusion that the Inland Revenue does not feel that its work could be helped if the taxpayer had a better understanding of the basis or methods of collection of the taxes involved.

Collection costs absorb about 2% of income tax receipts. While this proportion may not seem high, judged by either international or historical standards, it is a substantial figure. It is twice as great as in Sweden or Canada, four times as great as in the U.S.A.; and the U.S. Internal Revenue Service and the U.K. Inland Revenue employ similar numbers of staff although there are four times as many taxpayers in America. These calculations leave out administrative costs imposed on taxpayers (which are certainly higher in the U.S.A.) and on employers (which are probably higher in the U.K.). Sandford (1973) suggests that the total administrative costs of U.K. income tax are in the range of 4%–6% of revenue.

Why are costs so much higher in the U.K. than in the U.S.? One reason which is often given is that the U.S. employs 'self-assessment'. It is not clear to us exactly what people have in mind when they talk about 'self-assessment', but the American system is, at least at first sight, very different from the one which operates here. At the end of year, every taxpayer is responsible for completing a tax return, calculating the tax due, and posting a cheque, or more frequently claiming a refund, from the Internal Revenue Service (I.R.S.). But it is wrong to suppose that costs are lower in the U.S. because the taxpayer does the calculations instead of the taxman. In a world of microcircuitry, arithmetic is cheap, and indeed the I.R.S. checks the calculations on every return before it accepts it. To see what the significant differences between the two administrative mechanisms are we need to probe more deeply.

One reason why costs are so much lower in the U.S. than in the U.K. is that the I.R.S. makes extensive use of computers while the Inland Revenue does not. The continuing inability of the Inland Revenue to computerize the operations of P.A.Y.E. is a matter for considerable concern. In the 1960s, there were plans to build a network of regional computer centres. The first to be completed, at East Kilbride in Scotland, suffered extensive teething problems, while the second, at Bootle, was subject to interminable delays. Plans for further centres were abandoned. When a tax credit scheme was proposed in the early 1970s, computerization was deferred while the details of these proposals were marked out. These proposals were shelved in 1974. Work began on a new set of plans for computerization in 1977 and installation has begun. The present timetable would have the system in full operation by 1990—over 25 years after the introduction of computerized systems in other countries. It is worth stressing that income tax administration lends itself particularly well to the use of computers. Most people would now be amazed to receive a handwritten bank statement or electricity bill; but they will continue for some considerable time to receive handwritten notices of coding. And a bank which had failed to adapt to new technology would no longer be in business.

The second major reason why American administrative costs are lower is derived from a major difference of overall approach. In the U.S., the primary source of information is the taxpayer's annual return, and although there is an extensive network of reporting of income paid and of deducting tax at source this is for the purposes of detecting fraud and facilitating collection. In the U.K. payers of income are the primary information source, the system seeks to extract the exact amount of tax due at this stage, and the annual return of income is subsidiary (which is why many taxpayers are not required to make one). The origins of this difference are historical. Britain was the first country in the world to adopt an income tax, and it was then a flat rate

tax on certain kinds of income. Because there was considerable resist-
ance to the disclosure of personal affairs involved in making a return of
income it was natural to collect it from those who paid the income
rather than those who received it—and this indirect method of collection was how all taxes had hitherto been administered.

By contrast, the American federal income tax was introduced in
1913 and was conceived from the beginning as a progressive tax on the
total income of individuals. It was therefore an obvious procedure to
require an annual return of that income from the individuals concerned. The British income tax was in process of acquiring a similar
character. But there had never been a fundamental review of the suit-
ability of the whole administrative structure for the purposes of a
modern fiscal system, and there has still never been one. The
framework of tax legislation and administration is still based on
Addington's construction of 1803.

Thus Britain imposes extensive responsibilities on those who pay
income, and the administrative mechanisms seek to ensure that as far
as possible the exact amount of tax due is deducted at that stage. Most
other countries impose some reporting obligations on payers of income
and require some 'withholding' of tax to ensure that the tax is collected
before the associated income has been spent. But since they ultimately
rely on the taxpayer's own returns of income, they are not too concerned if the reporting mechanisms are occasionally imperfect or the
amounts withheld are inaccurate. The major contrast is between exact
withholding without general end-of-year assessment—the British
system—and approximate withholding with universal end-of-year
assessment—the American system, which is usually favoured elsewhere.

The principal merit of the British system is that it imposes minimal
demands on the taxpayer. He does not know how it is that he pays
what he does, but he does not need to. But there is a range of substantial disadvantages. If withholding is to work, it is necessary to have a
single basic rate for the vast majority of taxpayers—a company cannot
be notified of the different marginal rates of tax of all of its shareholders. We shall argue in subsequent chapters that this is not an unduly
serious restriction. More seriously, the absence of any general end-of-
year assessment constrains the solution to a whole series of problems.
How can we reform local authority finance? How can we achieve a sensible relationship between the tax and social security systems? How can
we establish independent sources of finance for devolved assemblies?
And the experience of other countries suggests very clearly that it is

more expensive to maintain the apparatus required to achieve exact withholding than to accept lower standards of withholding and process an annual return from every taxpayer. For these reasons, Eire is the only other country to have followed the British model.

We believe Britain should bring its procedures into line with the rest of the world. That requires, as a first stage, the abolition of the schedular system, by which different rules are applied to different kinds of income and liability is based on the sum of incomes which were received in a hotchpotch of different years. We propose instead that tax due in any year should be based on income in that year, with an annual assessment of an individual's total income. Many people will find it incredible that this does not already happen. If the present system did not exist, it is inconceivable that anyone would propose it should be introduced.

The second step is the abolition of the cumulative P.A.Y.E. system. Under a non-cumulative P.A.Y.E. system, an individual would be credited each week with 1/52 of his annual allowances, so that a person with a single personal allowance of £1,565 would be allowed up to £30·10 per week tax free. He would pay tax at the 30% basic rate on the excess, so that with earnings of £50 in a week the tax due would be £5·97. If income accrues evenly throughout the year, he will pay just the right amount of tax. With a progressive tax system, however, a worker whose earnings fluctuate from week to week may pay too much tax. If his 'good' weeks push him into a higher tax bracket, the rate at which he pays extra tax on his extra earnings will be greater than the rate at which his liability falls in the 'bad' weeks, and hence he would be due a refund of overpaid tax at the end of the year. Surprisingly, in countries where this operates this 'over-withholding' and consequential refund is generally rather popular with taxpayers (Barr *et al.*, 1977, p. 143). But we have already seen that to make the British withholding system work it is necessary that most taxpayers should pay the same basic rate of tax—which means that over-withholding would rarely arise. We can only operate a cumulative P.A.Y.E. system, it seems, if we do not need one.

We believe these reforms are necessary and desirable within the context of the present income tax system. We also think it essential that computerization be introduced as fast as possible. These administrative changes are prerequisites for the more fundamental structural reforms which we discuss in subsequent chapters. The Inland Revenue's principal administrative objection to our proposals for an expenditure tax is apparently that it would require annual returns from all taxpayers (Commissioners of Inland Revenue, 1979). We cannot imagine that they are unaware that this is currently the general practice in every other major country in the western world.

The black economy

There is evidence of increasing concern about the growth of the 'black economy'. The black economy includes the moonlighting plumber who expects to be paid in cash, the waiter who fails to declare his tips, the barmaid who is paid from the till at the end of the evening; all those areas of legal activity from which tax is properly due but from which it is not collected because the income in question is not declared. By the nature of the phenomenon itself, it is hard to find evidence on the extent of the black economy. But in research, as elsewhere, fools rush in where angels fear to tread. In order to protect ourselves from possible libel actions, we leave it to the reader to distinguish one from the other in the following account of evidence on the subject.

It is sometimes suggested that trends in the black economy can be inferred from movements in the use of notes and coin in payments. The most obvious point to be made is that for a long period the volume of transactions has increased more rapidly than the use of notes and coin. Thus the prima-facie case to be made from this data is that the black economy has been steadily declining. A much more likely explanation is that changes in money transmission habits in the legitimate economy, particularly the increased use of cheques and credit cards, have reduced people's needs for cash. With some strain on credulity, writers such as Feige (1979) have reinterpreted this information to assert that the black economy is large and growing. While that might be true, the problem of estimating demand for money functions has already produced one of the largest and least conclusive literatures in economics and the notion that this can be done with sufficient accuracy to enable trends in the black economy to be inferred from the residual is absurd.

The Central Statistical Office has claimed to have detected 'a glimpse of the hidden economy in the national accounts' by comparing income- and expenditure-based estimates of national product (Macafee, 1980). While at first sight this sounds promising, more careful consideration of how black economy transactions are recorded, if at all, suggests that some would be recorded as income only, others as expenditure only, and some as neither, depending on the precise measurement techniques employed. It is also unfortunate, if not surprising, that statistical revisions subsequent to the publication of the article have largely eliminated the discrepancies on which its findings were based. The article's title, though modest, is perhaps not modest enough. The Chairman of the Board of Inland Revenue suggested in 1979 that the black economy might be 7½% of national income, a figure subsequently modified to a 6%–8% range. This figure does not appear to be based on any survey or on other evidence and in the absence of any substantiation no real weight can be given to it.

A different approach was adopted by Dilnot and Morris (1981) who examined the income and expenditure records of households which spent significantly more than they claimed to earn. Discrepancies of this sort for which there was no other apparent justification were sufficient to account for between two and three per cent of recorded income. This painstaking micro-economic research seems to us much more likely to identify the black economy than generalizations based on broad aggregates or anecdotes, but it suffers from the difficulty that people engaged in large-scale tax fraud are unlikely to participate voluntarily in surveys of their income and expenditure, whatever guarantees of confidentiality they may be given.

Tax authorities have the great advantage that, unlike academic researchers, they can compel people to have their income surveyed. By far the most substantial study of the black economy is the American Taxpayer Compliance Measurement Programme (IRS, 1979). This computes the additional income recorded, and tax assessed, when households are subject to detailed audit of their affairs; and uses statistical techniques to estimate the total income and revenue which would be obtained if the whole population could be subjected to infinitely detailed scruitiny. The Internal Revenue Service concludes that between 91% and 94% of income from legal sources is reported to it.

These indications that the black economy may be quite small may come as a surprise to the many people who bore their friends, and the authors of this book, with endless stories about people who demand payment in cash, although the view that all cash transactions are outside the formal economy is as fallacious as the belief that all cheque transactions are reported to the Inland Revenue. It is a fact that most economic activity in the UK is in the hands of large organizations which as a matter of course comply with legal requirements to report income and output and to withhold tax. This concentration is not wholly a desirable fact; and the black economy, if kept within very limited bounds, is not necessarily to be regretted. The existence of small amounts of economic activity on which the marginal rate of tax is zero, much of which would simply not be undertaken at all if it were confined to the formal economy, may reduce the disincentive effects of taxation. When this achieves proportions which encourage large scale fraud or lead to a cumulative collapse of the moral force of the tax system, our reactions should be rather different; what is the honest taxpayer in Italy to do? But there is nothing more likely to encourage such fraud and such collapse than the wide circulation of exaggerated, and unfounded, reports of the extent of 'black' activities.

Nor, it should be stressed, is it worth spending £1 to collect £1 in tax. The money paid in salary to the revenue investigator, or the social security snooper, represents resources diverted from productive activity; the money they retrieve from the illicit window-cleaner is simply a transfer from his pocket to the wallets of better-disciplined taxpayers. The proper measure of the product of such expenditure is the cost—in administrative costs, in compliance costs, and in the resulting distortion of economic activity—of collecting that same revenue by other means.

Tax avoidance

Poor people who engage in the black economy are illegally evading tax. Richer people diminish their tax liabilities by legal tax avoidance. Like the black economy, tax avoidance has come under increasing scrutiny. The mechanisms by which Lord Vestey, the 'master butcher' and one of Britain's richest men, has avoided paying any significant amounts of tax over an extended period have been given much publicity. So too have the activities of Roy Tucker and his Rossminster Group, who were leaders in the construction of elaborate avoidance schemes in which convoluted series of artificial transactions were devised with no ultimate consequence other than the creation of a tax deduction for the customer, a profit to the inventor of the schemes, and a loss to other taxpayers. Extreme cases of this kind have now come to an end, under the twin blows of a—literal—frontal assault on Tucker's premises by representatives of the Inland Revenue and a ruling by the House of Lords that transactions which have no shred of commercial motive cannot give rise to a tax deduction.

We shall stress at other points in this book the importance of looking at how the tax system actually works, and that this is particularly important in examining its effects at the upper end of the income distribution. But we should make the general observation that, as Kaldor put it, 'the existence of widespread tax avoidance is evidence that the system, not the taxpayer, stands in need of radical reform' (Kaldor, 1980, p. 18). Tax avoidance cannot be defeated by appeals to the conscience of taxpayers—nor should it. The annual accretion of new provisions to deal with recently discovered avoidance devices is inevitably ineffective also; the Revenue put themselves in the position of men who go to shut the stable door every time they see a horse bolting.

THE TAXATION OF EARNINGS

THE most important changes to have occurred in the British tax system since we wrote the first edition of this book are the very substantial reductions in the higher rates of tax. Table 3.1 illustrates the effect of the changes at various salary levels. More concretely, the tax due on the salaries of around £100,000 of the chief executives of major companies such as B.P. and I.C.I. was reduced by £20,000 or £400 per week.

TABLE 3.1

Tax rates on high-paid employees, 1978–83

Gross income (£)	Marginal tax rate (%)		Average tax rate (%)	
	1978–9	1982–3	1978–9	1982–3
12 000	40	30	23·1	18·9
15 000	55	30	27·9	21·1
20 000	70	45	36·4	24·8
25 000	75	50	43·7	29·2
30 000	83	55	49·6	32·7
50 000	83	60	63·0	43·0
100 000	83	60	73·0	51·5

Figures are for a married man with £2,000 of other allowances.

In the last ten years, the maximum tax rate on earned income began at 91%, was reduced to 75%, raised again to 83%, and has now been cut to 60%. The top rate on investment income has been at various times 91%, 90%, 98%, and now 75%. Maximum rates of 60% and, more doubtfully, 75%, are realistic in a way that rates over 90% are not. We think it should be obvious to anyone who stops to think about the matter for a few minutes that it is entirely impracticable to tax things at 98%. The pressure to avoid tax becomes so strong that virtually any avoidance scheme becomes worth while, and no aspect of the activity is of any importance other than its tax implications. Even if as a result of measures for avoidance four-fifths of the receipts disappear, the after-tax returns have been multiplied tenfold; and if finding loopholes is so profitable it will prove impossible to stop them up.

We hope that the oscillations we have described above have come to an end, and these new moderate levels of maximum rates persist. But we doubt it; and suspect that further political changes will bring further changes in this part of the tax schedule. The reason is that this debate is conducted in a political fantasy world, in which one side professes to believe that these high rates have massive disincentive effects on economic behaviour and on innovation and enterprise in the U.K. economy; while the other asserts that they are a necessary mechanism for achieving redistribution and a fair distribution of the overall tax burden. There is very little evidence to support either of these propositions. They ignore the central fact about these apparently punitive rates; they are unenforced and unenforceable. They have principally been paid by senior managers in large corporations, and it is doubtful whether these people are primarily motivated by the likely effects of their additional effort on their after-tax earnings. Thus the disincentive effects are much less than often suggested. On the other hand, if one identified the wealthiest individuals in the U.K. one would find rather few senior managers among them. In consequence, these very high tax rates have had, and are capable of having, very little effect on inequalities in living standards. We argue these points in more detail in Chapters 3 and 4, and return in Chapter 5 to assess the consequences and point to needed reforms.

Taxation and effort

The effects of income taxation on work effort are a continuing subject of concern and discussion. This is not surprising—'reduce my taxes so that I can work harder' is generally a more winning argument than 'reduce my taxes so that I can be better off'. Unfortunately, this makes this an area in which it is hard to disentangle rhetoric from evidence.

In Chapter 1 we described how an income tax would affect work effort in two ways. The income effect describes the way in which tax reduces the taxpayer's real income. It leads him to take less leisure and to do more work, in order to maintain his standard of living, and is a function of the average rate of tax. The substitution effect depends on

the way in which tax makes additional work less attractive than additional leisure and is related to the marginal tax rate. This analysis
suggests that if we wish to identify those people on whom the effects
of taxation on effort is likely to be greatest, we should look at cases
where the substitution effect dominates the income effect—typically,
where the marginal tax rate substantially exceeds the average rate.
It is not necessarily there, however, that most economic damage is
likely to be done by taxation. This will occur at the points where the
marginal rate of tax is highest and hence the substitution effects are
greatest. The total damage done will depend on the numbers of people
falling into such categories as well as the size of the effect.

We now turn to the actual British tax structure. High marginal rates
are encountered in Britain at income levels where higher rate tax begins
to bite effectively—at incomes of £15,000 and above at 1982–3 rates—
and increasingly at higher incomes. But they arise also at below-average
income levels (those below £5,000 p.a.). The reason why this latter
group may pose a problem is not due solely to the operation of the
income tax—the rate faced by people in this category is much the same
as that for those on somewhat higher incomes—but to its interaction
with the wide range of *ad hoc* means-tested benefits which exists in the
U.K. Since these benefits are gradually (or in some cases suddenly)
withdrawn as income increases, there is an 'implicit tax rate' applicable
to each benefit. This 'implicit tax rate' is the proportion of any rise in
income which is lost as a result of an offsetting reduction in benefit.
These rates vary from item to item. They include 50% for family
income supplement (F.I.S.), 17–21% for rent rebates, and 6–7% for rate
rebates, and it is quite possible for several to be operating simultaneously. Each of these involves a different means test, with somewhat
different criteria, so that the actual marginal tax rate faced by a
low-paid worker may be anything between zero and a figure above
100% depending in an arbitrary way on his particular combination of
income and family and other circumstances. (This is the so-called
'poverty trap', discussed in Chapter 7.) But the typical rate is clearly
in excess of those applicable at higher incomes. So the function which
relates the marginal tax rate to the income of a U.K. employee is U-
shaped: the rate of tax he pays on additional earnings is high at low
incomes, falls as income grows towards average income, where it stabilizes at around 39%, before rising again with higher rates of tax.

Disincentive effects will therefore be most marked at the lowest and
the highest levels of income. It is to these—especially the former—that

most attention has been given in empirical work. There are a number of econometric studies of the effect of changes in wages on the number of hours worked and since taxation alters the effective wage we can infer its likely significance from them. These analyses raise rather difficult technical issues of interpretation, which are by no means fully resolved, and we refer the reader to the surveys by Stern (1976) and Godfrey (1975). Here we can only summarize the currently prevailing assessment, which is that the effect is not very large, and that it is probably negative—that an increase in a worker's wage leads him to do less work rather than more. This implies that the income effect of higher earnings in permitting increased leisure is greater than the substitution effect's encouragement to additional effort. This may seem startling, but it should not to anyone who has observed that better-paid workers tend to work shorter hours and receive longer holidays than those who are poorly paid: and that as the general level of earnings has increased over the last century or more hours of work have tended to diminish.

This does not, however, show that a progressive tax system has little disincentive effect nor, as we have argued above, that such effects are unimportant. A change in wages leads to both income and substitution effects, while it is the substitution effect which matters in assessing the welfare consequences of progressive taxation. By estimating the sizes of these two effects separately we can judge the likely impact of various taxation systems, and this distinction can be achieved with these econometric methods. Nevertheless, there is still little evidence for large substitution effects. This position is supported by some of the few experimental studies to have been undertaken in economics. The Penn–New Jersey N.I.T. (negative income tax) studies were undertaken in the late 1960s by the U.S. Office of Economic Opportunity, which offered a selection of low-income families fixed lump sum payments in return for a fraction of their earnings, and compared their activities with those of a matched control group. The results of these studies have been generally interpreted as indicating that the effect of taxation on work incentives is small.

Although this evidence is suggestive, it cannot be regarded as decisive. We have noted that there are technical problems involved in statistical studies of this kind and these may bias the conclusions towards insignificant results. Moreover, the studies are necessarily concerned with easily measurable dimensions of performance at work, such as hours of work or earnings in a particular occupation. If workers are deterred from seeking or accepting promotion by the effects of taxation, then this will not be adequately measured by these methods (though it seems improbable that incentive effects, if large, would be confined to those items which cannot easily be appraised). Further, the hours and the effort which people put in at work are closely related to group norms: if these norms are influenced by the existence of taxation, as seems quite likely, then there may be effects on group behaviour which are not fully observable in the actions of individual workers. Although an individual may not be able to choose to work a seven- or a nine-hour shift rather than one which lasts for eight hours, the reason for adopting some particular shift length will be related to the wishes of workers generally; if taxes were different, it is very possible that most people would want to work for longer or shorter periods and that the normal shift length would be changed.

A final, but very important, reservation is that all our discussion so far—theoretical and empirical—relates to what we might describe as 'primary' workers: people who may decide to work more or less but for whom the question of whether or not they enter the labour force is not in doubt. But there are also 'secondary' workers—married women are the most important group in this category—who may choose to work or not according to a range of considerations which will clearly include financial ones. For such workers, what affects their decision to enter the labour force is not any marginal rate of tax but the average rate of tax on the whole of their earnings. This may, depending on the treatment of the tax unit, be affected by the earnings of their husband (in the U.K. it is). The influences on these work/leisure decisions are rather different, although the operation of income and substitution effects may be similar in its end result—taxation by reducing the net earnings of the husband encourages the wife to work but by reducing the net earnings of the wife has a disincentive effect also. The empirical evidence suggests that this aspect of labour supply is much more sensitive to changes in wage rates or taxes than the hours or effort of primary workers: these are determined mainly by conventional expectations and fixed commitments of the family, while it is the wife's labour supply that provides the margin at which adjustments are made and where the main effects of changes in incentives are likely to be observed.

Somewhat different considerations arise in evaluating incentive effects at the other point in the income distribution at which they may potentially be important—near the top. Here we are primarily concerned with managers. We are also more concerned with the quality of effort than with its quantity. The performance of a senior manager may often depend less on how long he spends in the office than on how well he works when he is there—though there may, but need not, be some correlation between the two. His incentive to do better lies not in overtime payments for extra hours but in the hope of promotion and, to a much greater extent than for lower-paid workers, in the intrinsic satisfaction of the job itself. These factors mean that it is much harder, and more subjective, to assess the effects of taxation on managerial effort. Experimental studies are excluded, and there is no body of data which is even potentially available for econometric assessment. Such evidence as exists is derived from interview surveys, which are not (here as in many other economic contexts) a very satisfactory method of investigation: they can reveal attitudes to taxation, but these are not necessarily good indicators of what people actually do. Thus a recent survey (Opinion Research Centre, 1977) established that those with high incomes were more likely to consider the present income tax 'not sensible' but that is neither surprising nor very helpful.

The most carefully designed surveys of the impact of taxation on the higher-paid are those of Break (1957) and Fields and Stanbury (1971). Both these are studies of British solicitors and accountants. These groups are likely to be relatively well informed about the tax system, and are also in a better position than most to vary their effort and hours of work. Break found that only 13% of his sample made plausible reports of disincentive effects of taxation and that the proportion credibly describing incentive effects was almost as great. However, the former (though not the latter) proportion rose substantially with income, as the theoretical analysis would suggest it should, and reached 30% for those with incomes over £5,000 a year. (This is equivalent to between £30,000 and £35,000 at 1982 prices. In 1956 it implied a marginal tax rate of about 70%: the effective rate on such an income would now be 55%.) Fields and Stanbury replicated Break's work in 1968, and found that disincentive effects had significantly increased: the proportion of their sample reporting these was 19%, and this increase occurred primarily among those on moderate incomes: the fraction among the highest income group remained at 30%. These figures tell us the number of people who plausibly claim that taxation affects their work effort. They do not, however, tell us the magnitude of the effect on those who are influenced: and they are difficult to interpret adequately because they fail to distinguish income and substitution effects. Nevertheless, they are consistent with the hypothesis which was supported for low-income earners; disincentive effects exist, but they are not substantial. A further indication is provided by the observations both of Break and of Fields and Stanbury that the hours of work of those reporting disincentives differed little from the rest of their sample. They interpreted this as implying that those most affected were by nature more hard-working: there are alternative, and less disturbing explanations.

A somewhat different kind of interview study is that of Fiegehen and Reddaway (1981). A selection of companies were approached to ask what difficulties they had experienced as a result of the impact of taxation on their senior executives. They were particularly concerned with cases where managers emigrated, or refused to return from overseas postings, or where suitable candidates were reluctant to accept senior positions. They discovered that the incidence of such problems was negligible. This will surprise only those politicians and industrialists who have repeatedly asserted the opposite. It would be surprising if large numbers of men aged 45–55 were willing to tear up their roots and transfer their families to another country in order to earn larger salaries unless under very acute financial pressure; and even more surprising if people with successful careers in industry declined to join the Board because they thought the additional after-tax remuneration inadequate.

This does not demonstrate that high rates of tax on senior managers have no adverse effects. It is evident from Britain's economic performance that the quality of industrial management in the U.K. has been relatively poor, while Britain's international reputation in the professions, the provision of financial services, and in academic studies, is comparatively high. It is possible to argue that industrial management is intrinsically less attractive than these alternative careers, and that the British tax system has made it difficult to offer the material rewards which are used in other countries to offset this.

The high rate of tax may also have contributed to a decline in managerial morale in Britain in the 1970s. This decline is well documented—see, for example, Opinion Research Centre (1977). It is doubtful, however, whether tax was more than one element in a complaint about decline in real incomes; and it is likely that the average rate of tax (which was not so exceptionally high) is more important for this than the conventional disincentive effects of high marginal rates.

Our discussion of disincentive effects so far relates to the amount of work which people do, given that they choose some particular occupation. But the effects of taxation on whether they choose that occupation at all may be of as much or more practical importance. There are three levels of choice in this decision. First, there is the issue of whether people choose to live in the U.K. rather than in some more lightly taxed jurisdiction—the effects of taxation on the decision to emigrate. We defer a brief discussion of this issue to Chapter 14. Second, given that people live in the U.K. there is the question of whether they choose to work at all or not; we have already noted this possibility for 'secondary' workers, but retirement is also a decision which may be postponed or brought forward in the light of financial considerations influenced by taxation, and this was one of the effects noted by Break. There is a growing body of evidence to suggest that the retirement decision is sensitive both to tax rates and to the relationship between pension entitlement and earnings from work done after the official retirement age (the 'earnings rule' and similar provisions). (Zabalza et al., 1979.) Unlike most disincentive effects, which depend on marginal rates of tax, 'all-or-nothing' decisions to emigrate or to retire are principally determined by average rates of tax on the whole of earnings—it is difficult for most people to retire a little more or a little less and impossible to emigrate a little more or a little less.

A further issue is the way in which taxation affects choices between jobs. It is well known (for example, Goldthorpe et al., 1970) that car factories, as one example, tend to recruit workers who attach especially great importance to financial rewards and give low priority to a satisfying work environment. Income taxes reduce substantially the differential between jobs like these and others which are less well paid but more congenial. Some friends of the authors are badly paid academics rather than well-paid tax inspectors because they do not feel that the net addition to their income would compensate them for the loss of their friends and fulfilment in their work. High marginal tax rates will make it more difficult to recruit people to these less attractive occupations; though it is important to note that a society which feels it needs to recruit a certain number of tax inspectors will therefore be forced to raise their pre-tax salaries and thus part of the incidence of the income tax will fall on the employer rather than the employee.

Fringe benefits

Higher marginal rates of income taxation lead to income being sought and given in untaxed or lightly taxed forms. Thus the employers of well-paid workers in the private sector will tend to offer, not a salary, but a 'total remuneration package', which will include a range of fringe benefits. Such benefits are generally provided on a more extensive scale in Britain than in most other countries: and as a proportion of salary they tend to rise sharply at the same points in the scale as do marginal rates of tax.

TABLE 3.2

Total remuneration, excess over basic salary
%

Grade	U.K.		France	W. Germany
	1975	1978	1975	1975
Superintendent	18	18	7	8
Works Manager	23	29	7	21
Manufacturing Manager	26	33	8	27
General Manager	26	37	13	29

Sources: Diamond Commission, Report No. 7. (1979); Hay–MSL Ltd. (1976).

What are these fringe benefits? It is difficult to determine any sensible borderline between conditions of work and benefits. The employer who provides a congenial wash-room for his employees is presumably simply offering a reasonable working environment, while the one who installs a coloured suite in the bathroom of their homes is providing a fringe benefit; but there is a spectrum of benefits in between, and taxation will lead to a tendency for all of them to be substituted for earned income. The cruder forms of fringe benefit, such as the coloured bathroom suites, are liable to be taxed. Holidays are clearly a means by which managers can substitute leisure for taxed income, and their incidence increases with status and remuneration: 42% of top managers have over 21 working days' holiday in the year, compared with 4% of clerical workers and a negligible proportion of manual workers (B.I.M., 1974). Most companies provide meals in some form for their employees while on duty—indeed, large firms are legally obliged to do so. They are not obliged to subsidize them, but implicitly or explicitly most do. This benefit is generally available to all workers but tends to be on a significantly more lavish scale for the higher-paid.

Most firms provide some form of medical and life insurance benefits for managerial employees (and not, in the main, for lower-paid employees). But the most significant benefits provided for them are usually company cars and pensions. The expectation that an employer will provide a car for his top employees is confined to the U.K., where it is more or less universal: 94% of top managers were provided with a company car for their personal use in 1975 (Diamond Commission Report No. 3, 1976). A survey of company attitudes showed clearly that the main motivation for this is the provision of a tax-efficient fringe benefit rather than any transport requirement (B.I.M., 1974). Since 1978 such benefits have been somewhat more heavily taxed. More stringent provisions are now also applied to loans at low interest rates; the best known of these are the cheap mortgages provided by many financial institutions to their employees, although since the interest on these loans would generally be eligible for tax relief the tax advantages to such arrangements are limited. Nothing of the sort, however, applies to pension provisions. Contributions by employees are fully tax-deductible and no liability arises from the value of the employer's contribution. These benefits are limited only by a restriction of the pension which can be paid (before inflation adjustment) to a (tax-free) lump sum of one and a half times final salary and a pension of two-thirds (one-half if the lump sum is taken) of this salary, taxed as earned income.

These provisions are so generous that it is not surprising that the term 'deferred remuneration' has been coined to replace 'pension' as a description of these benefits at high income levels. It is now the case that at top managerial levels high salaries have become more important for the pension entitlements which they confer than for the net of tax value of the salary itself. An addition of £1,000 to the final salary of a 60% taxpayer is worth £400 to him in cash; but it permits the company (if his service with it exceeds twenty years) to make him a tax-free retirement payment of £1,500 and an annual pension of £500 p.a. thereafter (taxable, but in most cases at lower rates). We shall discuss pensions further below: but these provisions not only represent a significant erosion of the tax base but involve a restructuring of remuneration in a form whose impact on incentives is dismal. Whatever view one takes of managerial motivation, it is difficult to believe that it is encouraged in desirable directions by a system in which the most important form of payment to senior employees is their pension. And while it is clearly desirable that retiring employees should be provided with adequate pensions, there is nothing to be said for an outcome in which this becomes hopelessly confused with measures for tax avoidance.

This is reflected rather generally. Partly because incentive payments are often not pensionable, the British tax system encourages benefits such as cars and pensions which are status-related rather than incentives which are performance-related. Table 3.2 showed how Britain runs ahead of an international league in the former kind of supplement to salary; Table 3.3 shows how it runs behind in the latter.

How seriously should we take this proliferation of fringe benefits? It is an inevitable consequence of high marginal tax rates, and while the scope for it can be reduced it cannot be eliminated since in the end no tax authority can or should hope to prevent employers making the lives of their workers more congenial. These benefits do represent a significant erosion of the apparent progressivity of the tax schedule but it is probably only in small firms, where the distinction between personal and corporate expenditure is often unclear, that the erosion is very substantial. The most serious objection is their distorting effect on the ways in which remuneration is paid. First, since many employees do not greatly want these benefits and would, if they could get it, prefer cash in their pockets, they represent a straightforward source of economic inefficiency. Indeed the more stringent the tax regime is in outlawing more attractive fringe benefits the greater these losses are likely to be. But perhaps more serious is that by diverting money which might otherwise be paid as salary into conspicuous items of consumption—company cars, longer holidays, and lavish expenditure on offices, accommodation and travel for senior executives—high tax rates may well serve to increase the visibility of differentials and the extent to which they are resented. Many people would find it easier to see why their employer should pay more to those with greater responsibilities than why he should offer them larger desks and plusher carpets, and it is difficult to disagree. Pensions are a much more serious problem, and we return to this in the next chapter.

TABLE 3.3

Bonuses and incentive payments as % of basic salary, 1975

Grade	Median earnings, U.K. (£)	U.K	Australia	France	W. Germany	Canada	U.S.A.
Foreman	3200	2	5	1	0	1	2
Superintendent	5150	1	0	3	2	3	4
Production manager	7080	4	2	4	5	4	6
Works manager	9170	4	5	6	8	9	12
Manufacturing manager	13 200	5	4	6	16	13	18
General manager	16 950	6	10	13	11	15	23
Managing director	22 570	4	1	n.a.	n.a.	20	30

Source: Hay–M.S.L. Ltd. (1976).

THE TAXATION OF
INVESTMENT INCOME AND SAVINGS

WE noted at the beginning of Chapter 3 that the maximum rate of tax on investment income was reduced from 98% in 1978-9 to 75% in 1979-80. But anyone who paid an effective rate of tax on his investment income of anything resembling 98% should have sought competent professional advice. There are at least three major methods of getting round the taxation of investment income in this country, and together they enable those potentially liable to this tax to drive a coach and horses, or perhaps a large Rolls Royce, through the structure of the tax.

The first of these methods arises because capital gains are not taxed as income but at a maximum rate of 30%. Since many forms of investment income can be turned without difficulty into capital gains (and back again if desired), this is what any sensible higher rate taxpayer will do. Consider the case of a 75% taxpayer wishing to invest £100 for a secure return over a period of about five years. He might consider investing this in Treasury 12% Stock 1987 which could in August 1982 be bought for around £100 and which would have paid him £12 gross in interest in each of the next five years—on which he would have paid £9 in tax, leaving him a net £3 per annum—and have returned his £100 in 1987. Before doing this, however, he would have been wise to consult a competent stockbroker, who would have advised him to purchase Transport 3% Stock 1988 instead. £100 in nominal value of this stock yields £3 per annum till 1988 when it will also be repaid at £100. But because of the low interest rate it offers, the price of this stock is well below £100: it could have been purchased on the same day for about £75 per £100 nominal. Thus he could have purchased for his £100 stock with a face value of £133. This would pay £3·99 in gross annual interest, from which he would retain a net 99p which might help to cover the cost of the telephone call to the stockbroker. But he would make over the five years a capital gain of £33 (which on Government Stock is tax-free), since his stock will be redeemed in 1988 for £133. This is equivalent to an annual income of about £6. It is a minor nuisance to receive income in a lump sum at the end, but since the stock is readily marketable and can be relied on to appreciate steadily in value from 1982 to 1988, he can, if he wishes, receive an annual income by selling off each year sufficient of the stock to maintain at about £100 the capital value of the amount invested.

Thus by a suitable choice of investment, the 75% taxpayer could earn a perfectly secure annual income of between 6% and 7% per annum, or more than half the 12% which is available to someone who pays no tax. The effective rate of tax is therefore not 75%, but something in the range 40%–50%. Everyone connected with the investment business knows this, and indeed the Bank of England now issues stocks with low coupons like Transport 3% precisely because they will be attractive to higher-rate taxpayers. Better still, perhaps, for such taxpayers are the new indexed stocks: the 2% Treasury Index-Linked Stock 1988 will, if prices rise by more than 30% over the next five years, yield a greater capital gain than Transport 3%. The magnitude of the gain is less certain in money terms, but more so in real terms. Stocks issued by companies, rather than the government, may be subject to capital gains tax at 30% but it is unlikely that there will in practice be any chargeable gain.

Higher rate taxpayers not only buy stocks such as these, but also property and ordinary shares in companies. All of these investments are also held by tax-exempt institutions (such as pension funds), and since property and shares regularly provide an income yield (rent or dividends) which has recently averaged between 5% and 10% less than the secure fixed income from Government stocks it follows that these institutions must expect capital gains of at least that amount. If these expectations materialized, then the higher rate taxpayer could anticipate a total return (after both income and capital gains tax) of perhaps 5%. In fact he should do better than this, since he can invest in so-called 'growth stocks' which offer particularly low incomes but high opportunities for capital gain. Examples are to be found in rapidly expanding sectors such as electronics; thus G.E.C. or Racal yield less than 2% and the expected return on owning them is the capital gain expected from the expansion of their turnover and profits. Similar opportunities—such as reversions, properties with low current rents due for eventual review— exist in other fields. Investment trusts exist whose objective is to eliminate taxable income by turning it into capital gains (which are then favourably taxed), though these have not had the success for which their promoters or investors had hoped.

It is of course true that these capital gains are in the main less certain than the income yield from investment. Thus this part of the tax system operates so as more or less to eliminate the secure components of the returns from wealth while leaving the variable component unscathed. It is therefore a substantial inducement to speculative investment. Paradoxically, this is a factor which tends to increase inequalities of income and wealth. But it is likely that in recent years, with a volatile stock-market and collapsed property boom, it has destroyed more fortunes than it has made. In consequence, private investors have shown strong inclinations to seek greater security, and in all recent years the personal sector has been a substantial net seller of equities and a net purchaser of fixed interest securities, as individuals seek the safer haven of secure capital gains from stocks like Transport 3% 1988.

At present, at least £3,000 m. is invested in Government stocks which are clearly unattractive to anyone who is not a higher rate taxpayer: some examples are shown in Table 4.1. The tax system has, in effect, pushed private investors out of traditional 'middle-of-the-road' investments like good-quality equities, properties, and bank deposits and into fringe activities like 'performance shares', geared investments in property, and portfolio investment abroad, as well as higher rate taxpayers' stocks, which promise—but do not necessarily deliver—above-average capital gains. This is part of the general mangling of patterns of savings and investment in this country by the tax system, to which we shall return.

The second difficulty in the taxation of investment income is that a good deal of income accrues to institutions rather than to people, and is consequently taxed on a different basis. The most important of these institutions are life insurance companies, corporations, and trusts. Since the income of these is, for obvious reasons, taxed at much less than 75%, it is clearly convenient for higher rate taxpayers to arrange for their income to be accumulated by an institution rather than by themselves. This is less convenient if they actually wish to spend the income, since it cannot be distributed to the ultimate beneficiary without being subject to tax: but this difficulty can be surmounted if the taxpayer spends his *capital* while using the accumulated interest to replace it over time. This system is so easy to operate that its most extreme abuses have been checked: the investment income of bogus companies is liable to be attributed to its owners, as is the income of a trust which is permitted to pay money out to the person who put it in.

TABLE 4.1

Government stocks for higher rate taxpayers

Stock			Yield to 75% taxpayer*	Gross redemption yield	Yield on comparable stock
Exchequer	3%	1983	5·151	8·357	9·315
Exchequer	3%	1984	4·268	7·070	9·787
Treasury	3%	1985	4·549	7·333	9·598
Treasury	3%	1986	4·711	7·461	10·063
Treasury	3%	1987	4·515	7·151	10·244
Transport	3%	78/88	5·214	7·749	10·185
Gas	3%	90/95	5·225	8·299	10·785
Redemption	3%	86/96	5·211	8·387	10·720
Funding	3½	99/04	4·883	9·184	10·504

* Assumes income tax of 60% plus investment income surcharge of 15% on coupons received. Capital gains tax assumed to be zero.

All figures based on prices at 12 October 1982.

Source: L. Messel & Co.

But there are so many variations on the theme that there are still many that can be played.

A simple example of how this works is as follows. Consider someone with £1 m. of capital, on which he can earn 12%, but who is liable to the top marginal rate of tax. He could obtain a taxable income of £120,000. But he would do better to spend half his capital setting up a trust to accumulate for the benefit of his children. The income of such a trust will generally be taxed at 45% (30% basic rate plus 15% investment income surcharge), so that if the trust can earn 12% also it obtains 6·6% after tax and will in ten years time be worth around £1 m. so that he has maintained his wealth for his children. In the meantime, the settler can spend the remaining £500,000 and such interest as he can earn on it at a rate of almost £60,000 per year. If he failed to take action of this kind and simply invested for income, his income after tax would be £30,000 per year with a tax rate of 75%—half as much. With a tax rate of 98%, he would keep £2,400: this simple piece of tax planning would multiply his spending power by a factor of 25. For people who are not rich enough to set up trusts, life insurance policies can be used in a rather similar way.[1]

[1] These measures will also have effects (normally advantageous) on capital transfer tax liability. See Chapter 10.

The third loophole in the taxation of investment income is the simplest and probably the most widespread. This is simply to buy durable goods. If investment in shares, in bank deposits, or in investment property is very heavily taxed, it is not very surprising that many rich people buy large houses, or several houses, valuable pictures and furniture, cars, hobby farms, and so on. Such purchases yield no taxable income: their main return is the pleasure they give to the owner, his family, and his friends—which does not have to be very great to exceed the net of tax return they would obtain from more productive investments. These items can be expected broadly to maintain their real value in the long run: if they generate capital gains, these are lightly taxed, and then only if they are actually sold. Thus the tax system not only diverts private funds away from productive purposes, but into forms which encourage the kind of conspicuous display of wealth which its architects were presumably hoping to reduce.

The three methods we have described—the transformation of income into capital gains, the use of an institution to hide income while capital is spent, and the diversion of wealth into non-income-yielding forms—are by no means the only ways round the heavy taxes on investment income nominally imposed in the British tax system. But to list them is sufficient for our present purpose. This is to show that these taxes are entirely farcical, and despite the appearance of swingeing rates rising to 98% anyone who is paying an *effective* tax rate on such income of more than 50% ought to obtain better professional advice. Given that this is so, it is interesting to speculate on the motives of those who are responsible for imposing these taxes. It is possible that they do not know how little they correspond to reality, but it seems unlikely. It is possible that although the politicians and administrators most closely involved know that the appearance of immense progressivity is a sham, they believe that this appearance will deceive others into thinking that such objectives are being achieved. It is hard to imagine that the deception is successful, and the explanation is not one which flatters either group. The hypocritical nature of the present situation reflects little credit on the British tax system or on the British political system.

Taxation and savings

A major effect of the British tax system has been its effect on savings behaviour. Mill's dictum that 'no income tax is really just, from which savings are not exempted' (1865, p. 404), i.e. no income tax is just unless it is an expenditure tax, has not been generally accepted. But there are three forms of savings which do receive exemption or highly favourable tax treatment: investment in owner-occupied housing, pension funds, and life insurance. In consequence, these means of saving now account, in aggregate, for almost the *whole* of net personal saving in the U.K. (Table 4.2). We consider each of them in turn.

Owner-occupied housing is given favourable tax treatment in several different ways. The income which is derived from it is not subject to tax. This concept of income from owner-occupation puzzles many people, who see their houses as items of expenditure, not of income. If individual X rents a house from individual Y, the rent which is paid is taxable income in the hands of Y. But if X and Y happen to be the same person—i.e. if the owner of the house is also the occupier—no money actually changes hands and so the tax liability disappears. There is therefore a strong tax incentive for them to be the same person—a bias in favour of owner-occupation as against renting. At one time, tax was imposed on the notional 'income' from an owner-occupied house, under schedule A of income tax legislation. This tax was based on the rateable value of the house, a sum which was computed primarily for the purpose of levying local rates, and which purported to be the amount for which the property could have been rented in 1939. These figures became increasingly ludicrous, and when rateable values were revised in 1963 the Government was confronted with the option of either facing angry reactions to enormous increases in the amount of tax payable under schedule A or abolishing it altogether: they adopted the latter course. In addition to the exemption of this schedule A income the interest paid on loans of up to £25,000 for house purchase attracts tax relief. As we have noted, the anomaly here is not so much that this interest is deductible but that other interest payments are not. And finally, while capital gains in general are taxed those which are obtained on the taxpayer's principal residence are exempt.

It is the experience of most commentators on taxation that there is nothing more calculated to provoke a flood of apoplectic letters to the newspapers than the suggestion that the tax system is unduly favourable to owner-occupiers. Although the existence of the tax privileges we have described is incontrovertible, the writers of these letters have a point. What the tax system favours is owner-occupation, not owner-occupiers, and this distinction is not always made clear. It is not simply taxation which has led to the disappearance of private rented housing in this country—the existence of rent control and other legislation to

TABLE 4.2

Personal saving in the U.K. and U.S.A.

	1974	U.K. (£ m.) 1976	1978	U.K. average 1974–8	% U.K. 1978	U.S.A. 1976
Total personal saving	6655	10 256	12 962	100	100	100
Investment in houses	1702	2393	3199	24·5	24·7	34·2
Superannuation funds Life insurance	3493	5398	7976	55·6	61·5	26·4 10·5
Total, privileged savings	5195	7791	11 175	80·1	86·2	71·1
National savings	−11	592	1532			
Govt. stocks and local authority debt	1240	1977	123			
Co. securities and unit trusts	−1149	−1256	−1749			
Total, securities	80	1313	−94	4·5	−0·7	5·3
Building society deposits less lending for house	1969	3301	4906			
purchase	−2370	−3872	−5321			
Bank or finance house deposits	3037	1554	3855			
less personal borrowing	−186	−1035	−2420			
Miscellaneous financial assets	–	–	–			
Total net deposits	2450	−52	1020	14·2	7·9	25·5
Other and unclassified	−1070	1204	861	1·1	6·6	−1·9

U.K. average is average of 1974, 1976, and 1978 weighted to reflect change in prices using R.P.I.
Sources: CSO, *Financial statistics*, April 1979, Table 10.2; CSO, *Monthly Digest*, April 1979, Table 1.7; *Statistical Abstract of the U.S.*, 1977, Table 707.

protect tenants has probably been more important—but this has un-doubtedly been a contributory factor. The result is that the only widely available forms of tenure in this country are now local authority housing and owner-occupation, and people who are not interested in or not eligible for the former have little alternative to the latter.

They are then faced with buying houses at prices which have been forced up by the tax-stimulated demand for them: prices which reflect the capitalized value of the tax concessions, as described in Chapter 1. Because mortgage finance for house-buyers is not unlimited, it is unlikely that these concessions have been fully capitalized, and housing is still probably the best investment available to private individuals even now, but it is certain that house prices are higher than they would otherwise be. Thus current house-buyers obtain relatively little benefit from the concessions. Indeed they may be worse off, since young married couples are forced to save for deposits towards house purchase or to repay associated mortgages at a time in their lives when incomes are low, outgoings high, and large compulsory savings of this kind inappropriate. In a better-organized world, many people in this category would rent property, at least for a time, and that is what they do in many other countries.

The principal losers from these features of the tax system have been people who might have preferred to rent property—people who find mortgage repayments a very serious burden, people who have or would like to have jobs which involve frequent movement around the country. The principal gainers have been those who have owned houses in the past—or rather their descendants, since capital gains on the house you are living in are virtually unrealizable. Perhaps if it had been understood that the main beneficiaries of the policy of tax concessions to owner-occupation were the dead the policy might have been adopted somewhat less enthusiastically. (Their descendants will also benefit, and we consider in Chapter 10 whether it might be possible to achieve rather greater equity and recoup some lost revenue by imposing taxes when owner-occupied houses are passed on to the next generation.) But this account demonstrates why tax capitalization is such a dangerous trap—although we believe it would be better if the system had never incorporated these concessions it does not seem that it would now be either equitable or desirable to withdraw them. The losses from so doing would be principally borne by those who are currently struggling to meet the initial mortgage repayments on a house—people who have derived little benefit from the concessions and who may actually have suffered from them.

The second favoured form of personal saving in the U.K. is life insurance. The most important concession is that the Inland Revenue will contribute 15% of the premiums on a 'qualifying policy', provided total premiums do not exceed the greater of £1,500 or one-sixth of the payer's income. The funds of life insurance companies are favourably taxed. Although they are liable to corporation tax at 37½%, a rate substantially in excess of the basic rate of income tax, very little tax is in fact paid—in 1981, gross investment income on ordinary business was £4,670 m. and U.K. tax paid £263 m. (Life Offices Association, 1982). The principal reason for this is the treatment of expenses (Kay, 1982). Policies which qualify for these subsidies also exempt their holder from any liability for higher rate tax on the profits derived from them. Without these tax concessions, life insurance would be a thoroughly unattractive method of saving. Kay examined the results of 61 companies for a 10-year endowment insurance policy with profits maturing in 1976. The median proceeds for a man aged 39 who had invested £10 per month were £1,593, an effective rate of return of 6·1%. If he had simply deposited the money in a building society paying the standard interest rate recommended by the Building Societies Association, the same individual would have accumulated £1,621 over this period. He would also have been able to reduce, increase, or discontinue payments and to withdraw part or all of his savings at any time, so that it is likely that, given a free choice, he would have preferred to do so: and if he had saved regularly in this way almost all building societies would have paid him an enhanced rate of interest, increasing his proceeds by something between £50 and £100 and outperforming all but a handful of life insurance companies. The returns from 'without profit' policies were much worse: the median outcome from a sample of 46 companies was £1,306 (which should be compared with the £1,200 paid to the company over the period).

This picture is transformed by the tax subsidy: investment in a life insurance policy would have brought tax relief over the period totalling just under £200 while the building society could have offered nothing of the kind. The effect of this is to increase the number of insurance companies which 'beat' the building society from 19 out of 61 to 59 out of 61. (Even with this help, no non-profit policy gave an acceptable return.) It is very clear why life policies are an increasingly popular form of saving in the U.K., while in the U.S., where the tax advantages attached are very limited (see Goode, 1976), such contracts have steadily declined in importance: they comprised 11·7% of net personal financial assets in 1945 and 8·9% in 1970 (Bureau of the Census, 1976).

This discussion ignores the 'pure insurance' element of these contracts: the obligation on the company to pay a guaranteed sum in the event of the premature death of the policy-holder. However, the insurance content of the majority of contracts sold as life insurance policies is negligible. The actuarial value of the insurance element of the policies described above is about £8—less than 1% of the premiums paid and actually less than 5% of the tax relief obtained. Anyone substantially motivated to take out such a policy by insurance considerations was seriously misinformed—though in view of the selling efforts associated with the industry it is possible that some people were. This means that any justification of the present tax relief must relate to the desirability of contractual savings programmes, rather than life insurance as such—yet recent legislation has been explicitly aimed at denying relief to such plans unless they are disguised as life insurance policies.

The third form of privileged saving is through pension funds. Provided the fund meets a series of Inland Revenue criteria, pension contributions (whether made by employer or by employee) are excluded from income, and no tax is levied on the investment income of pension funds; but payments out of such a fund are taxable in full as earned income (except for the quarter which may be commuted as lump sum). In effect, savings of this kind are exempted from taxation while withdrawals are taxed, in just the manner which would be applied to all savings under an expenditure tax, which we discuss in Chapter 5 and 6. As a result, such schemes have been growing very rapidly. This growth is certain to continue, as social changes and legislation extend the coverage of occupational pension schemes to include manual as well as white-collar employees.

These factors have had very dramatic effects indeed on the structure and composition of personal wealth in the U.K. Over the twenty-year period for which data are available, the proportion of personal wealth which these three forms of privileged asset—houses, life insurance policies, and pension funds—comprise has risen from about 40% to over 65%. The details are set out in Table 4.3, and comparative figures are provided for the U.S.A. Since the rise in importance of housing overshadows the increasing role of life insurance and superannuation schemes, it is worth emphasizing that as a proportion of financial assets alone these two comprise 44% (U.K., 1979); 26% (U.K., 1957); 24% (U.S.A., 1976).

These privileged assets all have certain characteristics in common. They are all what one might loosely describe as civil servants' assets rather than entrepreneurs' assets. They are all well suited to people who have conventional intentions and predictable career prospects, but not to those who have no settled plans, who wish to take risks, or who have undertain incomes. They are all highly illiquid: none of them can readily be realized in an emergency, to tide over in the period between

TABLE 4.3

The composition of personal wealth
%

	U.K. 1957	U.K. 1979	U.S.A. 1976
Houses	26·6	—	50·8
(less mortgages)	(7·5)	—	(14·4)
Net housing	19·1	43·3	36·4
Life insurance	8·9	{25·0}	4·4
Pension funds	11·7		11·1
Equities	22·0	8·9	18·6
Bonds and Govt. securities	23·4	3·3	9·2
Deposits	21·6	14·4	26·7
Other wealth less borrowing	(6·6)	(5·1)	(6·4)
Total wealth per head (£, Dec. 1976 prices)	2980	5681	10 715

Notes: 1976 figures refer to 31 December. Estimates are based on balance sheet data.
Sources: Revell (1967); Financial Statistics: *Statistical Abstract of U.S.*; *International Financial Statistics*.

jobs, to start a business, or to buy or expand one. Two of them significantly reduce mobility between locations and between occupations. Indeed it is a notable feature that while it is normally part of the function of wealth to enhance economic freedom and personal security, these assets contribute very little to that. Each imposes contractual commitments which must be met even in adverse circumstances. Money in the bank increases an individual's ability to disagree with his employer: wealth which principally takes the form of accrued pension rights reduces it. (Although transferability of pension rights has been increased substantially, such rights are in almost all cases more valuable to those who remain with their present employer, and this is particularly true in the private sector.)

One result of this is that Britain now has the most attenuated small business sector of any country in the industrialized world. The Bolton Committee (1971) found that of thirteen countries it examined the proportion of manufacturing employment in small establishments (less than 200 employees) was lowest in the U.K. and was not much more than half that of the average of the other countries surveyed: and for very small firms the contrast is even more marked (Prais 1976, p. 160). Technological factors are of course an element in the decline of small firms but they can hardly account for the fact that while the number of small firms in the U.K. has halved in the last forty years it has almost doubled in the U.S.A. (Bolton, 1971, para. 6.9). Nor does such evidence as is available suggest that these trends result from the peculiar preferences of the British for large-scale organization. A recent international survey (*Vision*, 1977) showed that 61% of workers in Britain would prefer to work in firms with less than 500 employees. More significantly, Britain emerged as having much the highest proportion of the population who had thought about setting up their own business and the lowest percentage (after Holland) who had actually done so. And the finding that the median age of small firms in the U.K. is (at 22 years) three times what it is now in the U.S. and four times what it was in the late nineteenth century (Bolton, 1971, paras. 6.14–15) does not suggest that youthful vigour is characteristic of what remains.

The other side of this coin is the rapid growth in the size and significance of institutional investors. In the stock-market, personal shareholders have been persistent sellers of equities and financial institutions persistent buyers. In consequence, the distribution of holdings has been transformed as shown in Table 4.4. Not only are these institutional holdings large, but they are held in large units. Individual shareholdings of £100,000 or above represent almost 90% of the value of equities held by insurance companies (Erritt and Alexander, 1977). It is impossible to deal in quantities approaching this volume in the shares of any but a small number of large companies, and so the horizons of institutional investors are necessarily limited. Thus the growth of the institutional investor has not only channelled funds away from the smallest companies—in 1971 it was estimated that the total made available from these sources to companies with under 200 employees was about £7 m. (Merrett-Cyriax, 1971). It has also promoted concentration among very large companies, a process which has also gone beyond levels which have been achieved in other comparable countries or which are easy to justify on economic grounds (Hannah and Kay, 1977, Table 8.4 and *passim*).

But the influence of the institutional investor has not been confined to the market in company securities. Life insurance companies, and to a lesser but still substantial extent pension funds, are committed to paying or guaranteeing fixed monetary amounts at dates rather far in the future. These guarantees are intrinsic to the concept of conventional

TABLE 4.4

Ownership of shares by category of beneficial holder
(%)

Holder	1963	1969	1975	1980
Personal sector	56·1	49·5	39·8	32·8
Financial companies and institutions	30·4	35·9	48·1	54·1
Other	13·6	14·6	12·2	13·2

Source: Erritt and Alexander (1977), Economic Trends (July 1982).

life insurance contracts, though it is not obvious that they are of much value to investors, since the purchasing power of the amounts provided is quite unpredictable. The most successful recent developments in the life insurance industry have come from those who saw how the tax advantages of life policies could be obtained while this feature was abandoned (through 'unit-linked' life insurance). Nevertheless, it has been and remains true that insurance companies are anxious to invest a proportion of their funds in long-term fixed interest loans. Such loans are unattractive to most borrowers for much the same reason as they are unattractive to most lenders, but there are two main groups who are keen to borrow in this way—the Government, which can print money to finance repayment, and property developers, who were generally thought to be in a better position than industry generally to provide security of capital and income against such borrowings. In 1974 long-term loans financed 44% of the net assets of property companies; the corresponding figure for firms in manufacturing and distribution was 18%. (Business Monitor M3, 1977). The prominence of life insurance companies as willing holders of Government stock has made funding operations a good deal easier throughout the post-war period, though with more benefit to taxpayers than to policy-holders as such stock has lost the major part of its value during the period. These possibilities have also made life easier—indeed possible—for property developers, and those who feel that this activity has been somewhat over-emphasized in post-war Britain should note the central role of the availability of long-term mortgage finance and the origins of this availability.

Taxation and distribution

Consider the career of someone now retiring from a senior position on the board of one of Britain's largest hundred corporations. Such a person would probably have begun his managerial career just before, or just after, the Second World War and might in the late 1940s have been earning £200 per year. Moving rapidly ahead of his contemporaries he might twenty years later have expected to earn £15,000 per year; with promotion to the board and inflation in the 1970s this figure increases rapidly and he earns £30,000 or more for six or seven years before retiring with a peak salary of perhaps £50,000. Few people are as successful as this: there are perhaps twenty people starting work this year who can aspire to these heights.

Our hypothetical manager has fairly frugal tastes, and throughout his lifetime has reckoned to save around a quarter of his after-tax income. This means his maximum annual expenditure was around £12,000. On retirement, the accumulated wealth of such a man would approach £100,000. Feeling, with some justice, that he has been unusually fortunate in his career and unusually thrifty in his actions, he may be somewhat surprised to discover that there are in Britain at least 100,000 people richer than he is, and that they control well over 20% of all personal wealth. The example illustrates a central, but poorly realized effect of the British tax system—but one which is an inevitable consequence of a system in which high rates of tax on earned income are seen as the major redistributive device. There is a large number of very rich people in Britain, but the proportion of them who become rich as a result of personal savings from their own earnings is negligible.

If the much lower maximum rates of tax introduced in 1979 persist for the next thirty years—or even the next ten—then the results of the sort of calculation we have presented will look very different. But the picture we have painted is historically accurate—it is possible that in future senior managers will be able to accumulate really substantial wealth from their salaries but that has certainly not been true in the past. Where then does the wealth of the rich come from? It is likely that some are in fact professional managers, since as we have noted above the impact of taxation on high earnings is not quite what it seems—but it is nearly what it seems, and it is not likely that many top wealth-holders are in this category. There are virtually no employees in other sectors who are as well paid as such a manager—a handful of lawyers, accountants, actors, and sportsmen. The main sources of wealth are necessarily inheritance and capital gains, and most fortunes are the product of some combination of the two. Thus Harbury and Hitchens (1979) found that 60% of their sample of top wealth-leavers had fathers who were themselves in the top 1% of the wealth distribution, and over 80% had fathers who were in the top 10%. Industrial occupational categories do not, unfortunately, distinguish proprietors from professional managers: but the industrial breakdown given by Rubenstein (1974) suggests strongly that it is primarily the former who are the business men represented among the top wealth leavers.

Of course, to say that inheritance is close to being a necessary condition for wealth and that capital gains are the main route to increasing it is not to suggest that there is no relationship between wealth and personal exertion. Small business men are generally in the position of being able to turn part of the earnings of setting up or expanding their firms into lightly taxed capital gains, although it is important to recognize that it is difficult to realize these gains without relinquishing partial or complete control of their operations. In the study by Harbury and McMahon the two sectors in which the influence of parental wealth on the fortunes of the son is smallest are engineering and finance: the former is the area of the industrial economy where small firms remain most prominent, while finance embraces those sectors in which earnings can be most readily and conveniently taken in the form of capital gain. That the expansion of a small engineering firm is a major route to self-made wealth is not something which causes us concern. The prominence of the financial sector here is rather more disturbing, since one does not have to take a wholly unsympathetic view of the activities of the City to believe that the correlation between private gain and social benefit is probably less strong in this area than it is in manufacturing industry and within the sector itself it is generally easier to defend the utility of those actions which generate high earnings than those which generate major capital profits.

The normal justification of inequalities of wealth derives from the need to sustain enterprise and effort. But it is difficult to survey the kind of evidence we have been describing without feeling that only a rather small proportion of major wealth inequality in the U.K. actually serves this function. Under the present U.K. tax system it is not too difficult to stay rich, but it is distinctly difficult to become rich— though these difficulties operate haphazardly, and with a degree of differentiation between sectors which seems, if anything, the opposite of that which consciously determined social priorities might dictate. It is not surprising to discover that the degree of concentration of wealth in Britain has been declining, though slowly (Table 4.5).

But we attach importance not only to the concentration of wealth but to the mobility which underlies it. A concentrated structure is more acceptable if it is held by a changing group of people who are enjoying in their own generation the rewards of their own achievement than if it is owned by those whose families have always owned it—both because such a distribution should arouse less resentment and because such inequality is more likely to serve a function which is of benefit to the population as a whole. There is justice both in the left-wing criticism of the tax structure for its failure to shake concentrations of wealth and privilege, and in the right-wing criticism that it deprives people of the returns of effort and initiative. The present system has given us the worst of both worlds with maximal disincentive effect for minimal redistributive impact. It is not difficult to propose reforms which would lead to improvements on both counts, and these we will discuss in subsequent chapters.

TABLE 4.5

Trends in the distribution of personal wealth in the U.K.

| | Share of different percentile groups in total wealth (%) | | | | | | | |
| | England and Wales, adult population | | | Britain, over 18 | | U.K., over 18 | | |
Group	1911–13	1938	1966	1966	1971	1971	1976	1979
Top 1%	69	55	31	31	28	31	25	24
Top 5%	87	77	56	55	51	52	46	45
Top 10%	92	85	69	69	65	65	61	59

Taken as over 25 in 1911–13, 23 in 1923 and 1938, 19 in 1966. Figures for 1938 and 1966 (England and Wales) not strictly comparable.
Sources: Revell (1965); Atkinson and Harrison (1978); Diamond Commission
1979, Report No. 7, Tables 4.4 and 4.5; Social Trends 1982.

THE CHOICE OF THE TAX BASE

IT should be clear from the previous chapter that many of the weaknesses of the U.K. tax system arise from the absence of a coherent view as to what should constitute an individual's 'taxable income'. We have illustrated this by pointing to several difficulties in the existing structure of the tax system which have become increasingly evident in recent years.

Firstly, there is a case for shifting part of the tax burden from earned income to some wider measure of an individual's wealth, to reflect his total resources or consumption over his lifetime. Secondly, the present taxation of capital income, especially in an inflationary era, is most unsatisfactory. Thirdly, whatever view one takes about the appropriate tax treatment of savings in general, it is clear that the discrimination among different forms of saving has some undesirable effects. These considerations lead us to believe that it is time to take a fresh look at the basis of our tax structure.

Suppose we go back to square one and ask the question, 'What principles should guide the choice of the tax system?' In the theory of taxation two different lines of thought may be detected.

One traditional approach is to say that since taxes are levied to finance collective expenditure on services which either cannot be provided by the market, or which the Government of the day chooses to supply from public funds, then the amount of tax paid by an individual should be related to the benefit which he derives from public expenditure. This school of thought has become known as the 'benefit theory' of taxation. But it is very difficult to measure these benefits because people can rarely be excluded from enjoying the benefits of many forms of public expenditure. Financing national defence or public television by voluntary subscription is usually found to be impracticable, and the tax authorities and detector vans are called in to help out the state.

The objection to the benefit theory of taxation is not, however, based only on its impossible demands of human nature. We simply do not know the distribution of benefits of public expenditure, and there is little prospect of discovering it. How can we measure the benefits which any particular individual derives from defence, the police, or the Department of Industry? An alternative approach is to say that for a given level of public expenditure, the total cost of financing it should be divided among individuals according to their 'ability to pay'. The idea behind this is that an individual should make a contribution according to the 'sacrifice' which the tax burden imposes upon him, and that individuals should make equal sacrifices. This is not equivalent to saying that each individual should pay the same amount of tax because a rich man can pay much more tax than a poor man while being said to suffer the same 'sacrifice'. The evident difficulty of defining exactly what is meant by 'equal sacrifice' explains why the 'ability to pay' approach, like the benefit theory, has not contributed a great deal to the resolution of practical problems.

One reason for this is the confusion of two quite distinct issues. The first is the question of what is the best index of an individual's 'ability to pay.' Obvious candidates include income, wealth, and consumption. The second question arises once we have chosen a parti-cular index, income for example. How should the tax burden be distri-buted among people with different incomes? In other words, how pro-gressive should the income tax be? For the moment we shall consider these issues separately. In this chapter we examine the former, returning to the latter question in Chapter 14.

A natural way to measure an individual's ability to pay is his ability to earn. This, however, contravenes a basic criterion for a feasible index, which is that we must be able to *measure* it. What someone actually earns is not necessarily a good guide to what he could earn. A man who has the ability to produce a great deal but chooses to lie on a beach all year round will pay no tax. It would be difficult to prove that he had the ability to earn enormous sums, and impossible to measure at all accurately what he might have earned. Before this approach to the taxation of potential earnings is condemned as unjust and illiberal, we should recall the widely held belief that owners of property should pay full rates even if the property concerned is empty. The owner of an empty office-block is regarded as just as worthy an object of taxation as the owner of a building which is fully used.

Politicians and administrators charged with the responsibility for collecting taxes will be more interested in what measurable indices or tax bases they could use. At this stage we may distinguish three potential tax bases—wealth, income, and expenditure—the values of which measure how much an individual owns, earns, or spends respectively. Despite the fact that the idea of a tax on wealth is a relatively recent idea in the U.K. (as proposed by the Labour Government in a Green Paper in 1974, Cmnd. 5704), it has been used in many other European countries and was a favourite tax in times gone by. Representatives of the monarch rarely had the time to compute people's annual income or expenditure, and they would estimate an individual's visible wealth (acres of land of different types, numbers of servants and cattle), and levy a wealth tax at regular or irregular intervals depending on the Crown's needs. Such a tax is better described as a tax on assets than one on wealth in its widest sense, because there are important components of wealth which cannot be measured, such as the right to a future income or pension, or an entitlement to continue living in a subsidized house. The most important component of wealth which cannot be measured is simply the present day value of the future earnings which an individual may earn, sometimes described as 'human capital'. Apart from the special cases of slaves and football players there are no markets to enable us to put a precise monetary value on the stock of human capital. For this reason it is clear that wealth is not suitable as the index or base for the main source of tax revenue, a conclusion which is borne out by the current practice in all developed countries. Because of this we shall defer further discussion of capital taxes until Chapter 10.

Income and expenditure as tax bases

In more recent times, as we have seen in Chapter 2, income was used as the index of ability to pay and this has become the norm in all countries. Nevertheless, there has always been a strong intellectual tradition ranging right across the political spectrum including such figures as Hobbes, Mill, Fisher, and, more recently, Kaldor, which has argued in favour of the use of expenditure as the measure of an individual's ability to pay. In this tradition two arguments have been deployed for the superiority of a tax based on expenditure over income tax.

The first justification for taxing an individual on his consumption is that it is more just to tax someone on the value of what he takes out of society in terms of the goods and services which he consumes, than on the value of what he contributes to society, whether in the form of earnings in return for labour services or interest in return for the supply of capital services. This argument is usually supported by reference to the famous question of Hobbes,

What reason is there, that he which laboureth much, and sparing the fruits of his labour, consumeth little, should be more charged, than he that liveth idly getteth little, and spendeth all he gets: Seeing the one hath no more protection from the commonwealth than the other? (Hobbes, *Leviathan*, Ch. XXX)

The answer to Hobbes is twofold. Firstly, there is no obvious reason to regard a tax on what an individual actually consumes as evidently more *just* than a tax on the total economic opportunities of the individual which measure his potential consumption. A one-legged unemployed man who manages to maintain a low level of consumption by begging is unlikely to be seen as just as suitable an object of taxation as a wealthy miser who chooses to spend very little and counts his money each night. A tax on potential consumption has as much claim for the title of a fair tax base as a tax on actual consumption. Secondly, Hobbes's example is very misleading. The injustice arises, so it would appear, because one individual enjoys a good deal of leisure ('living idly' while his neighbour 'laboureth much') and this is not taken account of when his tax bill is computed. This, however, has nothing to do with the distinction between income and consumption. If we consider Hobbes's example and look a year or two into the future, then the man who had worked hard, saved, and now wanted to enjoy the fruits of his work and saving in the form of consumption would, under Hobbes's regime of an expenditure-based tax, find himself facing a heavy tax liability. Both an income tax and an expediture tax discriminate in favour of the 'idle', and unless we are prepared to tax people on the basis of what they *could* earn there is nothing we can do about it.

A more relevant distinction between an income tax and an expenditure tax is their treatment of saving, and this has been used as the second main argument for a tax on consumption. With an expenditure tax consumption incurs the same tax liability (for a given schedule of tax rates) regardless of the year in which the individual chooses to consume. There is no discrimination between those who prefer to spend while young and active, and those who prefer to spend in retirement. An income tax, on the other hand, is said to discriminate against saving because it gives rise to the 'double taxation of savings'. The reason for this is the following. Consider a world in which the only tax is an income tax, and two individuals who earn the same amount and hence pay the same tax. The first decides to spend everything this year and pays no more tax. The second decides to save up and spend the money next year. Because he saves he receives some interest on his savings, but under an income tax he is required to pay further tax on his interest income, and this has been described as double taxation. Although there is some force in this argument the position is more complicated than the simple label of 'double taxation' might imply. It should be obvious that what matters is not the number of times tax is paid (whether it be double, treble, or quadruple taxation), but the total tax burden. The important questions are whether taxing interest income discriminates between immediate consumption and deferred consumption, and whether this discrimination is a serious problem. On the first point, we have to decide whether the after-tax interest which the individual receives is less than the rate of return which the nation earns on investment which can be financed out of the individual's savings. In fact this is a complicated issue which depends on, among other things, the taxes and subsidies on investment by companies. Without delving further into these complications we may say that on average the U.K. income tax does provide a small incentive to immediate consumption and hence a disincentive to saving by individuals (see King and Fullerton, forthcoming).

Whether it is a first priority to remove this discrimination is another matter. There are certainly other distortions in the capital market which affect savings decisions. Access to opportunities for borrowing is not available to all, and in one important market, that for loans for housing, mortgages are rationed among those individuals who would like to borrow more at prevailing interest rates. But if we tried to calculate what would be the best way of taxing interest income, taking account of all the existing market imperfections, we would not only require an extensive and detailed knowledge of how these imperfections affected savings behaviour, but we would be most unlikely to come up with a system resembling the current tax treatment of saving. Hence there is a strong argument for not trying to introduce arbitrary elements of discrimination unless we are sure we are influencing decisions in the right direction. Although we believe that the 'double taxation of savings' implied by an income tax is an argument for an expenditure tax, it is not the only one nor even the most important argument. Indeed, it is necessary to correct a common, but mistaken, impression that the main argument for an expenditure tax is that it would encourage savings. We know little about the response of aggregate savings to changes in interest rates, and it is clear that, despite the large negative real rates of return on savings of recent years, people have gone on saving. Recent studies in the United States by Boskin (1977) and Howrey and Hymans (1978) yield conflicting evidence about the response of aggregate saving to interest rates, and it seems unlikely that changes in the tax system would have a major effect on savings. The important thing is not to distort individual decisions more than is necessary, and the attraction of an expenditure tax is not so much that it would remove a disincentive to savings in general but that it offers a practicable way of eliminating the differential taxation of particular forms of saving and capital income.

Given that it is unrealistic to think of calculating a special tax rate for each form of saving and each type of income, and given the anomalies which have been introduced into the present system by 'special concessions', there is a powerful case for choosing as the tax base either income or expenditure, but not a mixture of the two. The arguments in principle for choosing between income and expenditure, which we have discussed above, do not seem to us to lean heavily in one direction or the other. Either base can be defended and the decisive arguments come from a consideration of what the respective tax bases imply in practice. So we shall now examine in more detail the implications of an income tax and in the next chapter we shall turn our attention to an expenditure tax.

The definition of income and the 'comprehensive income tax'

It may seem too trite to observe that to operate an income tax it is necessary to have a clear definition of what constitutes 'income', but the sad truth is that no single definition of income commands universal assent. Those who either doubt, or are surprised by, this statement are referred to the voluminous literature on the subject (some of which has been brought together in the volume edited by Parker and Harcourt, 1969).

One of the most popular definitions of income remains that of J. R. Hicks (1939) who suggested that 'income is the maximum value which a man can consume during a week, and still expect to be as well off at the end of the week as he was at the beginning' (p. 172). Unfortunately, it is not an operational definition, either for an accountant or a tax inspector. The difficulty lies in the word 'expect'. How can other people possibly determine what I expect? And what are they to do if my expectations are unreasonable? Accountants and revenue officers must work with verifiable facts, and hence they must look, not at what I could have *expected* to consume during a week or a tax year, but rather at what I could *in fact* have consumed while still remaining as well off at the end as at the beginning.

Unfortunately, these two concepts are not the same. If things always materialized as I expected, then there would be no divergence between them: but of course things never do. Consequently, if events go well for me in some particular year—I win the pools, my shares prosper, and my forgotten rich Australian uncle dies—my receipts in that year will be greater than I could have expected them to be, or can expect them to be next year. My 'income', defined in terms of what I could have consumed in that year, will be greater than my income in the Hicksian sense of what I could have expected to consume, and greater than my long-run spending capacity. Conversely, if I have an unexpectedly bad year, in which my shares collapse, I lose my job, and my wallet is stolen, my receipts fall below my permanent income; anyone who looks at my accounts will see a gloomy picture, but an unduly gloomy one, because these unexpected adversities are unlikely to happen again. An omniscient auditor or tax inspector would seek to remove from the published figures the influence of such events.

Of course, there is no practicable method of doing this; but in raising the problem we can see why the taxation of capital gains, and capital receipts generally, has posed such difficulties for the income and corporation taxes of this and other countries. The problem is that capital gains may arise for a variety of reasons and we would wish to differentiate between the components of capital gains, some of which are equivalent to other components of income and others of which are not. This is clearly impossible and in practice we can only adopt some rather crude categorization which is based on things we can actually measure; accountants have attached importance to the distinction between realized and unrealized gains, while the Sandilands Committee (see Ch. 13 below) distinguished 'holding' and 'operating' gains. The reader may find difficulty with the latter distinction, as did the Sandilands Committee. These solutions are very unsatisfactory, and their proponents have compounded confusion by suggesting that their definitions gave the 'right' answer (for a further discussion of this see Kay, 1977). The distinction between the expected and the unexpected can never be observed, and after a careful consideration of the problems involved Hicks came to the following conclusion about concepts of income, including his own, 'They are bad tools, which break in our hands' (1939, p. 177).

British tax law initially took the view that all capital gains were windfalls and should not pay tax, unless they were obtained by traders in which case they were taxed as income. As we have seen in Chapter 4, it is rather easy to turn investment income into capital gains, and hence the view that capital gains are a different sort of animal from receipts of income has become more and more implausible. The result is the present unhappy compromise in which capital gains are taxed, although at lower rates than income.

Although similar procedures have been adopted in most other countries, there are advocates of the approach of treating all capital gains and most other windfall and capital receipts as income. This viewpoint has been especially popular in North America, but it also appeared in the Minority Report of the Royal Commission on the Taxation of Profits and Income in 1955. Its goal is to tax an individual on his 'comprehensive income', which is defined as the amount which an individual could consume without running down the value of his wealth. Simons has suggested that 'Personal income may be defined as the algebraic sum of (a) the market value of rights exercised in consumption and (b) the change in the value of the store of property rights between the beginning and end of the period in question' (1938, p. 50). It is this definition of personal income which has come to be known as comprehensive income and we can measure it by the value of what he does consume plus the change in the value of his wealth.

A comprehensive income tax (C.I.T.) would remove the present anomalies which arise from the differential treatment of capital gains, but only at the price of introducing substantial anomalies and administrative problems of its own. Capital gains under a C.I.T. would be taxed at full income rates, rather than the current concessionary rates, and, moreover, would be taxed each year as they accrued, unlike the present situation in which capital gains are taxed only when the asset concerned is sold. Such a proposal is clearly impracticable; firstly, it would require that all assets be valued every year; secondly, it would mean that people with illiquid assets (such as houses) would receive tax bills which they did not have the cash resources to meet. We are therefore thrown back on to the taxation of realized capital gains.[1] This is likely

---

[1] The Meade Committee (1978) did, however, suggest a method, albeit complex, for approximating the taxation of accrued gains.

to increase the likelihood of 'lumpy' capital receipts which arise sporadically rather than smoothly over time, and increase the need for adequate averaging provisions. On the other hand, the taxpayer benefits because he can defer payment of tax until the date when he chooses to realize the gain.

It also raises the question of what to do about capital losses. One can hardly tax capital gains without allowing losses to be tax-deductible. Yet this might result in some of the less bright or less fortunate City 'financial operators' being the poorest people in Britain in a particular year (such as 1974 when the stock-market collapsed), according to Inland Revenue statistics, even though they were also still among the wealthiest members of society. They simply cut their losses and sold out. Presumably, individuals of this kind, with low or very probably negative comprehensive incomes, would be helped by 'averaging provisions' so that their losses could be carried forward against future income. This, however, would mean that for one, or perhaps several, years certain individuals who would be both wealthy and enjoying a high level of spending would pay no tax. The prospect of finding City financiers who, on returning from a pleasant stay on a yacht on the French Riviera, were met at Heathrow by a chauffeur-driven Rolls Royce and a note from the Inland Revenue saying that their tax liability for this year had been waived, would send Fleet Street wild with excitement and M.P.s scurrying to put down awkward questions for the Chancellor. Comprehensive income is not an idea which it would be easy to put over at Question Time in the House of Commons.

One of the most serious difficulties with a comprehensive income tax is the adjustment of income measurement for the effects of inflation. We discuss what is involved in some detail in chapter 13; and all the problems considered there are ones which a comprehensive income tax would have to face.

A comprehensive income tax would also seek to deal with the other problems we discussed in Chapter 4 when looking at why the present tax treatment of investment income is so haphazard. It is necessary to ensure that all investment income currently earned by institutions is attributed, by one means or another, to the individual to whom it will ultimately accrue and is then taxed accordingly; only by this means can we reduce the large-scale avoidance of the present investment income tax and reverse the increasing institutionalization of savings. These procedures would have to be applied to trusts, to corporations, to pension funds, and to life insurance companies. This would mean that the income of a pension fund, for example, would be regarded as accruing to the individual who had rights in the fund, although most taxpayers would not appreciate a letter from the Inland Revenue demanding tax on income which they had never seen and which had been received by a distant pension fund. And how could we deal with unfunded schemes (such as that for Civil Servants) or inadequately funded schemes (such as virtually all U.K. occupational pension schemes)? The problems involved in 'unmasking' other institutions such as trusts are hardly less acute. In a rather similar way, but with equal difficulty, we could assess rich taxpayers on the 'income' which they derive from the durable goods which they presently buy in preference to more productive assets which yield taxable income; we might re-impose 'schedule A' on houses and extend it to other valuable items like pictures and jewellery.

It is true that what we have been describing is a rather idealized income tax, and that some of these difficulties could be avoided by not following the definition of 'comprehensive income' to the letter. After all, most of the countries which have a rather more successful record of economic management than Britain do manage to run an income tax, and it is clear that we could reduce some of the problems we have noted in Chapters 3 and 4 by moving in the direction of a comprehensive income tax even if that movement was only a partial one. But the pragmatic approach means that it is only too easy to lose sight of what it is that we are trying to tax, and to ignore the fundamental inter-relations between the different parts of the system or to be blind to their consequences. It is, after all, this pragmatism that has brought us to our present state, in which we are faced with high taxes on earned income which fail to tax spending out of inherited wealth, the almost random taxation of income from capital, the institutionalization of personal saving, and the gradual diminution in the tax base and corresponding increase in tax rates. But it may be inflation that provides the decisive argument. Britain's inflation rate is, and is likely to remain, higher than it has been in the past or in other comparable countries. Further *ad hoc* adjustments to deal with this are necessary, and we can expect that they will be made. But the full set of adjustments which are needed to deal satisfactorily with inflation are daunting, and it is this prospect which directs our attention most firmly to the expenditure base.

An expenditure tax

One advantage of choosing consumption expenditure as the tax base is that we require no valuations of an individual's wealth, and hence we avoid all the problems of measuring depreciation of assets (depreciation of consumer durables is less important and is discussed further in Chapter 6), of indexing for inflation, and of our inability to measure some important components of wealth, such as pension rights or human capital. It is no longer necessary to maintain what must inevitably be an arbitrary distinction between capital and income and this means that we can avoid the complexities involved in the indexation of capital gains and investment income, which, as we have seen, would involve major changes in the organization of capital markets as well as the tax system.

Problems of averaging are likely to be less severe also, because whereas an individual has little control over the timing of receipts of windfall gains he can choose when to spend his resources. Moreover, it seems likely that individuals prefer to maintain a relatively stable pattern of expenditure over a run of years, and not to enjoy a burst of spending in one year followed by relative deprivation in succeeding years. Averaging is achieved not by a set of provisions in the tax system, but by the individual's own voluntary decision on when to consume.

There are two important differences between a personal expenditure tax such as we have outlined, and existing taxes on expenditure often called 'indirect' taxes. A common objection to the imposition of indirect taxes is that they take no account of an individual's personal circumstances, and indeed are often, though not always, regressive. What progressivity does exist is achieved by taxing at higher rates of V.A.T. or excise duties those commodities which are consumed relatively more by the rich than by the poor. Since consumption patterns vary between individuals this is a rather arbitrary and haphazard method of redistribution, which is a blessing to the rich man who loves plain cooking and reading, and hard on the poor man who rejects conventional standards of attire and nutrition and adopts consumption patterns more usually associated with the rich by devoting himself to the consumption of whisky. It is important to realize that this objection cannot be levelled at an expenditure tax which is a tax on the total value of an individual's consumption expenditure during the course of a year. In itself it does not discriminate between consumption on different commodities, and can be as progressive as desired in exactly the same way as an income tax is progressive, that is by the existence of personal allowances and higher rates of tax. The degree of progression in the personal tax system is a quite separate issue from that of whether the tax base is to be income or expenditure.

The second difference between an expenditure tax and existing taxes on expenditure concerns the method of collection, and follows directly from the first. Because indirect taxes depend only on the total value of sales of a commodity and not on the identity and circumstances of those purchasing the commodity, they can be collected in the shops at the retail stage, or from the wholesalers (as was the case with the old purchase tax), or from the purchaser at the various stages of production (as occurs with V.A.T.). With an expenditure tax, however, the amount of tax depends upon the personal circumstances of the consumer, and the tax cannot be collected in the shops in the form of an addition to the bill.

How then can the tax authorities measure the value in any given year of an individual's expenditure? The first thing to say is that it does not require the taxman to follow housewives into the supermarket and surreptitiously observe the figures being rung up on the till. We can measure an individual's expenditure by observing what he does with the various cash receipts arising during the course of the year. He might receive amounts in the form of wages and salaries, tips, interest and dividend payments, gifts and bequests from other people, and he might receive cash from the sale of some of his assets (for example, shares or a house) or from borrowing money. Taken together these items form his total cash 'incomings'. We must also be careful to include items received not in the form of cash, but 'in kind', whether they be inherited goods (such as houses, paintings, or shares) or perks like free motor cars, lunches, and other fringe benefits. (These problems of identifying transactions and of policing the line between personal and business expenditures arise to the same extent and in just the same way with all taxes—income tax, expenditure tax, or V.A.T.) The total 'incomings' are matched by an equal total for 'outgoings' which describe what the individual does with his receipts. Some of these he may give away (to relatives or to charity), some he will use to meet the interest payments or repayments of the principal on loans taken out in the past, and some to save by placing his money in a building society account or by purchasing assets of various types (shares, for example). The remainder will be used to finance his personal consumption. In this way we can see that it is possible to calculate the value of an individual's expenditure by computing his various receipts and payments during the year, and we shall spell out in more detail how this would work in practice in Chapter 6.

It is also clear that some of the other problems associated with an income tax arise from the difficulty of defining an acceptable measure of an individual's *annual* income. In fact we shall now see that if we take a longer view and think of an individual's income over his lifetime, the difference between income and expenditure disappears. To see this let us consider an individual's lifetime accounts and imagine a very careful man who kept a complete record of all his receipts and all his expenditures. On the day after his death we enter his study and find in the left-hand drawer of his desk a complete record of all his receipts over his lifetime filed according to the year in which they were received. We will find his salary slips and notes of interest on bank deposits, perhaps some dividends, his pension while in retirement, and all the amounts which he inherited or received by way of gifts from others. In the right-hand drawer we find a similar set of notes, again filed by year, of all his expenditures and payments over the years, including gifts made by him to others. We also find a statement prepared immediately before his death of his net wealth (assets net of liabilities) which is to be bequeathed to his descendants. Into the left-hand drawer we then insert a file with the sale proceeds of the estate and into the right-hand drawer a file containing the same figure which is equal to the value of the estate passed on to his descendants.

Since the items of 'outgoings' in the right-hand drawer must have been financed in one way or another from the 'incomings' in the left-hand drawer, the total of all the figures in the left-hand drawer equals the total of the entries in the right-hand drawer. We enter the world with nothing, and we leave the world with nothing. Our lifetime accounts must balance. The total of the entries in the right-hand drawer is simply the total value of the man's own consumption and gifts and bequests to others over his lifetime. The total in the left-hand drawer consists of his lifetime earnings, gifts received from others, investment income, and the sum of the net sales of assets over his lifetime including the value of his estate. Since we enter the world with nothing the value of net sales is equal to the capital gain the man has made on his assets over his lifetime. Hence the total in the left-hand drawer can be said to measure the man's total lifetime income, and is equal to the total of what he spends on consumption and gifts to others.

From this we can deduce that the effect of collecting a tax on consumption and gifts made on an annual basis is to impose a tax on lifetime income. We might propose an expenditure tax (including gifts in the tax base) as a superior form of income tax!

In effect, what this tax does is to tax an individual on his lifetime use of resources and for this reason we may describe it as a lifetime expenditure tax (L.E.T.). The intellectual basis for the L.E.T. is different from that of the pure expenditure tax, although its operation is very similar. It is superior to a comprehensive income tax in that, although it can be described as a tax on lifetime income it avoids all the problems associated with an annual income tax which we discussed above, the unequal treatment of human and financial capital, the double taxation of savings, and the difficulty of measuring 'income' in times of inflation.

The arguments advanced in this chapter are the reverse of those normally associated with the debate over income versus expenditure. It is usual to argue that in principle expenditure has many conceptual attractions over income for the tax base, but that there are too many practical difficulties involved in measuring an individual's annual expenditure. We have argued that the choice in principle between income and expenditure is finely balanced, that we prefer lifetime income, but that to measure this the appropriate annual tax base is expenditure including gifts made, and that the compelling argument against a conventional income tax is the administrative complexity of measuring an individual's annual income.

To see how the L.E.T. would operate in practice, we now turn to a discussion of how an expenditure tax might be implemented.

A LIFETIME EXPENDITURE TAX

IN the preceding chapter we concluded that the most promising direction of reform of the U.K, personal tax system involved the transformation of the income tax into a direct tax on personal expenditure. Such proposals have been made before—we noted the distinguished intellectual pedigree of the concept—but it has been generally assumed that whatever the theoretical attractions of the expenditure tax the administrative problems of operating it were overwhelming.

Certainly the historical record is not encouraging. The only country to have recent experience of operating a personal expenditure tax—Sri Lanka—has abandoned it. The U.S. Treasury proposed such a tax in 1942, but the reception it received in Congress was so hostile that within a week the suggestion was withdrawn. N. Kaldor, distinguished dissentient member of the Radcliffe Committee of the early 1950s on the taxation of profits and income, invited consideration of the tax. The Committee consulted the then Chancellor of the Exchequer, and was doubtless relieved when he concluded that such a proposal was much too radical to fall within the terms of reference of a Royal Commission. Kaldor put forward his ideas subsequently (1955), but his work received more attention for its masterly analysis of concepts of income than for its description of taxes on expenditure. Only in India were his arguments found persuasive, but the tax was never a serious one (the number of taxpayers never exceeded 1,000) and was withdrawn in 1966 (Chawla, 1972). But we believe an expenditure tax is a practical proposition, and this is no longer an eccentric minority view. Official reports in Sweden, the U.S.A. and Ireland have shown how such proposals might be implemented in these countries (Lodin, 1967; U.S. Treasury, 1977 Irish Tax Commission (1982)) and the Meade Committee has analysed the possibilities and problems in the U.K. context.

We should stress that an expenditure tax does not operate by requiring an exhaustive listing of every purchase that has been made during the year of assessment. Many people will be familiar with the rueful reckoning of their expenditure on a foreign holiday. It is certainly possible to try to relive your experiences, recording everything you spent—counting the drinks by the swimming-pool, the tip to the taxi-driver, and so on. If your recollections are sufficiently comprehensive, the resulting total will be a good estimate of your total expenditure. But there is a much easier way of reaching a more accurate answer. You simply measure how much foreign currency you took with you, add the amount of currency you bought while abroad, and subtract what was left when you got back. You measure, not the expenditure itself, but the sources of the expenditure, and can thus achieve a simple and reliable measure on the basis of a small number of recorded (and readily verifiable) transactions.

A personal expenditure tax would apply just the same principle. It taxes the sources of expenditure rather than the expenditure. All receipts—whatever their source or nature—are taxable; but any part of them which remains unspent can be deducted in computing liability. We can regard currency you buy as a taxable receipt: the currency you sell back attracts relief. But one problem remains. Some of the things you bring back from holiday have a value that extends beyond the period of the holiday itself. Your expenditure on a bottle of duty-free sherry, or on the bullfight poster that permanently adorns the wall, is attributable not so much to the holiday as to the subsequent days and years in which you drink the sherry and admire the poster. An accurate measure of holiday consumption would require that you list and value every asset of enduring value which you purchased on holiday and subtract that valuation from the provisional estimate of your spending.

Clearly, this is a daunting administrative task, though a necessary one if an accurate measure of that particular period's consumption is required. But the key to devising a feasible expenditure tax is the realization that it is not important, nor even particularly desirable, that this valuation be comprehensive. Suppose a few pesetas are left in your beach shorts until the following summer; then the allocation of expenditure to particular years is inaccurate but nevertheless expenditure over a period of years is correctly measured. And the same would be true if you kept a wallet full of foreign currency for next year's holiday (or purchased a Picasso etching or a bullfight poster). This year's expenditure would be overestimated, and hence a liability to expenditure tax so computed would be excessive; but all you would have done would have been to make a prepayment on account of your liability next year or in subsequent years, and there is no general reason why a tax authority should take exception to that. Normally people would not want to prepay tax in this way, and indeed you can always ensure that your holiday expenditure is accurately measured by returning your unspent notes to the bank so that the amount you did not spend is recorded. But there may be good reasons why taxpayers may choose to make prepayments. It might simply be convenient to do so—and in the case of durable goods (the poster or the Picasso) such prepayment when the purchase occurs is much the easiest way to collect the tax due. Or they might wish to prepay because they expect to pay tax at higher rates in future as their expenditure rises, and they would rather incur liability at their lower current rates. In all these cases, prepayment of tax would be acceptable—and indeed desirable, since it provides an opportunity for those with uneven patterns of expenditure to average their taxable expenditure. The objective of progressive taxation is to impose a higher average rate of tax on those with a higher average level of income (or expenditure). An incidental side-effect is that those whose average income (or expenditure) is no higher but is more variable also pay a higher average rate of tax. The possibility of prepayment diminishes this inequity.

An annual expenditure tax, which seeks to measure an individual's spending in each separate year of assessment, poses very serious administrative problems, because it requires that his assets be assessed annually. A lifetime expenditure tax, under which payments over the lifetime depend on spending during the lifetime but where payments in any particular year are not necessarily related to spending in that year, is a much more feasible proposition. It is also potentially a fairer tax than either an annual income tax or an annual expenditure tax, even in their idealized versions. We now consider more specifically how such a tax would operate.

The introduction of a lifetime expenditure tax would involve the creation of a class of 'registered assets'. These would include business assets and negotiable securities; some deposit accounts with banks, building societies, and other financial institutions would be registered, though we anticipate that current accounts with banks and balances held for day-to-day requirements and short-term savings would not normally be registered assets. The basic principle is that all receipts obtained during a year would be subject to tax, but after summing these receipts the taxpayer would deduct his net purchases of registered assets during the year. The resultant figure would be his taxable expenditure. The structure of the tax is illustrated in Fig. 6.1. Arrows

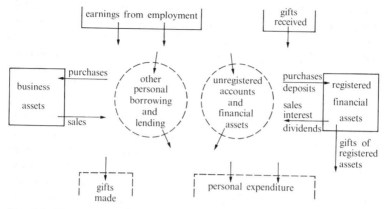

Fig. 6.1. The sources of personal expenditure

indicate flows of receipts and payments. Transactions which cross unbroken lines are the subject of tax payments or deductions, and it is these transactions and these only that the tax collector monitors. Those that cross broken lines do not interest him. It is important to note that these criteria relate simply to cash flows, and that there is never any inquiry into or distinction between flows of capital and flows of income. The tax base is simply the sum of all net receipts which come across the unbroken lines; earnings and gifts, net surpluses from trading, and net receipts from dealing in registered assets. Since lifetime accounts balance, this is equal, over the lifetime, to the sum of all personal expenditures and gifts to others.[1]

The easy questions on the present income tax form would go over to an expenditure tax form more or less unchanged. The first question would still be 'How much did your employer pay you during the year?', and people with incomes only from employment and negligible savings or dissavings would notice no real difference. It is the treatment of savings and investment income that is drastically altered, and the changes mostly represent simplifications. At present, the taxpayer must record the proceeds of sales of securities during the year of assessment, and obtain from his records the corresponding acquisition costs at various different dates in the past: additionally, he must declare his

---

[1] If both registered and unregistered assets exist, and either (a) returns on unregistered assets are certain or (b) the tax is proportional, the lifetime expenditure tax is exactly equivalent to a lifetime income tax, as discussed in Chapter 6. If neither of these assumptions holds, there may be divergences.

purchases during the year so that these can be recorded and related to his subsequent disposals. The gains thus computed are then taxed on a separate basis with a number of available optional treatments and complications. Under an expenditure tax he would simply write down the gross figures for sales and purchases during the year and the net proceeds would be added to his other receipts. The questions would relate to his year's transactions alone.

Similarly, the tax treatment of his trading activities would be much simplified. Tax would be based on the cash accounts of the business, and the proprietor would simply pay tax on the net amount which he withdrew from the business during the year. Life insurance policies would generally be registered assets, so that the whole of any premiums paid would be deductible against tax, but all receipts from policies would be taxable. This would seem to impose a heavy liability when a policy matured, and if the proceeds were spent there would (and should) be such a liability. But if they were not all dissipated immediately tax could be deferred until they were used for expenditure by depositing them in registered accounts, and life insurance companies would no doubt be quick to facilitate such arrangements. Figure 6.2 gives some impression of what an expenditure tax return might be like.

There would be two new sets of questions. One would ask for details of gifts received during the year, including gifts of valuable assets, subject of course to some exemption limit. Receipts would no longer escape tax simply because they had not been earned. Details of accrued interest would not be requested (so those with forgotten bank accounts would no longer be embarrassed when they or the Revenue remembered). Instead, institutions authorized to operate registered accounts would at the end of each tax year notify both taxpayer and revenue of the amount of net additions or withdrawals, and the form would ask for this information.

The simplifications involved in moving from an income basis to an expenditure base arise principally from the shift from an accruals base to a cash flow base. It does not matter whether a receipt is an item of capital or income. It is unnecessary to determine the date of the *transaction* to which any particular item relates; the issue is simply when and whether a particular cash payment occurred. Every question on the expenditure tax form asks only about actual cash payments which took place during the year of assessment. The result is that for taxpayers with simple affairs, the procedures involved in completing an E.T. form would differ very little from those which are required at present;

and for those with more complex circumstances, people who participate in businesses and have substantial investment incomes, the return in Fig. 6.2 would be easier to complete.

Nevertheless, the form raises difficulties through its unfamiliarity, and this is not a negligible consideration. Unsatisfactory though the present income tax system is, a few individuals and most accountants have experience and understanding of its operation. No such expertise is presently available for an expenditure tax system. Taken too seriously, of course, this argument would imply that no change in the tax system could ever be made, however miraculous the expected improvement. But it does highlight the central administrative difficulty raised by the expenditure tax. This is not the traditional 'How would it work?'—the answer to that is 'better than at present, at any rate'—but 'How do we get there from where we are now?'

A radical transition to an expenditure tax

This transitional problem is a serious one. We have described how an expenditure tax could be operated by simply monitoring those transactions which cross the solid lines of Fig. 6.1, and once the new tax system were fully functioning this would indeed be true. Expenditure could only be financed out of sources which were either the subject of a tax charge now, or which had been the subject of such a charge at some date in the past; present or past employment income, trading surplus or gifts, or withdrawals from registered assets. But this would not be true on the day when the expenditure tax was introduced. On that day there would exist a substantial stock of assets which could, unless some procedure were devised for recording its existence and monitoring ing its subsequent disposition, be used for subsequent consumption, and which could be spent without involving its holder in any liability to expenditure tax at any time. Indeed the whole of existing personal wealth would potentially be available for this purpose.

Although the owners of this wealth would not have paid expenditure tax on it, they might in accumulating it have paid income tax: and it would be fair and consistent with the spirit of the tax that this should be regarded as prepayment of expenditure tax. If savings had been derived from taxed income, it is unjust that expenditure from them should be taxed also. As we saw in Chapter 4, however, the proportion of personal wealth in the U.K. which has been accumulated from taxed income is probably rather small. Nevertheless, some of it has been:

Fig. 6.2

Expenditure Tax: Assessment Year 1988

Receipts

1. *Employments* Enter here the total of all payments from
                  your employer (attach form E2)

☐

                  Taxable benefits in kind: see note X

☐

2. *Businesses*   Enter here the gross sales proceeds of all
                  businesses owned or operated by you (list
                  details on form B1)

☐

3. *Partnerships* If you are a partner in any business, enter
                  here the total of all distributions to you

☐

4. *Gifts*   Enter the total of all gifts and inheritances
                  received. You may neglect the first £100
                  from any person (list details on form G1)

☐

5. *Pensions, social security and national insurance benefits.*
                  See note 5.

☐

6. *Securities*   Enter the total sales proceeds of securities
                  sold during the year

☐

                  Enter here the total of all dividends and in-
                  terest payments received
                  (list details on form S1)

☐

7. *Registered accounts* Total of net withdrawals from each
                  account (list on form R1 and attach forms
                  R2)

☐

8. *Life insurance policies* Total of maturities (attach forms
                  L2)

☐

9. *All other receipts* See Notes

☐

10. *TOTAL RECEIPTS* (Total of lines 1–9)

☐

Payments

11. *Employments* All admissible expenses connected with
                  your work (see note Y) (list on form E1
                  unless you claim the standard deduction)

☐

12. *Businesses* Total admissible expenses of businesses
                  owned or operated by you (give details
                  on form B1)

☐

13. *Securities*   Total acquisition cost of securities purchased (list on form S1)   ☐

14. *Registered accounts* Total net deposits in registered accounts (list on form R1 and attach forms R3)   ☐

15. *Life insurance policies* Total premiums paid in the year (if the policy is a new one, attach form L3)   ☐

16. *Other payments* See notes. Give details on form P1   ☐

17. *TOTAL PAYMENTS* (total of lines 11–16)   ☐

18. *NET TAXABLE EXPENDITURE* (Subtract line 17 from line 10)   ☐

Extracts from notes to taxpayers

4. Gifts of registered assets which you have received must be listed on form G1 but need not be included in the total.

5. If you received a pension or social security or national insurance benefits in 1988, you should have received form SS1 at the end of the year. If so, enter the total from it in line 5. If you have not received SS1, contact your local tax or social security office.

6. Gifts of registered assets which you have made count as disposals for this purpose.

9. You must list here all other receipts in 1988 unless (i) they are returns of or on money you have yourself already paid and (ii) you have not claimed tax relief on that payment in this or any previous year (e.g. tips and bonuses must be entered; receipts of principal or interest on loans need not be included *unless* you claimed tax relief when you made them).

11. You may claim a standard deduction of £50. If you wish to claim more you must provide full details on form E1.

Notes to reader

Forms B1, G1, S1, P1 etc. are supplementary statements which need be completed only by those who have items in these categories: the total is then brought forward to the main form.

Forms E2, R2, SS2 etc., are supplied by the institutions involved, and the taxpayer need only transfer the total figures to his tax return.

and the smaller the total amount of the wealth, the larger the proportion of it which is likely to have been subject to income tax at some
time. But there are no rules by which we can hope to distinguish
between wealth which was saved out of earnings and wealth which
originated from capital gains or from ancestors who picked the right
side in the Wars of the Roses. It is possible that one could attempt,
as the Meade Committee (1978) did, to devise some very crude rules
for separating 'life-cycle' and other components of wealth: capital up
to some rather arbitrary figure, perhaps related to age, could be deemed
to have been derived from earnings, and amounts in excess of that a
proper object of taxation, so that a credit of that amount would be
given against future expenditure. But the rough justice which would be
done would be extremely rough.

Combined with this problem of equity is a straightforward problem
of enforcement. Wealth which is concealed on the appointed day for
the transition can be spent thereafter without involving its owner in a
liability to expenditure tax, and indeed can even be a source of tax
relief if it is subsequently converted into registered assets: wealth which
attracts the attention of the tax inspector would be substantially less
valuable. Thus there would be a strong temptation as the transition
approached to convert assets into inconspicuous forms: jewellery, gold
coins, banknotes stuffed under the mattress. Kaldor (1955) was prepared to deal with the last problem by calling in the currency on the
appointed day, noting that if the threat were believed it would be
unnecessary to carry it out. But devices of this kind are very far fetched.

Moreover, the problems of equity and enforcement are by no means
unrelated. If measures are thought to be fair, then they will be less
widely evaded and there will be general support for effective action
against those who try to get around them. There seems to us no possibility of devising transitional arrangements which would not be grossly
inequitable in many particular cases, and which would not be seen to
be inequitable in many particular cases. This is not only a serious objection in itself, but one which more or less precludes effective action to
enforce whatever transitional rules might be devised. It would be a
remarkably selfless opposition political party which, faced with the
manifest injustices of the transition, did not promise to abandon the
tax or to undermine whatever specific transitional arrangements were
proposed. If this is the only route by which an expenditure tax can be
reached, then however alluring the prospect at the end may be, we shall
never go down it. We therefore devote the remainder of this chapter to

an analysis of evolutionary proposals by which, in time, the present tax system might be transformed into an expenditure tax.

Towards an expenditure tax

In Chapter 2, we suggested a number of administrative reforms which were desirable if income tax were to be operated more efficiently and effectively. In particular, we advocated the abolition of cumulative P.A.Y.E., the schedular system, and the institution of a single annual return of the whole of a taxpayer's income. We would favour these reforms whether or not any other changes are made in the structure of income tax. They would certainly be desirable and probably necessary if progress were to be made towards an expenditure tax, since only by means of an annual return would it be possible to be confident that individuals obtained the reliefs to which they were entitled and paid the tax to which they were liable. We assume that such changes would be accompanied by extensive computerization of U.K. income tax administration, which has already occurred in most comparable countries and is slowly being introduced in Britain (although the schedular system makes the process more difficult).

At the same time, we would like to see progress in the following directions: firstly, in acknowledging that expenditure is the most appropriate base for the main direct personal tax; secondly, in assimilating the existing unsystematic reliefs for saving to the expenditure tax arrangements; and thirdly, in extending these arrangements to other forms of saving. We have described the three main forms of 'privileged' saving in the present U.K. tax system: life insurance, pensions, and housing. As we move to an expenditure tax, new life insurance policies would obtain full tax relief on premiums paid, and proceeds of the policy, whether by surrender or maturity, would be taxable in full. As we noted on page 86, this would probably lead to some changes in the institutional arrangements made by companies to deal with policy maturities, so that the whole sum due need not be drawn from the policy proceeds immediately it matured. Unfortunately, it would be necessary to continue the present very complicated rules for existing policies, at least for some years, since otherwise current policy-holders would suffer the disadvantage of the new procedures (the tax on proceeds) without having received the benefits (relief on premiums and accumulation).

We have also described housing as a 'privileged asset'. The Meade

Committee has discussed in detail the most logical treatment under various tax arrangements. But it is not clear that tinkering with the tax treatment of housing would improve the efficiency of the much-distorted housing market, and because tax concessions in this area have been largely capitalized, as we noted in Chapter 3, any change in the *status quo* would be likely to involve major inequities and hardships to particular individuals. If we were to describe what might be done about the U.K. housing market we should need to write a book, and this is not it. The U.K. is by accident or design committed to an outcome in which those who can buy their own homes and those who cannot are housed by local authorities, and no foreseeable tax changes will alter that situation.

Pension funds are already taxed on L.E.T. principles—contributions are exempt but the proceeds are taxed—and therefore no change in these arrangements would be required. But there are at present substantial restrictions on the benefits which can be provided from schemes that qualify for Inland Revenue approval: these restrictions could be abandoned and the associated administrative machinery abolished, since if people can save in this way for themselves there is no need to limit the amount they save in this way via a pension fund. Equally, once people have the opportunity to save in this way for themselves there is little reason to compel them to make such provision through a pension fund. Under an expenditure tax, it is very much easier for people to make 'life-cycle savings' to ensure that part of their income is available to them after their retirement. So we expect that there would be less demand for extensive occupational pension schemes, and people who were offered good schemes of this kind would no longer be at a great advantage relative to those who were not. We expect that state and private schemes would continue to provide basic pensions to ensure against poverty in old age: but would envisage that more elaborate provisions might become voluntary. If this happened, the present extreme complexity of pension fund administration could be reduced, and the proportion of personal wealth which was held in pension funds would diminish while that held directly by individuals would rise.

In addition to these changes, it would be essential to bring other types of savings into the expenditure tax framework. The procedure for dealing with land and negotiable securities would be as follows. After some appointed day, A day, the new rules would be applied. Purchase costs would be deductible and proceeds would be taxable. (Some limits on the purchase of registered assets which would qualify for a deduction would be necessary during a transitional period.) Any seller of securities subsequent to the appointed day would therefore be liable to tax on the whole of his receipts from the sale, unless they were reinvested in other securities or registered assets. If he had purchased his securities after A day, he would obtain no relief against this liability, since he could already have claimed their cost as a tax deduction: but if he could show that they represented a pre-A-day acquisition, he might be allowed to deduct the purchase price from the proceeds. This means that for securities which he had purchased under the previous income tax regime, he would be taxed on the capital gain as at present but at income tax rates. This means that in spite of the relatively conservative nature of the transition to an expenditure tax involved in these proposals, many people spending out of accumulated wealth would pay more tax than they do under the present tax structure right from the start.

Changes would also be needed in the taxation of unincorporated businesses. The base for taxation would be shifted from the profit of the business to the net amount withdrawn from the business during the year by the proprietor, since all sales proceeds would be taxable (whether capital or current in nature) and all expenses would be deductible (whether capital or current in nature). The small business-man would pay only on that part of his profit which he chose to with-draw for his own consumption, and would be fully relieved of liability on what he reinvested in the future growth of his firm. He would therefore obtain the twin benefit of a system vastly more conducive to the expansion of small business (aided by an increase in the impor-tance of personal saving relative to that of institutions) and a sub-stantial reduction in the administrative burdens involved in preparing tax accounts. There are opportunities to make similar simplifications in the taxation of incorporated businesses: we discuss these further in Chapter 12.

The other major category of personal saving is deposits in accounts with banks, building societies, and other financial institutions. In general, it seems to us undesirable that current accounts and balances used for transactions purposes should be registered assets: monitoring the balances on accounts which are the subject of frequent small trans-actions would be a nuisance for the taxpayer, the financial institution, and the Revenue alike. But both the logic of the tax and the desirability of allowing as much freedom of choice as possible in savings behaviour suggest that taxpayers should have the opportunity to make deposits in registered accounts. All payments into such accounts would attract relief: all withdrawals would be taxed. But these accounts would mainly be intended for long-term and contractual savings, not for day-to-day purposes. These objectives can be achieved by requiring that basic rate tax be withheld from withdrawals from registered accounts, with provision for rapid refunds from the Revenue in cases of hardship. This would have the effects of making it inconvenient to operate frequently on registered accounts, and of ensuring that people who did so did not end up with tax liabilities which they could not pay because they had already spent the full amount which they had withdrawn. In due course it would be desirable to assimilate unregistered accounts fully to the expenditure tax system by abolishing tax on the interest derived from them: registered accounts would then fall within the right-hand box of Fig. 6.1, unregistered accounts into the central circle.

Once all these changes had been made, the British income tax would have been transformed into a direct tax on personal expenditure. It is interesting to note that, with two exceptions (the more extensive monitoring of gifts and the treatment of registered deposit accounts), every change involved is a simplification. The taxation of life insurance policies and companies is much more straightforward. Most of the burdensome aspects of pension fund administration disappear. The tax treatment of capital gains and of small businesses, which are the most difficult parts of the present income tax system to understand and to administer, is greatly simplified. Why do so many people believe, as we used to believe, that an expenditure tax might be fine in theory but could not work in practice, when in reality it is likely to be rather easier to operate than the existing income tax? We think there are two reasons. One is that the expenditure tax has not been explicitly compared with the present tax structure, but rather with some idealized income tax system which was not too precisely defined but which was assumed to be working smoothly and efficiently. We had simply forgotten how complicated and unsatisfactory the system was at the moment.

The other reason is that it is common to view any proposed change to the tax system in isolation. If we take for granted that every other aspect of the tax structure is to be operated more or less as it is now, then it is almost inevitable that any change will seem difficult and expensive to make. But if we take a broader view of the system as a whole and look at sets of interrelated changes, a much wider range of possibilities is feasible. For example, we shall observe that there are many changes (such as the introduction of local income tax) which are costly with cumulative P.A.Y.E. and cheap without it. This is one reason why it is essential, even for an understanding of the administration of taxation policy, to be aware of the underlying principles of taxation involved, since only then is it possible to see these inter-relationships and the effects of the system as a whole. It is also for this reason that a tax system which is to be fair, simple, and efficient in administration must stick closely to a well-defined set of underlying principles. When we depart from these—for good or bad reasons—we begin to generate anomalies and loopholes: these demand *ad hoc* solutions which give rise to further anomalies and loopholes: and so on down a path of ever-increasing complexity. A principal merit of an expenditure tax is that it really can be operated in a way which is close to such basic principles, while as we saw in Chapter 5 a comprehensive income tax presents many more problems; spending is easier to measure than income, and cash flows are easier to recognize than accruals. A satisfactory annual income tax would be difficult to operate even in a perfect world, which is why it does not work very well in the U.K.

SOCIAL SECURITY AND TAXATION

The origins of the present British social security system are to be found in the 1942 Beveridge Report. Most cases of poverty can be attributed to one of a small number of specific causes—sickness, unemployment, or old age. Beveridge proposed a scheme of 'social insurance' against these various contingencies. Individuals would make payments, like insurance premiums, to a national insurance fund. If they become sick, unemployed, or old, they would then be entitled to claim on the fund. Everyone would pay the same contribution and all claimants would receive the same benefit. If a scheme of family allowances to meet the needs of large families were also introduced—and one was in fact implemented in 1948—Beveridge expected that most households would be assured of a level of income sufficient to avoid hardship.

Some people might slip through the net. They might not have paid sufficient contributions to be entitled to claim on the national insurance fund, or they might have exhausted their right to benefit, or their poverty might not result from an insured contingency. For these people there was to be a means-tested scheme of national assistance, which would guarantee a basic standard of living to all. This would be available only to those who were not in work, and who had insufficient resources of income or capital from any other source.

The development of the scheme in practice differed significantly from Beveridge's intention. There were three main reasons for this. The contingent benefits were set at lower levels than he had planned, and this meant that someone who received sickness or unemployment benefit or an old-age pension, and had no other income, was normally entitled to national assistance. It followed that national assistance, instead of being a fallback scheme, became the normal method of income support for a large number of households. Under the Beveridge scheme, families getting national insurance benefits would normally neither need nor be entitled to national assistance. In reality increasing numbers of people could claim both. In 1966 national assistance was renamed supplementary benefit. This change was mainly intended to remove the stigma attached to receipt of 'national assistance'. The alternative title chosen demonstrated the change which had occurred in the function of the benefit.

Secondly, the proportion of pensioners in the population increased rapidly, and this meant that the flat rate contribution needed to supprt a given level of retirement pension rose to levels at which it became a disturbingly high proportion of the earnings of low paid workers. To avoid this, an earnings related element of contributions was introduced, and in partial compensation limited earnings related benefits were provided. By 1975 contributions had become strictly proportional to earnings (up to a ceiling which is at present £220 per week). Finally, there was increasing concern that a scheme based on Beveridge principles was inadequate for the needs of those who were in work—and hence ineligible for benefits—but whose earnings were low. There was therefore a growth in the number and size of benefits paid to working households. Rent and rate rebates and family income supplement were the most important of these.

For all these reasons, the British social security system has moved a long way from the principles laid down by Beveridge. But because there has been no subsequent comprehensive review, the language of the Beveridge Report still governs much policy discussion and formulation even though it is now largely irrelevant to the reality of the modern system. The contributory 'principle' is still affirmed—most eloquently by employing 10,000 people to maintain and check contribution records—although the 'contributions' are simply a tax on earnings and it is the means-tested supplementary benefit system which determines the income level of most unemployed households and of many other beneficiaries. Unable to decide whether we have, or want, a system based on principles of social insurance or on a general income maintenance scheme, we maintain the full administrative machinery needed to operate both.

The present system

The principal contingent benefits are those for sickness and unemployment, and the retirement pension. Earnings related supplements to the first two of these were abolished in 1982, so that they are once again flat rate benefits. The earnings related component of retirement pensions is increasing, as a result of the development of SERPS (the State Earnings Related Pension Scheme). The rates of these benefits are shown in Table 7.1. Other contingent benefits include, among others, widow's, maternity, invalidity, and disability benefits.

All those not in work are entitled to have their incomes brought up to the supplementary benefit level. There is a 'long term' rate—mainly for pensioners and single parent families—which is higher than the short term rate for other households. Housing costs, rent, rates, and mortgage interest are normally paid in full, and the figures in Table 7.1 include a 'typical' payment of £15 a week for a single householder and £20 for a couple. Others with low incomes—those with low earnings or who receive national insurance benefits without supplementation—are eligible for rent and rate rebates. Only for very poor households do these rebates cover the whole of rent or rates.

From 1983 rent and rate rebates have been replaced by a 'unified' housing benefit. However, unification refers to the administrative procedures, which are now mainly undertaken through local authorities, and not to the basis of calculation of the benefits. There remain different, and more generous, procedures for those out of work than for those in it; and in fact a new formula has been introduced for those pensioners who are poor enough to be entitled to housing benefits but not poor enough to qualify for a supplementary pension.

TABLE 7.1

Rates of Benefit, November 1982 (£)

	Single person	Married Couple
Retirement pension	32·85	52·55
Unemployment and sickness benefit	25·00	40·45
Long term supplementary benefit	32·70	52·30
(including rent and rates)	47·70	72·30
Short term supplementary benefit	25·70	41·70
(including rent and rates)	40·70	61·70

Rent and rates are assumed to be £15 for a single person, £20 for a couple

All families receive child benefit at the rate of £5·85 per child. There is a premium for single-parent families, and those on sickness or unemployment benefit receive a small extra payment of 30p per child. Supplementary benefit recipients obtain, as well as child benefit, an additional payment of between £2·90 and £9·95 per child, depending on its age. Poor families, whose head of household is in work, are entitled to family income supplement. This is half of the difference between the household's actual income and its calculated 'needs allowance', up to a maximum of £23 per week for a family with two children.

There is a wide range of other means tested benefits—in 1977 the National Consumer Council (NCC, 1977) counted 45, although some of these, such as that for National Health Service wigs, are unlikely to be relevant to many people. This complexity is reduced somewhat by a 'passport' system, in which receipt of one benefit automatically confers entitlement to others. For example those who obtain family income supplement or supplementary benefit are immediately qualified for free school meals for their children and for free prescriptions.

Some of the benefits we have described are strictly contingent benefits—everyone with a particular characteristic is entitled to them regardless of their income. The richest man in Britain can draw child benefit for his children, and if he is an employee, receive sickness benefit when he is ill. Many social security payments are income related, however, and the majority are both contingent and means tested. For family income supplement, for example, there are two tests, one of each kind. Are you the working head of a household which contains at least one child? Is the household income sufficiently low?

The effectiveness of the system

It will be apparent from the above description that one of the present difficulties is the sheer complexity of the system. The number of benefits and the intricate formulas for computing the amount of benefit, involving 'needs allowances' and 'prescribed amounts', are enough to confuse the dispassionate student and must seem bewildering to potential claimants. It is worth bearing in mind that one reason the poor are poor is that they are not qualified as chartered accountants.

Partly because of this complexity, and partly because many people perceive some stigma attached to claiming means tested benefits, by no means all those who are entitled to benefits actually claim them. Such failure to claim may also be the result of a rational decision that the amount which would be likely to be paid would not compensate for the time and trouble involved. Data on the extent of take up are poor—as with the black economy, if the information to measure the problem accurately were available it would yield the information needed to solve it. There are two main sources—estimates based on apparent entitlements in household surveys, and local estimates by organisations helping those potentially eligible to claim. Table 7.2 gives official estimates of the rate of take up of some of the principal benefits.

TABLE 7.2

Take-up of Means-tested Benefits

Benefit	Date	Take-up (%)
Supplementary benefit[1]	1977	74
Family income supplement[1]	1978–9	51
Housing benefits[2]– rent rebates	1979	72
rent allowances		50
rate rebates		70
Free school meals[3]	1978–9	61

Sources: (1) SSAC (1982)
          (2) Parliamentary written answer, 1980.
          (3) Wilson (1982)

Most people would see the relief of poverty as the principal objective of the social security system. There are others. Families whose income falls through some misfortune such as sickness or unemployment may suffer hardship even if they are not poor and it may be a legitimate function of a state insurance system to provide assistance in such circumstances, especially since it may be difficult to insure privately against risks such as unemployment. But it is mainly in terms of its impact on poor households that the effectiveness of the social security system is judged. To measure the numbers in poverty and the effect of tax and benefits on these numbers we have to define poverty, and there is no unique way of doing this. Two broad approaches may be distinguished. The first is to lay down an *absolute* level of income below which a family is defined as being in poverty. This approach—adopted first by Rowntree—might attempt to define minimum households needs for food, shelter, clothing etc. and to measure the budget required to satisfy them. An alternative approach changes the poverty standard each year in line with some measure related to the living standards of the rest of the community. This represents a way of measuring *relative* poverty. We might examine this by looking at the number of people whose incomes fall below some specified fraction of the average. This level would change over the years and so there is a difference between the numbers of those in absolute poverty and the numbers in relative poverty. Most people's conception of poverty contains both a relative and an absolute component. We are more likely to contribute to a collection on behalf of the poor of Bangladesh than we are for the poor of Sweden; but we might also regard inability to afford a television set as a mark of poverty, a view which would have been surprising in 1958 and incredible in 1938.

The very different implications of a relative and absolute standard are shown in Table 7.3. If we adopt the standard of 1953, then the poverty which existed in 1953 had been all but eliminated by the 1970s. If we choose a relative measure, then the decline in poverty is much less dramatic; in 1973, 2.3% of the population—over one million people—were still 'poor'. Conversely, however, if we were to apply the 1973 standard to the distribution of income in 1953 we would find that almost a quarter of the population were poor.

TABLE 7.3

Numbers in poverty in Britain, 1953–1973

	Standard of 1953		Standard of 1971	
	% of population	Number (m.)	% of population	Number (m.)
1953	4·8	2·4	21·0	10·6
1963	1·4	0·8	9·4	5·0
1973	0·2	0·1	2·3	1·3

Source: Fiegehen, Lansley, and Smith (1977), Table 3.4.

Thus there is unlikely to be general agreement on the extent of poverty. It is common to count 'the poor' as those with incomes below the supplementary benefit level. This is a measure of relative poverty if benefits are raised in line with earnings (as has tended to be the case in the long term); a measure of absolute poverty if they are linked only to prices (the present legal requirement). It is a criterion which requires some care in use, in order to avoid the absurd implication that a rise in the supplementary benefit scale—a measure designed to relieve poverty —increases the number of people who are poor. The number of people whose incomes fall short of the S.B. scale is perhaps better regarded as a measure of the effectiveness of the benefit system than of the incidence of poverty.

Even this criterion, however, is not free of ambiguity. The most recent general study of poverty in the U.K., by Beckerman and Clark (1982), defines between 1 m. and 2·7 m. people as poor, depending on how this S.B. scale criterion is interpreted. We examine the causes of poverty on the basis of Beckerman's narrow definition (the others would not give substantially different qualitative results). Even if 'the poor were always with us', at different times in history they have included very different groups of people. When Seebohm Rowntree began the systematic study of poverty with his survey of York at the end of the last century, poverty was mainly the result of low earnings. In the 1930s, most of those in poverty were the unemployed and their dependants. Now, most of those who are poor are poor because they are old.

Table 7.4 provides supporting information. In 1974–6 almost half of all poor households were pensioner households. Fewer families were poor than in the 1960s, and large families were a much less significant cause of poverty than old age. In examining the causes of poverty it is, however, important to look also at contingencies which carry a high risk of poverty when they occur, even if they do not affect many people. Single parent families come into this category. We can all expect to be old but most of us can hope not to be single parents—and a high proportion of single parent families are poor.

The state earnings related pension scheme (SERPS)

It appears that old age is a principal cause of poverty today. In 1978 a major reform of state pension provision in Britain came into operation. The effect of the scheme builds up only gradually, since rights to the more generous pensions which it offers are earned only by work which is done after April 1978. By the end of the century, however, the scheme will have made considerable progress to maturity.

Its operation is of staggering complexity. The earnings related pension which is paid is based on the following calculation. Take earnings in each tax year of your working lifetime since 1978, up to the national insurance contribution ceiling (currently £220 per week). Revalue each of these annual income figures in line with the movement of average earnings between then and your retirement date. Take the average of the best twenty of these figures, and subtract from this the national insurance contribution floor at the date of your retirement. Your earnings related pension is then one quarter of the figure which emerges from this calculation.

TABLE 7.4

Numbers in poverty, 1961-3 and 1974-6

| | No of poor persons (000) | |
	1961-3	1974-6
Pensioners—single	290	515
couples	210	250
	500	765
Non pensioners—single	45	40
couples, no children	110	90
1-2 children	330	210
3 or more children	220	230
Single parents	30	70
Other households	490	260
	1225	900
Total	1725	1665

Source: Beckerman and Clark (1982), Table 5.6.

Things are only as simple as this if you are not contracted out of the state scheme. If you are a member of a good occupational pension scheme, your employer can choose to 'contract out'. About half of all employees, including most of those who work for the public sector or for large companies, are contracted out. This means that both you and your employer pay lower rates of national insurance contribution. In return, you will probably have to pay something towards your occupational pension, and this occupational pension must be at least as good as the guaranteed minimum pension (GMP) calculated by the Department of Health and Social Security according to another complicated formula. Most occupational pensions are in practice likely to be better than the GMP. Whether this is so or not, the amount of the GMP will be subtracted from your state earnings-related pension. This means that you will have at least as good a pension, in total, as you would have had if you had not been contracted out; and if your pension from your employer is more than the GMP then the sum of his pension and the state pension will be more than you would have had from the state scheme alone. Widows generally inherit the whole of their husbands' SERPS entitlement and part of their GMP's.

It is clear that checking that your pension has been correctly calculated is a task which can while away many otherwise happy hours of
retirement. Perhaps the most important observation to be made about
the scheme is that its design appears to owe more to the political need
to offer something to each of the many interest groups concerned with
pensions than to the economic need to find a fair, effective and predictable system of provision for retirement in the twenty-first century.
Low income pensioners will be better off under the scheme *either* if
they are not at present claiming supplementary pension *or* if the
amount of earnings-related pension they will obtain is sufficient to take
their total pensions above the supplementary benefit level. This second
condition will be met, broadly speaking, if their earnings related
pension entitlement is more than their rent and rates. It seems likely
that when the scheme is mature this will in fact be the case for most
households, although not by much if past incomes were low; lifetime
earnings of around £100 per week would yield a pension sufficient to
match the supplementary benefit entitlement of a household with a
rent and rate bill of £15 per week. Families with sustained experience
of unemployment would be little, if at all, better provided for than
at present.

It follows that full operation of SERPS will substantially reduce the
number of pensioners in poverty, as measured by criteria based on an
S.B. scale, although the net transfer of resources to poor pensioners is
rather small. This result is achieved at enormous cost.

SERPS is a 'pay-as-you-go' scheme. This means that benefits are
paid out of current taxes—principally national insurance contributions.
Most private pensions are funded, so that when pensions are being
earned money is set aside and invested to pay for the pensions when
they fall due. Although there is something called the National Insurance
Fund, it is not a fund in this (or any other) sense, and no assets have
been set aside to meet future claims to state pensions. The only backing
for current promises is the hope that future governments will levy
sufficient taxes to pay for them.

The moral force of a pledge from today's politicians that our children
will pay us more generous pensions than we are willing to pay our
parents may reasonably be said to be weak; and it is a striking example
of the humbug to which a spurious 'contributory principle' leads. The
potential cost of SERPS is very high. If resources are to be made available to the elderly on the scale which SERPS implies, then estimates
by Hemming and Kay (1982) suggest that they would be capable of

financing a 70% increase in the flat rate state pension. This would virtually eliminate poverty among the old and substantially increase the incomes of all pensioners, including the poorest. The benefits of SERPS are distributed in an arbitrary and capricious way and mostly accrue to the better off.

Tax and social security

The interaction between the tax and social security systems is a difficult issue. For many, it may seem surprising that there is any inter-action at all. Is it not absurd that people with incomes below the supplementary benefit level should be liable for income tax? Surely it is nonsensical that many households are simultaneously paying income tax and receiving means-tested benefits? The interrelationship appears to be the product of some administrative muddle in which the left hand of government—the Department of Health and Social Security—does not know what its right hand—the Inland Revenue—is doing.

Although there is no shortage of administrative muddle, in this or other areas of the tax system, this picture is somewhat over-simplified. If the tax threshold were raised to a level at which no one who was poor was liable for tax, this would benefit not only the poor but every-one who paid income tax, whatever their income level. As a result, increasing the threshold is a very expensive method of helping the poor. We might try to claw back the gains from those with incomes above the tax threshold, but this involves sharply increasing the marginal rate of tax paid at this point in the income distribution. This would make it difficult for poor households to escape poverty by increasing their earnings—it would exacerbate the poverty trap, which we discuss below. Related difficulties would arise in trying to eliminate the overlap between tax and means-tested benefits. It is important to recognize that most of those taxpayers whose incomes are at or a little above the tax threshold are not poor at all. The tax thresholds—around £30 per week for a single man and £47 for a married couple—are very low and very few bread-winners have incomes as low as that. Most of the people who do are secondary earners—married women working part time, juveniles, people moving into retirement (Morris and Warren, 1980). There is nothing necessarily irrational about collecting tax from all of these people and refunding part or all of it through family income supplement to the small minority of them who do indeed have house-hold responsibilities. It may therefore be a perfectly economical administrative procedure to have some people who both pay tax and receive benefits.

Nevertheless, some aspects of this interaction of tax and social security are clearly unsatisfactory. The poverty trap is one of these. As income increases, entitlement to means-tested benefits falls, and this imposes an implicit marginal tax rate on extra earnings additional to the explicit rate imposed by the tax system itself. This rate can be 50% for Family Income Supplement, 25% for rent rebates, 8% for rate rebates. These rates cannot simply be added to each other because there are interrelations between them. The combined effect is shown in Table 7.5. A household in these circumstances earning £50 per week has to increase its gross income by £50 per week in order to increase its net income at all, and over part of this income range the implicit marginal tax rate is over 100%—by earning more you actually make yourself worse off.

These implicit marginal tax rates are very difficult to work out, not least for the individual concerned. Means-tested benefits are not awarded at the same time as tax is collected, and the periods over which they are calculated differ from the fiscal year. Some benefits such as FIS and free school meals run for up to twelve months once eligiblity has been determined. Consequently, an increase in wages does not neces- sarily affect benefits received for several months, and a temporary increase might not affect them at all, or alternatively might affect them for a very lengthy period. This complexity makes it possible that many people are unaware that their marginal tax rate is so high, and hence the disincentive effects are reduced. Whether a system which works only because people do not understand it is desirable is another matter. Although the income range in which the poverty trap applies is wide, the number of people affected by it is not large. The poverty trap applies in acute form (implicit marginal tax rates of well over 60%) only to those houseolds which receive family income supplement; in 1980 there were about 100,000 of these. In its strict form, therefore, the poverty trap applies only to a small number of households. But there is a large number, perhaps over half a million, with marginal tax rates in excess of 50%. This results mainly from withdrawal of rent and rate rebates as earnings increase. In this broader sense, housing rebates are a more significant cause of high tax rates than family income supplement. It is also rather intractable. We have shown how it is possible that a man with gross earnings of £100 per week is no better off than someone with £50 per week. We can reduce the poverty trap

TABLE 7.5

The Poverty Trap, November 1982
(£ per week)

Gross Income	50·00	80·00	100·00	120·00
Plus: Child benefit	11·70	11·70	11·70	11·70
Rent rebate	13·84	10·09	7·32	3·91
Rate rebate	4·55	3·35	2·41	1·21
FIS	20·75	5·75	—	—
Free school meals	5·00	5·00	—	—
Less: Income tax	−0·89	−9·89	−15·89	−21·89
National insurance	−4·38	−7·00	−8·75	−10·50
Net Income:	100·57	99·00	96·79	104·43

Note: Data are for a married man with two children. There are no other tax allowances. Rent is £15 and rates £5 per week.

either by making the £50 a week man worse off or by making the £100 a week man better off. The first of these is presumably unacceptable—it relieves the poverty trap by exacerbating poverty. The second of these can only be done at reasonable cost if we avoid making people with incomes a little over £100 a week any better off—which means extending high marginal rates of tax into a broader range of the income distribution, and one in which much larger numbers of households are to be found.

The poverty trap and the unemployment trap are often confused. The poverty trap affects households in work; the unemployment trap affects households out of work. The poverty trap reflects the lack of incentive for low income households to increase their earnings. The unemployment trap reflects their lack of incentive to find a job at all. This affects people who have high *replacement rates*. The replacement rate is the proportion of your net income which will be 'replaced' by the benefit system if you lose your job (or, for someone who is already out of work, the ratio of current income to expected net wage). A simple illustration of how a replacement rate is calculated is given in Table 7.6. Since there are usually costs associated with holding a job such as travel to work and meals while there, someone with a replacement rate of 90% or more is probably better off on the dole. Of course, many people dislike work and might welcome the opportunity to give it up even if they were somewhat (but not too much) poorer, and the benefit system attempts to restrict the entitlement of people who quit jobs voluntarily or refuse or do not seek reasonable offers of employment; there are other people who might want to work even if it made them worse off. In assessing the disincentive effects of the unemployment trap, it is necessary to look at the whole distribution of replacement rates and not simply at the number of people for whom it exceeds 90% or 100%. At high levels of unemployment these disincentive effects do not matter very much—though some suggest that high replacement rates are the cause of high levels of unemployment (Minford, 1982)— but an issue of equity remains. Most people would think it wrong that people should be better off on benefits than in work, and this would remain true even in no one gave up employment as a result of it.

TABLE 7.6

Incomes In and Out of Work, November 1982
(£ per week)

In Work		Out of Work	
Wage	100·00	Unemployment benefit	41·05
Child benefit	11·70	Child benefit	11·70
Rent rebate	7·32	Supplementary benefit	6·45
Rate rebate	2·41	Rent and rates	20·00
Tax	−15·89	Tax rebate	1·97
National Insurance	−8·75		
	96·79		81·17

$$\text{Replacement rate} = \frac{81.17}{96.79} = 84\%$$

Careful calculation of replacement rates is an extremely complicated exercise. The figures in Table 7.6 reflect a snapshot of an early week of unemployment, which may be misleading. Because both earnings and benefits are taxable, but in different ways, a spell of unemployment can have effects on tax liabilities after it has ended (or before it started). Benefit entitlements are themselves a function of the length of the spell of unemployment. To measure a replacement rate accurately, it is necessary to specify the length of time for which a household is unemployed, past work experience and to measure its effect on net income over a period which may extend for several years.

Estimates of the distribution of replacement rates on this basis are given in Table 7.7. The short-term rates relate to a four week spell of unemployment; the long term rates to indefinite unemployment. In 1978 short-term rates were very high—18% of the working population would have continued to obtain 90% of their net earnings during a short period of unemployment—and were much higher than long-term rates. Since then, the position has changed substantially. There has been a marked fall in short-term rates and these are now close to long-term rates. There are three main reasons for this. The level of benefits has fallen somewhat, relative to wages. Earnings-related supplements to national insurance benefits have been abolished. Most importantly, unemployment benefit became taxable in 1982. This does not mean that large amounts of tax are now collected from the unemployed— someone who is out of work for a lengthy period will not normally receive enough in benefit to incur a tax liability. But for someone who had both earnings and unemployment benefit receipts in the course of a fiscal year, the fact that additional earnings might be taxed at around 40% while benefits were not taxed at all made short term replacement rates high for many taxpayers, and this anomaly has now been removed.

TABLE 7.7

Distribution of Replacement Rates for the Working Population

Working Households with Replacement Rates Below	November 1978		November 1980		November 1982	
	Short-Term	Long-Term	Short-Term	Long-Term	Short-Term	Long-Term
40	2	10	3	25	14	23
50	7	31	10	47	36	45
60	21	56	28	67	59	65
70	43	75	51	84	78	83
80	65	88	72	93	90	93
90	82	94	86	96	96	97
100	92	97	95	98	98	99
110	97	98	98	99	99	99
Average Rate	74	60	71	53	58	54

Source: Morris (1982)
Notes: 1. Short-term means 4 weeks unemployment; long-term 52 weeks or more.
2. These calculations reflect the maximum that replacement rates can reach, as they relate to the position just after a benefit uprating. Prior to the November uprating in 1982, for example, the average long-term rate will be 52 per cent.
3. The methodology employed in the estimates is that reported in Kay, Morris and Warren (1980).

In consequence, the unemployment trap—once a serious problem—has now largely disappeared. There is now more cause for concern about the number of people for whom replacement rates are very low.

Both the poverty trap and the unemployment trap affect families with children and high housing costs. The poverty trap arises because the benefit system gives more support to low income than to high income families—it is withdrawal rates from benefits such as FIS and, particularly, rent and rate rebates which give rise to high marginal tax rates. The unemployment trap arises because the benefit system tends to give more for children and housing to those out of work than it does to those in it. These points suggest that both traps could be eased by a better-integrated system of support for children and housing costs. We discuss this further below.

Fundamental reforms

The British social security system is complex, is not very effective in eliminating poverty, and is not particularly generous to many groups while reducing or eliminating the incentives given to others to find employment or to increase their earnings. It is hardly surprising that there are many proposals for root and branch reform.

We noted earlier that benefits might either be contingent, or income related, and that many which we have at present are both. Reform proposals fall into two main categories. There are those which reduce the number of contingent benefits, and rely on a single means-tested system to deliver support to those with inadequate resources. Tax credit proposals, social dividend, or minimum income guarantee, and negative income tax schemes are in this group. The opposite direction of reform is to plan a more generous and extensive network of contingent benefits and to reduce the number and extent of means-tested benefits. This would follow more closely the principles of the Beveridge Report and has been described explicitly by some (Meade 1978) as a 'back to Beveridge' plan.

Before considering either of these groups of proposals in more specific detail, we should note a fundamental problem common to both. The merit of contingent benefits is that it is easy to see that the unemployed, or the old, have, as a class, greater need for income support than the working population. The merit of income-related benefits is that within any of these categories there are some people who need state support to achieve adequate income levels and others who do not. It follows that a move to a system which predominantly relies on one kind of benefit at the expense of the other involves discarding information about either means or status which enables the social security system to be targeted more effectively on those with the greatest needs.

For this reason both types of proposal tend to be less cost-effective than the present system. Moreover, schemes in the negative income tax or social dividend group tend to hurt the poorest people in needy categories—such as the old or unemployed with no other source of income —and to help poor people in less needy categories—such as households in work but with low incomes. Conversely, back to Beveridge type schemes tend to favour rich people in needs categories—affluent pensioners or large families—and to hurt poor people in less needy categories—low income working households. For these reasons, those who support predominantly income-related schemes often retain some contingent benefits, and those who favour contingent benefits recognize that adequate levels are difficult to achieve if they are paid to all. Proposals which begin as fundamental reforms therefore tend to become modified in ways which lead to results not necessarily much less complex, than, or different in effect from, the present system.

The appeal of one single comprehensive scheme of income maintenance is obvious. One such proposal (originally put forward by Lady Rhys Williams during the last war) is to scrap *all* existing social security benefits and replace them by a single payment for each member of the household. This payment would be a kind of 'social dividend'. It would be paid automatically to all households regardless of circumstances, and would be tax-free, thus representing a guaranteed minimum income for each household. All personal tax allowances would disappear and income tax would be imposed on all income other than the social dividend. We shall assume for purposes of exposition that all income is taxed at a single basic rate. The operation of a social dividend scheme is illustrated in Fig. 7.1. This shows how a family's income after tax depends on its income before tax and the social dividend. If there were no tax or benefit system at all each family would find itself on the dashed 'no-tax' line on which income before tax equals income after tax. With the social dividend scheme a family receives the guaranteed minimum, shown by the distance OA in the figure. As its earnings rise, part of the increase is taxed away and so net income rises less fast than gross income—the slope of the line AD is less than the slope of the no-tax line. At some level of income, shown in the figure at OC, the amount

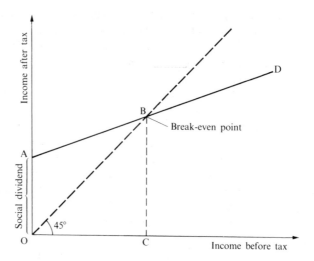

Fig. 7.1. A social dividend scheme.

of tax paid equals the social dividend received. This is the break-even level of income. Below this level of income families are net recipients and above it they are net contributors to the public purse.

A universal tax credit scheme would have just the same effect. The idea of a tax credit is that instead of receiving a personal income tax allowance of £30 an individual would be given a weekly tax credit of £9 (which is simply the value of a £30 allowance to someone who pays the basic rate of 30%). All income would be taxable but he could off-set the credit against his liability: so that if his income for the week was £80 he would pay £24 − £9 = £15. For someone who earned as much as this the system would work just as it does at present; the difference is that those with low incomes could reclaim the credit, so that a man with an income of £20 and a tax liability of £6 would receive a refund of £3. If the scheme were extended to the whole population, then it is exactly equivalent to a social dividend for everyone of £9.

An alternative approach, but one which is again the same in its effects, is a negative income tax. The basic idea behind this is to extend the tax system to cover people whose incomes are below the tax threshold. With a negative income tax, their liability would become negative; while others continued to have tax deducted from their earnings they would receive weekly additions to their income from the government.

The amount of these payments would be the basic rate of tax multiplied by the shortfall of the taxpayers' income from the tax threshold. The equivalence of negative income tax and social dividend can be seen from Figure 7.1. The tax threshold is the point at which no net tax is paid, and is therefore the break-even point of the social dividend scheme. This is at income OC. Above this point tax is paid and net income increases along the line BD. Below the threshold a family receives payments of negative tax which help to offset the fall in its earnings and it moves down the line AB. A family with no income has a negative tax payment of OA, equal to the tax rate multiplied by the tax threshold. This is precisely equivalent to a social dividend of OA.

These systems appear simple, easy to understand, and capable of providing a minimum income for all. Their drawback is obvious. The existing personal income tax allowances imply a universal tax credit, or social dividend, or maximum payment of negative income tax of £9 per week for a single person and £14 for a married couple. This is quite inadequate for subsistence of any kind; the corresponding supplementary benefit rates (including average housing costs) are £41 and £62. In order to bring these rates into line, it is necessary to be enormously more generous to those in work, or very much more parsimonious to those out of work; the system either becomes much more costly, or is much less effective in relieving poverty. We must either contemplate basic rates of tax of 50–60%, or be less ambitious in our view of what the social security system can achieve.

Regarded as a social dividend scheme, the present system in effect pays a much lower social dividend to those in work than to those out of work. Since most people are in work, this saves a great deal of money; but it is unfavourable to those in work with very low earnings. Anyone with earnings of less than £40 per week is likely to be better off on supplementary benefit; but because virtually no one in full time work does in fact earn as little as this the anomaly is not particularly serious.

For these reasons, the Meade Committee contemplated a 'two-tier' social dividend scheme, under which a lower rate of dividend would be paid to those in employment. This illustrates the general point made at the beginning of this section. By making the rate of social dividend contingent, rather than universal, we can make the system offer better value for money. We begin to consider different rates of social dividend for the old, for single parents, for the chronically sick, and so on. We move steadily back from the pristine simplicity of the social dividend to a system of partly contingent benefits much closer to the present system.

The alternative radical reform proposal is 'back to Beveridge'; this implies raising purely contingent benefits to levels which ensure that those who receive them always have incomes above the supplementary benefit level. National insurance benefits would be set clearly above S.B. scale rates, and child benefit would be increased (broadly doubled) in line with the provision for children in the S.B. scale. There are two main difficulties with this approach. The first is its cost. Raising pensions, or child benefit, is very expensive; and it is expensive because the money is distributed to all pensioners, and all families with children, most of whom are not poor. Just as discarding contingent information raised the cost of relieving poverty by means of income support mechanisms, so discarding information on incomes raises the cost of relieving poverty through contingent benefits. It is cheaper to support poor families by providing higher payments to the children of the poor—as happens with FIS and S.B.—than to support all children. One suggestion for financing higher child benefits is to abolish the married man's allowance, and we discuss this in Chapter 14.

The second difficulty is the treatment of housing costs. The principal reason S.B. scale rates are above national insurance benefit levels is that the former includes payment for housing while the latter does not. If there were a competitive housing market national insurance benefits could be raised by some average price of housing services of a certain minimum standard, and the Beveridge principle adopted. But the housing market is in such a mess that any average allowance for housing costs would, on the one hand, leave many families with inadequate resources to meet their actual housing costs, and, on the other hand, be much too generous to many families living in heavily subsidized accommodation. The only real solution is reform of the housing market, but in the absence of this those responsible for running the social security system have to carry on as best they can, and one can only sympathize with them.

Improving the present system

Even if fundamental reforms have less to offer than appears at first sight, there are substantial advantages to be gained from a more rational interaction between the tax and social security systems. First, the opacity of the present position is an obstacle both to claimants obtaining their rights and to policy-makers seeking improvement. Secondly, the extent of poverty and unemployment traps is a serious issue. Poor households may take actions which appear to them to be beneficial, which it is desirable that they should take, and by a series of outcomes which they may not understand leave themselves worse off. Marginal tax rates over 100% are not acceptable in a tax structure with any claim to equity or justice. Thirdly, there ought to be possibilities of administrative rationalization. Fourthly, the operation of the tax system is much more automatic than that of the benefit system; bringing the two together should offer prospects of delivering benefits in ways which would reduce or eliminate the problem of low take-up.

A pre-condition for integration is a reduction of the number of means-tested benefits. Part of the reason for this proliferation is well-intended attempts to protect the poor from the consequences of particular price increases. It should be a normal principle that such assistance is provided by general income support rather than by benefits related to consumption of specific commodities. This will be to the disadvantage of those who need National Health Service wigs but it is by no means clear to us why we should be more concerned for poor people with thinning hair than for poor people with large appetites. The principal means-tested benefits which remain are those for child support and for housing. The first of these is required to long as we are not prepared to finance benefits for *all* families at the level implied by current rates of supplementary benefit, family income supplement, and free school meal provision; the second so long as the housing market remains as disorganized as at present. The objective should be to provide these benefits on a common basis for those in and out of work, and to deliver them to those in work and possibly to some others through the income tax system. To do this requires a more flexible income tax coding and assessment procedure. It must also confront the difficulty that income tax is levied—for good reasons—on annual income while benefits are—also for good reasons—based on weekly resources. It is impossible to tell someone with no money to wait until the end of the fiscal year to see whether he is entitled to benefit.

There are two principal ways in which this might be achieved, both of which involve the abandonment of the cumulative PAYE system. One is to levy income tax on the basis of weekly or monthly income. If this assessment implied that benefit was due, rather than tax payable, then people in work would receive that benefit automatically through their pay packet. This procedure was the administrative principle behind the tax credit scheme proposed in the early 1970s, and it has obvious advantages in securing possibilities of rationalization and of the automatic delivery of certain benefits.

There are two major disadvantages. One is that levying income tax on a short term basis only works satisfactorily for people with regular incomes from employment. It is necessary to retain a different system for people who have business activities or investment income—even of a quite limited kind—or whose incomes or tax affairs generally are in any way complicated. A second problem is that even for employees the procedure only works satisfactorily if everyone is covered by a single basic rate of tax. If this is not so, then people with fluctuating incomes may be heavily penalized. We shall argue in chapter 14 that this restriction is not as serious as it might appear. But it does limit the flexibility with which resources can be distributed to people with very low incomes. Most people would think it intolerable to have a basic rate of tax about 50%; but it is also unsatisfactory if very poor households have only 50% of the shortfall of their income below acceptable levels made up through the tax and benefit system. It is therefore necessary either to have a system less effective than at present at relieving poverty, or to retain much of the existing range of benefits for households in work.

An alternative approach is to retain an annual basis of assessment for income tax, but to move to a weekly basis for deductions, and to integrate many of the principal means-tested benefits at this point. This involves abandoning the cumulative PAYE system, and would mean that an annual assessment of income would be needed for most households. People with incomes which were very low in particular weeks of the tax year would find that a high proportion of their needs in these weeks were met; but if the annual assessment showed that their income over the year was quite high than some additional tax might be due from them and this would be collected if their income returned to its previous levels. The amalgamation of means-tested benefits with non-cumulative PAYE might allow a combination of flexibility in meeting individual needs with a much more automatic procedure for giving support to poor families. As in many other areas of the tax system, the administrative change involved in restructuring the ways in which income tax is deducted from wages offers a flexibility which is the key to unlocking more fundamental structural problems of the tax system.

8

INDIRECT TAXES

Direct and indirect taxes

THE *Oxford English Dictionary* defines an indirect tax as one which is 'not levied directly upon the person on whom it ultimately falls, but charged in some other way, especially upon the production or importation of articles of use or consumption, the price of which is thereby augmented to the consumer, who thus pays the tax in the form of increased price'. We argued in Chapter 1 that the economic analysis contained in this definition is shaky, and in general such a distinction cannot be made. We mean by indirect taxes only what is usually meant by them and attach no special significance, and particularly no economic significance, to the classification.

Nevertheless, many people do. Indeed, it almost became part of the conventional political wisdom of the U.K. that the tax structure relied too much on direct taxation—especially income tax—and too little on indirect taxes. In a period of inflation, a progressive income tax takes an ever-increasing proportion of real incomes while the real yield of indirect taxes (which are in many cases levied as fixed monetary amounts) declines. This shift was not intended, and it reinforces the case for indexation, which is the only way in which inflation can be prevented from accidentally bringing about changes which no one wants to bring about by design. So it is not surprising that the balance of direct and indirect taxation should have been a subject of attention.

But some of the reasons which people had for believing that the balance of direct and indirect taxation was wrong were bad ones. One is that it is thought that the disincentive effects of high rates of direct taxation can be reduced or avoided by a shift to indirect taxes. This argument is quite simply false. Let us ignore for the moment the role of savings, since it is the incentive to work rather than the incentive to save which is at the centre of this concern: we have dealt with savings incentives at greater length in Chapter 5. Then anyone considering whether to work longer hours or assume more responsibility will weigh the obvious costs against the benefits in terms of increased consumption which he (or she) would derive: the additional effort would, we shall assume, generate additional earnings of £10 per week. Now compare a 50% tax on all income with a 100% tax on all expenditure—since that is the rate which is needed to maintain the same revenue. Then our worker would discover that the extra £10 per week was reduced to a net £5 per week by the income tax: with taxes on expenditure, it would remain £10 but would only buy the same bundle of goods, the additional £5 being absorbed by the indirect taxes. The reality of the final outcome is exactly the same in both cases. It is possible that for a time people might be misled into working harder to earn larger monetary amounts before they noticed the reduced purchasing power of what they were receiving; but it is improbable that this irrationality would persist for long. If it did, then inflation—which puts larger quantities of less valuable money into wage-packets in just the same way—would have precisely the same beneficial effect on incentives to work, and few people would find this easy to believe.

The hope that the disincentive effects of high marginal rates of taxation can be reduced by recasting direct taxes as indirect ones is therefore quite chimerical. We should note also that the view that shifting from income tax to a pay-roll tax (like employers' national insurance contributions) would confer benefits, or even make a significant difference in anything but the short run, is erroneous in just the same way and for just the same reasons. A pay-roll tax on all forms of employment will lead partly to employers being unable to pay the same money wage as before —and hence to lower earnings than would otherwise have occurred—and partly to an increase in labour costs which will be reflected in higher prices for all goods and services. It is not easy to say which of these effects will be predominant, but this determines only whether we have (in the first case) slightly lower wages and lower prices or (in the second case) somewhat higher wages and higher prices, and the disincentive effects will be the same regardless of whether its incidence resembles more that of an income tax or a general commodity tax. One cannot remove the disincentive effects of taxes by disguising them under a different name, and those who look at our E.E.C. neighbours and are attracted by the combination of lower rates of income tax and higher pay-roll taxes are guilty of an error which is certainly not made by Continental managers and trade-unionists. What matters is the relationship between take-home pay and prices in the shops and this seems to be understood much better by the ordinary person than by many tax experts.

There are, however, two possible grains of truth in these arguments. One is that people may be more resentful of the fact that over half of the product of their extra effort goes in tax if this fact is intimated to them on their pay-slip than if the same money is extracted by their shopkeeper in a slightly more roundabout way, and that this resentment itself leads them to do less work—that people are willing to deprive themselves if they can also see that they are simultaneously depriving the taxman. (Musgrave (1959) describes this as the 'spite effect'.) Some people may have this psychological make-up, but the Social Survey (Radcliffe, 1954) found that more people cited high prices than high taxes as an adverse influence on their incentive to work, and it is a weak argument for a particular tax structure that it would help to conceal the realities of the tax system from people who have pathological views about it.

The second point is that indirect taxes are generally less progressive than direct taxes—mainly, though not entirely, because there is a threshold of income which is exempt from income tax while all expenditure, however small, is vulnerable to commodity taxation: we pay commodity taxes on every penny of expenditure but not on the first £1,565 of income. This means that the marginal rate of income tax is generally substantially above the average rate, while for commodity taxes there is little difference between the two. Thus indirect taxes can yield the same revenue from lower marginal rates, and hence disincentive effects (which depend on these marginal rates) would be reduced if this were done. This argument is perfectly valid, but it rests on the reduction in progressivity, not on the shift in the structure of taxation, and this reduction could be equally well—and more honestly—achieved by altering the rates of direct tax than by changes to different kinds of tax.

The second bad argument for preferring indirect to direct taxes suggests that the former are voluntary in a sense in which the latter are not: this notion is reflected in an older terminology which distinguishes 'escapable' and 'inescapable' taxes. It is true that any particular indirect tax can be avoided by any particular individual who chooses not to consume the taxed good. But it is also true, given that a certain amount of revenue is required, that taxes in general cannot be avoided by individuals in general. So an 'escapable' tax leaves the person who escapes it worse off—since he would have preferred, in happier circumstances, to have consumed the good which is taxed—and it makes everyone else worse off too, since it requires a higher rate of tax on those who continue to consume the good. Thus the tax structure to which this argument would lead is the worst possible in terms of economic efficiency—it maximizes the welfare loss which is additional to the basic and inescapable burden of the tax.

Principles of indirect taxation

What then would an efficient system of commodity taxes be like? A first principle is that there should be no taxes on intermediate goods—on items like sheet steel or turbo-generators which are sold to other producers rather than to final customers. Taxes on things must of course ultimately be paid by people, so that levies on producers must finally be borne by taxpayers generally in one capacity or another, as consumers, workers, or owners of firms. Hence the imposition of taxes on producer goods does not reduce the tax burden in any way; in fact it will actually increase it by inducing producers to make different and (from a social viewpoint) less efficient choices of inputs. Essentially, the principal objectives for indirect taxes—raising revenue, achieving some distributional aims, or encouraging or discouraging particular consumption patterns—can all be more efficiently achieved by the imposition of taxes on final goods alone (Diamond and Mirrlees, 1971).

The burden of commodity taxation should therefore be confined to final goods: how should it be distributed among them? Economic efficiency requires that indirect taxes should be cast so as to minimize the distortion of consumer choice involved—that as far as possible, the revenue should be raised without diverting taxpayers into less preferred patterns of consumption in their (collectively unsuccessful) attempts to avoid tax. At first sight, it might appear that this implies that all commodities should be taxed at the same rate and this has often been assumed, but there are at least two reasons why such an argument is false. First, while a uniform tax on all commodities will minimize distortion of the consumer's choice between different commodities, it will nevertheless have disincentive effects on his choice between leisure and work. So if a heavier tax is levied on commodities for which demand is inelastic—goods which the consumer will buy in any case— a lower rate of tax can be imposed on other goods and the disincentive to work reduced with little consequential distortion of choice of commodities. And if heavier taxes go on goods which are in some respects substitutes for work—like camping, sports, and yachts—and lighter ones on complementary activities—like overalls, travel to work, and this book—then this too will tend to ameliorate the disincentive effects of commodity taxation. These considerations underlie the 'Ramsey rules' (Ramsey, 1928; Baumol and Bradford, 1970) which say, very roughly, that commodity taxes should have the effect of reducing demand for all commodities in the same proportion.[1]

But these rules overlook the second weakness of the case for uniform commodity taxation—that it ignores the distributional impact of such taxes. This is a basic objection not only to uniform taxation, but to the Ramsey rules themselves. These are the answer to the question, 'If we are not concerned about the source of tax revenue, but simply aim to raise a given amount of revenue with minimal disincentive effect, what commodity taxes should we impose?' But if we are really not concerned about the source of our tax revenue, we should not impose commodity taxes at all; we can simply divide public revenue requirements equally among the whole population and raise them by means of a universal poll tax which avoids distortion altogether. Of course, the distributional consequences of this would be unacceptable, and that is why we adopt income and commodity taxes instead. But this means we cannot choose rates for these taxes independently of our view of distribution, so that commodity taxes must be chosen according to principles which take account of the distributional characteristics of goods as well as their demand elasticities.

Since the commodity composition of expenditure changes as income rises, indirect taxes can be used to influence distribution by imposing higher taxes on goods which attract a higher proportion of the expenditure of the rich. It need hardly be said that this too cannot be accomplished without disincentive effects—if managing directors spend a larger fraction of their income on caviar than their deputies then a heavy tax on it will discourage the latter group from aspiring to the positions of the former. And further analysis suggests that there may not be much advantage in using commodity taxes in this way. Adjustments to income tax can achieve similar effects more sensitively, and without diverting rich and poor alike into celebrating festive occasions with cider and fish paste rather than champagne and caviar. We might still, however, see some case for taxing 'prestige goods', such as Rolls Royces, whose attraction is derived not so much from their intrinsic utility but from the prestige which their limited availability confers on the owners.

Differential commodity taxation does not look a promising method

[1] The rules take this precise form only for small tax revenue and compensated changes in demand.

of redistributing income, but there is a further possibility we should consider. We saw in Chapter 5 that an ideal tax system might be one which avoided disincentive effects entirely by taxing not earnings but the ability to earn. If we look at the kinds of goods which are consumed in relatively large quantities by the affluent, we might try to distinguish two categories. There are goods like large houses, expensive motor cars, and yachts, which most people would like to buy if they could afford to. But there may also be other goods which are consumed only or mainly by people with high earning ability. Books and opera tickets might come into this category. We have seen that it is impossible to levy taxes on the first kind of good without disincentive effects; but it is possible to avoid them by taxing the second. Taxes of this kind represent a method—the only method—of relating tax liability to earning capacity as distinct from earnings. For example, if certain social groups send their children to public schools and if appointment to lucrative jobs in the City is made from this group, then we would wish to impose a heavy tax on public school fees. We might also redistribute by subsidizing goods which people with high earnings potential tend not to buy at any price—such as bingo sessions and certain Sunday newspapers. The difficulty with such a policy is immediately evident. We are confident that readers of this book have above-average earning capacity. But are they reading it because this is the kind of book which people of superior intellect and ability like to read: or is it that they have acquired their superior intellect and ability as a result of their taste for reading books like this one? Probably both are true; but in the former case we should wish to tax the book heavily and in the latter case to subsidize it heavily.

Whatever category readers actually do comprise, they may by now share our scepticism as to whether there are in fact large gains to be obtained by departures from a general principle of uniformity in commodity taxation. The administrative arguments against doing so are substantial. In order to exploit differences in the distributional characteristics of goods, it will be necessary to adopt a rather fine commodity classification—to distinguish not only cheese from other dairy products but Cheddar from Camembert and White Stilton from Blue. (The 1974 cheeses subsidy scheme attempted just that.) Such distinctions are likely to lead to administrative nonsense and to large and pointless distortions of consumer choice. It is not easy to believe that the information required to devise an optimal scheme is likely to be available, or likely to be used to good effect if it is.

There remain some arguments for taxes or subsidies on particular commodities. One is simple paternalism—I, as Chancellor of the Exchequer, think that people (presumably other people) drink too little milk or too much beer and seek to remedy the situation by fiscal incentives. Another justification for these corrective taxes can arise if they allow prices to be adjusted so as to ameliorate the effect of inefficiencies elsewhere—if electricity for space-heating is too cheap, then one way to stop excessive use of such electricity is to impose a tax on space-heaters. As the example suggests, it is usually preferable (though not always possible) to tackle such problems directly rather than to adopt 'second-best' policies of this kind. A slightly different argument concerns goods whose production or consumption imposes costs or benefits on those who are not themselves directly involved in buying and selling them—goods which are made in smoky factories, transported in juggernaut lorries, or grown in attractive orchards. The 'external effects' of these goods are not fully accounted for by the person or organization who provides them. Hence they will tend to be over- or under-supplied—there will be too many juggernauts and too few orchards. Economists have long argued (with rather little practical effect) that these problems might more appropriately be dealt with by means of taxes and subsidies on the products concerned than by administrative regulation. Taxes of these kinds are an exception to the general rule that taxes on intermediate goods should be avoided.

A further reason for indirect taxes may be to act as a tariff; to improve the balance of payments by discouraging imports and to give advantages to British producers of competitive goods. An effect of E.E.C. membership has been that duties which were formerly wholly or partly tariffs have been recast as indirect taxes. This is not a substantive change, since domestic production of tobacco and wine (from English grapes) is insignificant. The relative prices of (foreign) wine and (domestic) beer are unaffected. This consideration may also have been one motive for the so-called 'luxury' rate of V.A.T. (p. 127 below), which fell heavily on imported goods.

Indirect taxes in Britain

If we examine the structure of commodity taxes in the U.K., we find one general sales tax—V.A.T.—and heavy duties on three products—tobacco, alcoholic drinks, and petrol. Table 1 (p. 4) shows their relative contributions to revenue. We consider these major indirect taxes in turn.

The basic principle of V.A.T. is that it is a sales tax chargeable to the sellers of all output, with the proviso that in computing their liability firms may deduct any V.A.T. which has been levied on inputs into their products. We can see how this works by considering a simple example with a standard rate of V.A.T. of 10%. Suppose a man discovers a block of iron which with the aid of a magic wand (provided free of charge) he turns into steel worth £100. Adding V.A.T. at 10% he sells this to a motor-car firm for £110. The firm buys additional components which cost £500 to make and on which it is charged £50 V.A.T., and employs labour at a cost of £400. It sells the car for £1,300, charging 10% V.A.T., to make up a total price to the purchaser of £1,430 and secure a profit of £300. The firm now assembles its accounts for this set of transactions, which are

	Revenues			Costs	
	£			£	
		V.A.T.			V.A.T.
Car	1300	130	Steel	100	10
			Components	500	50
			Labour	400	
			Profit	300	
				1300	60

It must now account to the Customs and Excise for the difference between the V.A.T. levied on its outputs (£130) and the V.A.T. charged on its inputs (£60) so that it makes a payment of £70. This amounts to 10% of the £700 of *value added* in the car factory: the difference between the values of inputs and outputs, made up of £400 of labour costs plus £300 profit, and indeed it would be possible to compute the tax in this way. (This would be an *accounts* basis for the tax, in contrast to the *invoice* basis which is what we are describing and which is used in the U.K. and in the E.E.C.) At the same time as the V.A.T. man receives the car firm's cheque for £70, he also gets £50 from the component manufacturer and £10 from the steel producer, so that in aggregate £130 (10% of the value of the final output) is levied on the sequence of transactions involved in the production of the car. It is easy to check that this amount would remain the same however few or many transactions are involved in the chain of production.

Thus the main advantage of V.A.T. is that it is a method of levying a tax on all commodities that enter consumption while effectively exempting all intermediate goods—those who buy goods for further processing receive a refund of the tax which they have been charged, and only those who are the final consumers of the goods actually pay it. Thus it seems an ideal tax judged by the first of the principles of indirect taxation described above—the taxation of producer goods is systematically avoided. The price paid for this is a high one, however. As will be clear from the exposition above, the tax is complex and, as is inevitable if a charge is levied on every transaction in the economy and refunded on most of them, it is very expensive to administer. Initially, V.A.T. cost about twice as much to collect per £ of revenue as did the purchase tax which it replaced (cf. Customs and Excise, 1976, and estimates of Richardson Report, 1964). The near doubling of the rate in 1979 made this picture look less bleak. Since it costs little more to collect V.A.T. at this higher rate, the outcome was a reduction of nearly one-half in cost per £ collected. If rates of purchase tax had been doubled, then much the same would have happened. But the administrative burden is much greater than this. V.A.T. is a self-assessed tax—forms must be completed and tax paid or refunds claimed by the taxpayer himself, subject to random checks by control officials. Total compliance costs were put by Sandford *et al.* (1982) at 10% of revenue collected. This figure predates the increase in the rate in 1979 and is also likely to have fallen considerably, but it remains a disturbingly high proportion. The number of taxpayers increased from 74,000 in the last year of purchase tax to 1–2 m. under V.A.T.: and the number of collectors rose from 2,000 to over 13,000 (Parr and Day, 1977).

The Richardson Committee concluded in 1964 that V.A.T. had no merits sufficient to compensate for these acknowledged administrative problems, and proposals to introduce it were rejected at that time. Two developments led to its implementation in the U.K. The first was the adoption of the French V.A.T. by West Germany and subsequently by other members of the E.E.C. In both France and Germany, V.A.T. replaced unsatisfactory turnover taxes, levied cumulatively at each stage of production, which were both expensive to run and inefficient in economic effects (the rate of tax depended only on the number of stages in the production process). In Britain, however, purchase tax, a single-stage, broadly based commodity tax levied on wholesalers, had developed into a relatively cheap and simple fiscal instrument. But the adoption of V.A.T. became part of the process of harmonization to

E.E.C. institutions. Such harmonization would have substance as well as form only if two further conditions were fulfilled; first, if there was similarity between countries in tax base and rate structure, and second, if they ceased to refund tax on their exports and levy it on imports, as at present (i.e. if the tax had an 'origin' rather than a 'destination' basis). The second development was the failure of an attempt to tax services (purchase tax was levied only on physical commodities). S.E.T. (selective employment tax) was a weekly tax per employee, chargeable to firms in service industries, and administered by levying it on all employees and refunding it to manufacturers. The case for S.E.T. was poorly presented (mainly in terms of a desire to transfer labour from service to manufacturing industry), the definition of the borderline between the two sectors gave rise to constant anomalies, and the tax proved wildly unpopular. V.A.T. offered a mechanism by which the taxation of services could be integrated into a general system of commodity taxes, and when it was introduced in 1973 S.E.T. disappeared, unlamented. If a more acceptable method of imposing a general tax on services could have been devised—and possibly S.E.T. might have developed into such a tax if the base had been shifted to payroll, as was proposed, and the anomalies had been ironed out—then the administrative advantages of a purchase tax/services tax system, especially for small firms, would suggest that arrangements of this kind might be superior to the present V.A.T.

TABLE 8.1

Rates of V.A.T.

Zero	15%	Exempt
Food	All other	Land
Water	commodities	Insurance
Books		Postal services
Fuel and power		Betting
Construction[1]		Finance
Exports		Education
Transport		Health services
Children's clothing		Burial and cremation
Protective clothing		
Large caravans		

[1] New construction is zero-rated. 'Improvement' is zero-rated, but 'repair' standard-rated: the distinction is obviously unenforceable.

There are two rates of tax—zero and the standard rate of 15%. A 25% 'luxury' rate was introduced in 1975, reduced in 1976, and abolished in 1979. Additionally, some products—such as financial services, education, and funerals—are exempt. Exemption is not the same as zero rating, since while the exempt trader need pay no tax on his outputs his zero-rated colleague can reclaim the tax paid on his inputs as well: so it is always better to be zero rated than exempt, and (if the value of output sold to final consumers is less than the value of taxed inputs) it may even be more beneficial to be standard-rated than exempt. Consumption of food does not rise in proportion to income (Fig. 15.1, p. 241) and because it is both zero-rated and a substantial part of the budgets of poorer families the distributional impact of V.A.T. is slightly progressive.

As Table 8.2 shows, the difference between the rates of tax imposed by V.A.T. on the major part of consumers' expenditure and the rates on these selected items is very great: tax accounts for the major part of the price of cigarettes and whisky, and the effective rates on beer and petrol, though lower, still mean that the prices of these commodities relative to others are wildly different from what they would be if the structure of indirect taxation were non-discriminatory. The taxes on alcohol and tobacco are not, of course, imposed for reasons which are recognizably economic in character. There is some talk of the inelastic demand for these commodities (demand for tobacco is inelastic—a 10%

TABLE 8.2

The incidence of tax on various commodities, 1982

	Cigarettes	Whisky	Beer	Petrol
Factor cost	24·5	1·09	31	76
Specific duties	38·1	4·08	13	63
Ad valorem tax	20·0	—	—	—
V.A.T.	12·4	78	7	21
Retail price	95·0	5·95	51	1·60
Tax as % of factor cost	288%	446%	65%	111%

Cigarettes. pence per packet king size tipped.
Whisky. £ per bottle blended whisky.
Beer: pence per pint of bitter.
Petrol: pence per gallon four star.
Source: Reports of Customs and Excise; own estimates.

price rise might reduce consumption by 1½%–and the same may be true for beer, but consumption of wines and spirits is rather sensitive to price. see Deaton, 1975). The unpleasant consequences which their consumption has for others may also be cited (although smokers make reduced demands on public services by dying prematurely and alcohol as social lubricant has beneficial as well as adverse external effects). But the real reason these taxes exist is that it is rather easy to induce feelings of guilt about these forms of consumption: and as a result it is more acceptable to raise revenue in this way than in others. Taxes on alcohol were raised very sharply during and immediately after the First World War, and those on tobacco during and just after the Second World War, in periods when such moralistic sentiments were particularly easily aroused.

The adverse consequences of smoking on health have drawn attention to the tobacco tax. A common view is that the Government 'cannot afford' to discourage smoking because of the loss of tax revenue which would result. A reduction in smoking would affect the Government budget in a rather wide range of ways. The most immediate secondary consequence would be a reduction in medical costs and in claims for sickness benefit. These savings would grow, but over time a number of other factors would become important. Because reduced consumption of cigarettes would significantly increase life expectancy, there would be a rise in revenue from income tax, but an increase also in the cost of retirement pensions and medical treatment for larger numbers of elderly people, partly offset by a reduction in widows' pensions and benefits. Atkinson and Townsend (1977) have quantified a number of these items, which are substantial, and the effects on revenue from tobacco duties are not the only, or necessarily the dominant, element in the calculation of the effects of changes in smoking habits on the Government budget.

But as this discussion should make clear, to evaluate these factors simply from the standpoint of their effect on Government revenue and expenditure is to take an extremely–indeed offensively–narrow viewpoint. What is required is a much wider cost-benefit analysis, and the framework of this has been set out by Atkinson and Meade (1974). Recent work by Atkinson and Townsend (1977) leaves little doubt that an increase in the tax on tobacco would yield an increase in both Government revenue and social welfare. But the force of these arguments has not influenced policy sufficiently to prevent a substantial cut being made in the real burden of the tax. On the (low) estimate of demand elasticity cited above, simple indexation of the tobacco tax over the period in which the relationship between smoking and lung cancer has been known would have reduced deaths from this cause by between 1,500 and 2,000 per year.

The structure of tobacco tax has been revised as a result of EEC harmonization proposals. A duty based on weight of tobacco has been replaced by a specific tax of 2·1 p per cigarette and *ad valorem* tax of 30% of the retail price. Because the overall incidence of tobacco taxation is so high, the structure of the tax regime has major effects on the structure of the cigarette market. Cigarette coupons have disappeared (because they are now effectively subject to the 30% tax). Britain used to have shorter cigarettes than other countries, because the weight-based regime gave a strong incentive to reduce tobacco content: now king-size cigarettes dominate the market. The predominantly *ad valorem* tax regimes of France and Italy mean that a saving of 1 centime in manufacturing cost may reduce the retail price by 5 centimes, and hence give an artificial incentive to the use of low quality tobacco and packaging which are characteristic of French and Italian tobacco products. Kay and Keen (1982) show that in general specific commodity taxation creates less distortion of consumer choice per £ of revenue.

Expenditure on alcohol and tobacco as recorded in the Family Expenditure Survey (FES) is substantially below the estimates of consumption based on output data. One reason for this is probably the embarrassment some respondents feel about revealing their true consumption, but it is also possible that people with high alcohol consumption and high incomes have a lower response rate in such surveys. Figure 8.1 shows the available data on expenditure on tobacco and alcohol as a percentage of average houshold expenditure. It appears that the tobacco tax is regressive (that is, it takes a higher fraction of income from the poor than from the rich), and there is some indication that this regressivity has increased over a period of time because tobacco consumption seems to have fallen more among high-income groups. This tendency is strongly confirmed by evidence on smoking trends in different social classes (see Table 8.3). By contrast, the tax on alcohol appears to be progressive. Figure 8.1 shows that expenditure on alcohol increases more rapidly than income, and higher-income groups consume relatively more wines and spirits which are more heavily taxed.

It is much less easy to see why petrol should be considered a suitable subject for expecially heavy taxation, though there are arguments for a somewhat higher tax than that on other commodities. Some rationale

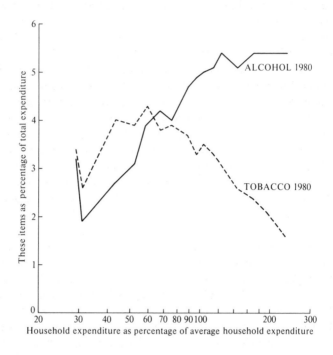

Fig. 8.1 Spending on alcohol and tobacco related to household expenditure.

TABLE 8.3

Percentage of cigarette smokers by sex and social class

		Men		Women	
	Social class	1958	1978	1958	1978
I	Professional	54	25	43	23
II	Intermediate	48	38	43	33
III	Skilled	60	49	42	42
IV	Partly skilled	54	53	42	41
V	Unskilled	61	60	42	41

Source: Tobacco Advisory Council.

can be derived from the second-best and external effects arguments described above. Motorists impose disutility on each other and on the population at large: and since road space is costly to provide but can be used free of charge, provision will be excessive if all demands at a zero price are met. In addition, the imposition of a tariff on oil may be a rational response by O.E.C.D. countries acting collectively to the O.P.E.C. cartel. To the extent that the case for petrol tax rests on these arguments, the usual objections to the taxation of intermediate goods do not apply: the demands of industry for road transport are clearly not less offensive or less pressing than those of private motorists. But it is difficult to decide what levels of tax would be justified by these considerations. Taxes on vehicles and on petrol amount to more than 150% of related public expenditures, but in the light of the arguments above it is not clear that this figure is too high.

We have already noted that the structure of indirect taxation occasions much less criticism than do the present direct taxes, and we share this view. But we do not consider that the weaknesses of the present direct tax system would be significantly alleviated by a shift from direct to indirect taxes, and we think that the proper balance between the two is actually one of the less important questions facing current British tax policy. The prominence of this issue in current debate is, we suspect, the product of a failure to understand fully the implications of one of the basic principles of public finance which we described in Chapter 1 — the irrelevance of the formal incidence of a tax to its effective incidence. It follows from this that one cannot make major improvements, or indeed large changes, simply by changing the identity of the payer of a tax. Nevertheless, there are reasons for supposing that the U.K. would do better to rely rather more on indirect taxes than it does at present. The most important of these is the problem of enforcement. Any tax is subject to difficulties of defining the base, of policing, or preventing avoidance and evasion. These problems increase more than proportionately with the rates of any particular tax, and indeed we have seen how at very high rates of tax they become overwhelming. If this is so, then if we are to have two broadly based taxes it is better to have two 'medium' taxes rather than one high and one low tax.

LOCAL TAXATION

Rates and local authority finance

LOCAL authorities levy rates on immovable property—houses, shops, offices, factories (though not farms)—within their area of jurisdiction. The basis of the tax is the 'net annual value' of the property. This figure is assessed from time to time and is intended to be the amount for which the property might be let if the tenant were responsible for all repairs. The rate is then fixed as a poundage, so that with a rate of 70p in the £ the owner of a property assessed at an annual value of £500 would pay £350 each year in rates. Although in general there is more than one local authority exercising functions in any area, a system of 'precepting' means that the lower tier authority is responsible for all rate collection.

We distinguish domestic rates—levied on houses—from industrial and commercial rates. In 1981–2 the total yield from rates was £10,926 m. of which 60% came from industrial and commercial property. Only 40% of local authorities' receipts of rates consisted of domestic rates although these represent a substantial tax on housing. The yield of domestic rates in 1981–2 was £4,437 m. and consumers' expenditure on housing in 1981 was estimated by the C.S.O. to be £24,366 m. including rates. This is a rather arbitrary and unreliable figure but it suggests an effective tax rate on housing (rates divided by expenditure on housing excluding rates) of 22%. A tax of this magnitude is greater than the standard rate of V.A.T. thus providing some justification for not imposing V.A.T. on housing. But this is only part of the story because the disincentive effect of rates is offset by subsidies to all major forms of tenure—tax concessions to owner-occupation, subsidies to local authority tenants, and rent controls in the private rented sector. Although the total value of these subsidies, and their effect on the demand for housing, is unclear, they certainly exceed domestic rates in their amount.

Since no free market in rented housing has existed for many years, it is difficult to measure satisfactorily the rental values which are supposed to be the basis of the tax. Two post-war revaluations have been conducted (in 1963 and 1973). In these, assessed values for house property have in practice been determined in relation to other assessed values, and it is obscure how the process ever got started: it is clear that any future domestic revaluations will have to be based on the capital value, rather than the rental value, of the house, and a divisor might be specified to produce comparability between domestic and non-domestic valuations. As an economy measure the next revaluation has been postponed indefinitely. Revaluations change, often rather radically, the relative tax burden on different ratepayers; and both revaluations have led to extensive discontent with the rating system and the establishment of Committees of Inquiry. The Allen Committee, reporting in 1965, identified the regressive impact of the rating system. This arises at the lower end of the distribution largely because many people (especially pensioners) live in houses which reflect their past, rather than their current, income; while at the upper end rateable values increase less rapidly than either the capital value of houses or the incomes of those who live in them. As a result of the Allen Report, a system of rate rebates was instituted. It was much extended in 1974 and in 1974-5 rebates were paid to 2·2 m. claimants. Additionally, rates are paid for recipients of supplementary benefit. These measures would largely have eliminated the problem of the rate burden on low-income households were it not that the number claiming is thought to represent only 70% of those eligible for rebate (see Table 7.2). The Layfield Committee, which reported in 1976 (Cmnd. 6453), had a broader brief which enabled it to investigate local government finance as a whole.

TABLE 9.1

Sources of local authority finance

	1966–7		1981–2	
	£ m.	%	£ m.	%
Government grants	1457	51	15 716	59
Non-domestic rates	804	28	6489	24
Domestic rates	611	21	4437	17
	2872		26 642	

Source: Chartered Institute of Public Finance and Accountancy.

Many people think of rates only as domestic rates, and it is not widely realized that domestic rates are not the most important component of the total rate burden nor rates the most important source of finance for local authorities. Industrial and commercial rates are not paid by the buildings themselves, though this impression is sometimes given; thus one commentator on local government finance has written 'industry and business will have to pay more. This is right and proper; such hereditaments can obviously afford to contribute more to the public purse' (Ilersic, 1973, p. 104). The formal incidence of rates falls on the occupiers of property, the businesses which make use of it; the effective incidence is much less certain. Rates are borne by the owners of commercial and industrial property to the extent that they are capitalized, i.e. reflected in a lower capital value for the rated property (see Ch. 1). Where land prices are a principal element in property values, this is likely to be the case: thus if the rates were removed from Central London office property, competition could be expected to bid rents up to very nearly the present level set by rent and rates together and the main effect would be an increase in property prices. This will be partly true for commercial property in other city centres. Outside these areas, however, rates primarily represent an addition to the cost of one factor of production—buildings. The result of this will be that offices and factories will tend to be more cramped, less well fitted, and less well located than they would otherwise be, and since the tax is an extremely heavy one (in 1978-9 it averaged 86% of 1973 rental values) this effect is likely to be substantial. The incidence of the tax will largely fall on final consumers, in these cases, but since they will not be willing to pay more for goods produced in highly rated areas deviations from the over-all average level of rates will be reflected in different local levels of profits, earnings, and employment opportunities. Industrial and commercial rates are a worse tax, not a better one for being a poorly perceived and understood tax on intermediate goods. The incidence of rates on a factory will fall partly on those who buy the products it makes, partly on those who work in it, and partly on those who own shares in the companies that own and operate the factory. The proportion of that total rate burden which falls on people living within the boundaries of the authority which levies the rate will vary widely from case to case, but will on average be small.

The purposes of the grant system

We have seen that the bulk of local authority revenue comes not from rates but from central government grants. It is therefore impossible to understand the development of the rating system in isolation from the grant system. Why should central government support local services in this way? There are four major reasons. 'Spill-overs' are benefits of local expenditure which arise outside the area of the authority which undertakes the expenditure. Local governments which are principally concerned for their constituents will not undertake enough of such activities, and those which do extend them will impose an 'unfair' burden on local residents. This problem can be dealt with by specific central government subsidies to certain activities, and in the U.K. Government grants to local authorities originated in this way with payments towards the cost of 'national services' such as main roads and education which were thought to generate 'spill-overs'.

A second function of central grants is to alleviate 'fiscal imbalance'. If taxes are raised by that level of government which is able to levy them most efficiently, while expenditures are determined at the level of government which is able to administer *them* most effectively, there is no reason to suppose that the resources and needs of any particular tier of government will match. It is the experience of the U.K. and of most other countries, that tax collection has become more centralized than expenditure decisions, and there is therefore a need for offsetting grants from the centre to local units (revenue-sharing).

Grants can also be used to redistribute revenue among local authorities. We might ask why it is necessary or desirable to redistribute among governments rather than directly to persons. Local authorities differ in terms of resources; some represent poor areas, while others—such as the City of London— have a large local tax base because they contain concentrations of commercial property which yield far more in terms of rateable value than they demand in local services. Local authorities also differ in their needs. Some may have large numbers of children or old people who make extensive use of the facilities which local government provide. It may be more expensive to provide the same frequency of refuse collection or to keep the roads clear of snow in a scattered rural area than in a densely populated urban environment. (Although it is not obvious why town dwellers should pay for this.) An individual who lives in an area with low resources, or extensive needs, will need to pay more in order to secure the same level of local services as someone who is more favourably located. This is not only inequitable, but may lead to movements between areas which exacerbate the initial problem (as may have happened in the USA).

Designing an equalization scheme to deal with these problems is by no means easy. If resources are measured by rateable value, then areas such as London will appear to have greater than average resources not because Londoners are especially rich but because property in London is relatively expensive. Although the Layfield Committee clearly identified the problem, successive governments appear not to have understood. Nor can the needs of a local authority be objectively determined. Although there is now extensive statistical analysis of the spending patterns of local authorities, the choice of explanatory variables and the legitimacy of particular needs is inevitably a matter of subjective judgement and ultimately of political whim. And what exactly is it that a redistribution scheme should equalize? Perhaps local authorities should each be able to provide the same level of services at the same cost to local residents. But what level of services should be chosen? How much of any increase or shortfall should be borne locally and how much should be reflected in changes in grant? What is meant by cost to local residents?

Yet another objective—and one which has acquired increasing importance—is control over the overall level of local authority spending. This can be done by offering carrots and sticks to induce local government to conform to central government wishes. But why should the national government be concerned to control the level of local spending, as distinct from the level of its own contribution to that spending? The difference, after all, is something which local authorities will have to raise for themselves. It is natural that I should monitor carefully my own donation to the Red Cross; less clear why I should want to restrict the amount which the Red Cross obtains from other people. If there were some rigid limit to taxable capacity, then every pound a local authority raised would reduce the revenue available to central government by a pound; and hence central and local expenditures would be directly competitive. But while it is true that the higher the level of taxation the greater is the cost of raising additional taxation, the magnitude of this effect is small. The burden of taxation rises steadily with its level, rather than reaching some fixed ceiling. If local authorities are required to raise the revenue for additional expenditure from their own resources, there is really no more reason for central government to be concerned with their expenditure levels than for it to be concerned about the expenditure levels of any other agents in the economy.

The development of the grant system

Grants were initially related mainly to 'spill-overs'—to encourage the provision of services which benefited the population at large rather than the residents of a particular authority. For this reason, they were 'hypothecated' grants—the government met a proportion of expenditure on specific approved items. As time progressed fiscal imbalance became more an important rationale for government grants. In the 1960s local revenue sources were much less buoyant than local expenditures and the government greatly increased the proportion of local spending which was met from central funds. As the level of local authority spending rose, so did the need for redistribution of resources between authorities. Specific grants were substantially replaced by an unhypothecated general grant, which contained elements related to both the needs and the resources of particular authorities.

The Layfield Committee reported in the mid 1970s. It identified incompatible demands on the British local government system. On the one hand, local autonomy and control of local services is jealously asserted; and on the other, we want central government to procure appropriate service levels, to restrain both local and national tax demands, and to achieve equity between different local authorities and between different groups who receive services from local authorities or finance them. We cannot achieve all these objectives simultaneously; and if we insist on trying to do so we move, as we have, to an even more irrational and incoherent system of local authority finance. Layfield therefore proposed that the system should move either in the direction of greater central control of local services, or towards more real independence of local government. The second alternative—which was clearly preferred—required new sources of local revenue in order to increase the financial autonomy of local authorities. A local income tax was proposed as a means of achieving this.

The government buried the Layfield Report under a mountain of platitudes, favouring instead a 'middle way' between the Scylla of central control and the Charbydis of local autonomy. Subsequent events have confirmed the Layfield analysis, and demonstrated that there is no middle way. Either you drive a car yourself, or you allow someone else to do it, possibly under instructions as to the general direction he is to take. If you appoint a driver but insist on dictating every change of gear or steering to him, you will end up off the road; and this is what has in fact occurred. Relations between central and local government have deteriorated rapidly. This has followed from the introduction in 1980 of a new block grant system and from increasing— and generally unsuccessful—attempts to plan the levels of spending both of individual authorities and of local government in aggregate. Under block grant, a grant related expenditure (GRE) is defined for each authority. This is based on a central government assessment of its spending needs. The basic principle is that each local authority should be able to fund its GRE from its block grant and the notional rate income which it derives from a standard rate poundage. If an authority's expenditure is equal to its GRE, then it has a notional rate income equal to its rateable value times the standard rate poundage. Its block grant will then be equal to the difference between the GRE and the notional rate income.

If block grant were fixed at this level, then local authorities which spent more than their GRE would have to find the balance from their local resources, and those who spent less would be able to refund the difference to their residents. However block grant varies as actual expenditure differs from the centrally determined GRE. This variation has two purposes. Central government acts to some degree as ratepayer for councils with low rateable resources of their own, and hence makes some contribution to overspending and retains some of the benefit of underspending. At the same time, the government seeks to penalize high spending and discourage low spending. These two objectives are directly contradictory. It follows that deviations from the GRE may be either taxed or subsidized depending on how the balance of them chances to fall, and additional expenditure of £1 may cost local residents more or less than £1.

The basis of grant for an authority whose spending differs from its GRE is fixed by a 'poundage schedule'. The poundage schedule defines the rate which should be levied to fund any specified excess or shortfall from the GRE. Once the relationship between GRE and actual expenditure is known, a 'grant-related poundage' (GRP) can be determined from the poundage schedule. The GRP increases, and at an increasing rate, as expenditure above the GRE increases. The notional rate income —the amount the authority is expected to raise from its own resources— is now equal to the GRP times the rateable value. Block grant is once more equal to the difference between actual expenditure and notional rate income. It follows that if the system operates as it should, two different authorities with actual expenditures which are the same proportion of their GRE would each be charging the same rate poundage, if their other resources were the same. By varying the poundage schedule the government can vary the inducement or penalty for under or overspending.

If the reader finds this difficult to understand then his bewilderment is certainly shared by many local councillors. This very complexity can lead to perverse incentives. If an authority is overspending its GRE modestly, then additional expenditure may be very costly because it leads to substantial loss of block grant. Once grant has been lost altogether, however, the penalty disappears, since you cannot get less than zero grant. The cost to ratepayers of *further* spending falls. It follows that if you overspend at all it may make sense to overspend hugely, and a number of major authorities—such as the Inner London Education Authority—are in precisely this position. The problem is compounded because the inevitable arbitrariness of the expenditure assessment leads to GRE figures which are in many cases quite unrealistic.

But perhaps the most serious consequence is that, as the chief financial officer of the GLC has commented, 'our financial performance is determined more by the changes in grant than by any action which the Council takes' (Stonefrost, 1982). Table 9.2 shows how tenuous the relationship between changes in expenditure and changes in rate levels has become. If changes in grants have a larger effect on the financial outcome than changes in expenditure, then it is hardly surprising if local authorities devote more attention to lobbying for the former than controlling the latter. If an excessively sophisticated system of incentives and disincentives has the consequence that changes in rate bills mainly result from factors outside local control then the effect is entirely counter-productive.

Alternatives to domestic rates

The government's rather surprising response to the crisis in local government finance has been to conclude that what is needed is a substitute for domestic rates, and a green paper 'Alternatives to Domestic Rates' was published late in 1982. Domestic rates occasion much criticism. Often this criticism is less than coherent, and it sometimes seems that a principal reason for the volume of protest is simply that

TABLE 9.2

Expenditure changes and rate changes, 1982–3

Local Authority	Increase in planned expenditure, 1982–3 over 1981–2 (%)	Increase in average domestic rate bill, 1982–3 over 1981–2 (%)
GLC	42·6	42·8
Nottingham	21·9	33·4
South Northants	21·4	13·5
Kingston upon Hull	8·3	46·5
City of London	5·9	31·8
Lambeth	5·5	−2·9
Richmond	1·8	28·3
Basingstoke	−6·5	14·0
North Norfolk	−13·2	14·1

Source: Financial Times, 21 July 1982

rates are an unusually transparent tax; there are few other cases where individual taxpayers are personally and directly responsible for making payments. The major objections expressed are that the burden of rates is independent of the number of earners in a household; that they bear heavily on people (such as pensioners) who live in property which is large relative to their incomes; and that they are inequitable as between individuals who live in different parts of the country with different property prices. The essence of all these criticisms is that domestic rates are not an income tax; and any attempt to modify domestic rates to respond to these criticisms would have the effect of turning them into something close to an income tax. If this is the basis of the argument on which domestic rates are to be replaced, then there is one and only one alternative tax that meets the bill, and that is local income tax.

These arguments against the rating system are not as strong as they might at first sight appear. Income is a measure of taxable capacity, but it is not the only one or necessarily the best. Income, supplemented by information about housing consumption, may well give a better guide to a household's standard of living than either of these variables alone and this is what a tax system which includes both national income tax and domestic rates achieves. The argument stresses the importance of looking at the impact of local authority taxation as part of the tax system as a whole, and not in isolation.

Local income taxes are used to finance local services in many other countries. There are, however, peculiar administrative difficulties in implementing a local income tax in Britain. The reason is that while almost all other countries make rough and ready deductions of income tax from pay and assess liability by means of an end-year tax return and assessment, the British system attempts to secure exact deductions of the tax due and exempts most taxpayers from an annual return. It is easy in other countries to incorporate the assessment and collection of local income tax in the annual return; in Britain it would be necessary to establish place of residence in a separate inquiry and notify this to employers for each one of their employees individually. Even on the modest proposals of the Layfield Committee, it was estimated that this would require a 15% increase in Inland Revenue staff and expenditure.

There is an obvious alternative, which is for Britain to move over to collecting its income tax in the same way as everyone else. The Green Paper notes this possibility, but observes that 'Major issues of tax policy and administration would be raised which would need to be examined thoroughly and in detail on their own merits before any change of this kind could be made' (para. 6.23). If this statement was intended to be a preliminary to such a thorough examination, it would have been one of the most encouraging statements in the Green Paper; but there is no indication that it is anything of the kind. The reference to thoroughness and detail appears not as a prelude to action, but as a reason for inaction. The best test of the sincerity of the government's intention to seek alternative sources of finance for local authorities is the date and speed with which it begins detailed consideration of the implications of a universal end-year assessment system.

The second alternative to domestic rates is a poll tax. A poll tax could not replace rates, unless levied at unimaginably high levels, but it could supplement existing sources of local authority finance. There are two major objections to it. The first is that it is regressive. This could be overcome by adjusting the national tax and benefit system by increasing income tax allowances and benefit rates. What matters from the point of view of social and economic policy is not the progressive or regressive impact of every individual element of the tax system, but the impact of that system as a whole. It is perfectly possible, and may be necessary, to have a regressive local authority tax system within an overall progressive tax structure.

The second problem follows closely from the first. A general poll tax could be a cheaply administered revenue raiser for local authorities. But would it be possible to implement such a tax while resisting pressure to exempt old age pensioners, low income earners, pregnant women and so on? If not, we could easily end with a tax system that presented all the administrative burden of a separately administered local income tax with none of the advantages of equity and flexibility which an income tax itself would offer.

The reform of local government finance

It is odd that the subject of reform of domestic rates should have been pushed to the front of the stage. Each of the three main sources of local government finance—domestic rates, industrial and commercial rates, and government grants—is properly the subject of considerable criticism; but the case against the present structure of domestic rates is the weakest of the three. A more urgent reform is one which would make local authorities more effectively responsible for raising their own revenue from their own constituents. This would, as Layfield argued, both restore local autonomy and secure more effective financial control over local authority spending. The grant system, and the structure of non-domestic rates, require more urgent attention.

A programme of this kind demands substantial reductions in the average level of block grant. Non-domestic rates have little merit as a tax and less as a local tax. There are enormous disparities between authorities in the size of the commercial and industrial rate base, and it is clear that many councils have—perhaps mistakenly—seen it as a milch-cow which can be exploited indefinitely without detriment to the local economy. If non-domestic rates are to be retained—and any sudden abolition would create extensive and arbitrary disruption in the property market—then these deficiencies would be removed by transforming them into a national tax at a fixed poundage.

These two changes—reducing grants to local authorities and transforming industrial and commercial rates into a national tax—would lead to the loss of most existing local authority revenue, and its transfer to the national exchequer. Assuming no major change in the range or level of local authority services, the only possible source of finance on the required scale would be a local income tax at a high average rate. This could be offset by corresponding reductions in the level of national income tax, so that no overall increase in the burden of income taxation need be implied. If local income tax were to finance most local authority expenditure, it is likely that the typical rate of local income tax would be higher than the residual national income tax. We might see local tax rates of 15-20% and a national tax of 10-15%. This programme sounds a revolutionary one; but the revolution it requires is mostly the revolution of established arrangements in Whitehall, and the impact of these changes on the man in the street would actually be quite small. By far the most important implication for him is that he would become aware of the scale of local authority expenditure, of its potential impact on his standard of living and conscious of the implications of its control. That is the objective of the change.

CAPITAL TAXATION

AS yet we have not considered a group of taxes which can best be
described as capital taxes. These include taxes on the value of property
owned or transferred to another individual, but it is both difficult and
misleading to attempt a clear-cut distinction between taxes on income
and taxes on capital in just the same way that we have argued against
making a rigid distinction between income and capital. For example,
we have already examined capital gains tax when discussing the
taxation of unearned income, and rates (a tax on the value of property)
when looking at the structure of indirect taxes. There is one group of
taxes, however, which would immediately be recognized as constituting
an example of capital taxation, and that is taxes levied on inheritance,
gifts, and the transfer of wealth from one generation to another. Another example of a capital tax is an annual wealth tax.

Taxes on capital have a longer history than taxes on income. This
may seem surprising to those people who regard the idea of a wealth
tax as a recent left-wing idea, but rulers found it easier to measure their
subjects' wealth than to perform the more sophisticated calculations
necessary to compute their income. The idea of death duties goes back
many centuries. Modern legislation dates from the introduction of
probate duty in 1694 which lasted until the famous budget of Sir William
Harcourt in 1894 which brought in estate duty. In the eighteenth and
nineteenth centuries two other taxes on transfers at death were
enacted, legacy duty and succession duty, and these survived until
1949. These two latter duties embodied the principle that the tax paid
should reflect the circumstances of the recipient, or donee, rather than
the size of the estate. Estate duty related the tax paid on transfers of
wealth only to the circumstances of the donor. There have been many
suggestions for replacing estate duty with a tax on the receipts of beneficiaries. Such a tax is often called an accessions tax and in 1972 the
Government published a Green Paper (Cmnd. 4930) to stimulate discussion on the idea of moving towards inheritance taxation. But when
estate duty was finally overhauled in 1975 it was transformed into

capital transfer tax which continued to relate tax liability to the size of the estate.

Capital transfer tax did, however, bring one very important change to the system of taxing transfers of wealth in Britain. For the first time it extended the taxation of estates to cover gifts. Under the old estate duty the principle was not to tax gifts at all, but in order to prevent gifts made 'in contemplation of death' avoiding tax altogether it was necessary to include gifts made just before death in the taxable estate.[1] If the only loophole were death-bed gifts then a rule including gifts made within a few weeks of death would be sufficient. But wealthy individuals and their wealthy advisers are sufficiently ingenious to plan to give away at least part of the estate well before the expected date of death, and by so doing they were able to avoid tax altogether. The Government responded by extending the length of the period before death within which gifts made were taxable from nothing to three months, then to a year, three years, five years . . .! Before it was replaced, estate duty covered gifts made within seven years of death. Clearly, the taxman favoured the healthy, wealthy, and well advised.

The addition of gifts to the base of the transfer tax was a logical and necessary step, although since the introduction of capital transfer tax the Government has seen fit to reduce the tax rate on gifts to considerably less than the rate applying to transfers on death. Allegedly this was to help ease the problems of the transfer of small private businesses, but it increases the possibility of tax avoidance and reintroduces the creation of rules to prevent deathbed gifts which are now defined to be those made less than three years before death. Another change which followed the inclusion of gifts was the decision to levy tax on the *cumulative* lifetime total of gifts and bequests made. Instead of being an annual tax, capital transfer tax was designed to be a tax on lifetime transfers. But in 1982 the government changed this principle to basing the tax on transfers made within a ten year period. Hence when a gift or transfer is made, the tax charged is based on a cumulation of transfers over ten years. Although there is a good case for lifetime cumulation, and some case for an annual tax, it is difficult to conceive of any economic justification for basing a tax on transfers cumulated over a period of ten years. Rather, this change, like others introduced in recent years, appears to be aimed at nibbling away at the base of the tax thus reducing the burden and eroding receipts of revenue. The

[1] The technical phrase '*Inter vivos* gifts' is used to describe gifts made before the date when they would become taxable as transfers on death.

amount which may be given away tax free within any ten year period is (1982-3) £55,000 and in addition there is an annual exemption of £3,000 per individual. In 1982 it was announced that the threshold for capital transfer tax would in future be indexed (over-indexed in fact because the adjusted threshold each year will be rounded up to the nearest £1,000).

The move to replace estate duty by capital transfer tax was inspired by the evident failings of estate duty. Avoidance of estate duty became so easy that it was sometimes described as a 'voluntary tax'. There have been so many changes to the detailed tax legislation, all designed to stop up the loopholes, that the tax avoidance industry has grown as rapidly as any. Yet despite these efforts the tax has done little to bring about a more equal distribution of wealth, and seems relatively unimportant in comparison with the effects of high rates of inflation which we discuss later. The easiest way of avoiding estate duty was simply to hand on wealth to the next generation and hope that you lived for another seven years. That way you would never pay tax at all. In a study of the importance of tax avoidance by *inter vivos* gifts Horsman (1975) found that in the late 1960s the values of gifts made upon which duty was never charged was probably of the order of £330 m. a year. The amount of tax avoided was estimated by Horsman to have been £177 m. in 1968 compared to actual receipts of death duties in that year of £382 m. Given the importance of avoidance by this means it is strange that the Government gave way to pressure and introduced lower rates of tax on *inter vivos* gifts under capital transfer tax.

Gifts were not the only method by which it was possible to avoid paying estate duty. Lower rates of duty were charged on agricultural land and property, assets of private business, growing timber, and works of art. No doubt a good case was made out for the special treatment of each of these classes of assets in turn, but these arguments almost always overlook the basic principle of the capitalization of taxes of which we have given several examples in this book. If a concession is made to the taxation of growing timber then wealthy individuals will switch at least part of their wealth from other assets into growing timber. This extra demand will bid up the price of timber until there is no net advantage in passing on wealth in one form rather than another. Tax revenue falls, and those who gain are the people who happened to own the timber when the concession was announced. It is hard to see what is achieved by this, and in the case of farming it can have perverse results. The reason for giving concessions to agriculture is to help farmers continue in the profession. But all that happens is that farms become much more valuable than would otherwise have been the case (thus making farmers even more concerned at the prospect of paying tax) and it becomes even more difficult for the genuine small farmer to borrow enough to purchase his own farm. On top of this, many farmers become millionaires, a fact which they find puzzling because there is no change in their standard of living. The only way in which they can enjoy the benefit of their good fortune is to abandon farming, at which we hope they were skilled, sell out, and go and live in the South of France. We suspect many farmers would be happier on their farms than in the casino in Monte Carlo.

We would have hoped that the introduction of capital transfer tax would have seen the end of these anomalies. Not a bit of it; reduced rates apply to gifts *inter vivos*. Although this concession was given to reduce the 'threat' to small businesses, it applies to transfers of *any* kind of asset. We shall return to the subject of small businesses later in the chapter. Agriculture too receives special treatment. It is zero-rated for V.A.T., exempt from rates, receives concessions for capital gains tax, and the value of agricultural property is reduced by 50% for the purposes of capital transfer tax. There are restrictions on those who may benefit from agricultural relief but the definition of 'working farmer' is not too difficult to satisfy. There is also special relief for gifts made to charity and for works of art and historic buildings.

Another method of avoiding tax has been for the wealthy to set up trusts, the trustees of which could distribute the income and capital of the trust in any way they wished to individuals on a list of potential beneficiaries. This sort of trust, called a discretionary trust, could (provided it satisfied certain minimal conditions) escape estate duty altogether and hence was an attractive way of handing on family wealth down the generations without paying tax. It was clearly important to stop up this loophole. Some steps were taken in 1969 and the switch to capital transfer tax also brought with it changes in the tax treatment of trusts. It may be that in due course these changes will be seen to have stopped up some of the more serious loopholes. The prospect of this was diminished when in June 1979 the new Conservative Government postponed for two years the date when discretionary trusts will be taxed under the full C.T.T. provisions. This was later postponed further until 1983. But the rewards for successful ingenuity in this area are great, and the use of trusts, many of which are set up for the sole purpose of tax avoidance, seems likely to remain a vehicle for the rich to hand on their wealth. Indeed, a leading authority on the subject has written, 'in Great Britain it is probably true to say that 95% of all discretionary and accumulation trusts are created solely for tax-saving reasons' (Wheatcroft, 1965, p. 136).

Although there are high nominal tax rates at the top end of the scale, the numerous possibilities for avoidance mean the system raises little revenue and average tax rates are rather low. As Atkinson has commented, 'Where those with good tax advisers—and perhaps few scruples—can pay little tax while others pay tax at rates up to 80%, there can be little respect for the equity of taxation' (Atkinson, 1972, p. 129). The failure of capital transfer tax to remedy the deficiencies of estate duty can be seen from Table 10.1. From 1963–4 to 1973–4 the revenue from estate duty rose 32% in contrast to the rise in money G.D.P. of 139% and in total tax revenue of no less than 166%. But since 1973 the revenue from transfer taxes has hardly risen in nominal terms. Between 1973–4 and 1981–2 the combined receipts of estate duty and capital transfer tax rose 21% in a period during which prices rose by 218%!

It is possible for individuals who are obviously far from being paupers to die leaving estates for tax purposes which bear little relation to their real wealth. It is generally believed that the largest sum ever paid in death duties, by a considerable margin, was the £11 m.

TABLE 10.1

Revenue from transfer taxes
(£ m.)

	Estate duty	Capital transfer tax
1963/4	312	—
1973/4	412	—
1974/5	339	—
1975/6	212	118
1976/7	124	259
1977/8	87	311
1978/9	46	323
1979/80	32	401
1980/1	27	425
1981/2	17	481

Source: Inland Revenue Statistics, 1982, Table 1.1.

paid on an estate estimated at between £40 m. and £60 m. on the death of the third Duke of Westminster in 1953. On the subsequent death of the fourth Duke, his reported estate was a little over £4 m., on which estate duty came to around £1 m. In fact not even this sum was paid, since after a protracted legal case it was resolved that the Duke (who was partially disabled by war wounds received in 1942 and who died of cancer in 1967) was entitled to the benefit of an exemption from estate duty for those killed on active military service. The fifth Duke died in 1979, and press reports then estimated that the family fortune controlled by the new Duke of Westminster was between £300 m. and £800 m. Again the reported estate was expected to be less than £5 m. (Daily Telegraph, Feb. 20 1979).

Another major cause of the failure of death duties to produce revenue is the rate structure. At first sight this may seem surprising because the 'enormously high' rates of up to 8% imposed by Harcourt in his 1894 Budget have steadily risen and the top marginal rate today is 75% (50% on gifts). But to pay an average tax rate of even 30% requires the transfer of an estate of £200,000 and that is before taking any account of the special concessions to gifts or particular assets described above. If the money is handed on as a gift (provided it is made more than three years before death) an average tax rate of 30% would need a gift of £750,000, and if the gift consisted of a small business the maximum tax rate would be 25%. On a gift of a small business worth £5 m. the average tax rate (in 1982/3) was 19·8%. In 1982/3 a single person on average earnings pays income tax (including national insurance contributions) at an average rate of almost 30%. We should also note that transfers between husband and wife (whether during life or on death) are completely exempt from tax. Gifts to charities are also exempt from tax.

The reason for this disparity between high marginal and low average rates on capital transfers is the very high exemption level below which no tax at all is paid, £55,000, and the slow build-up of marginal rates (see Table 10.2). With good advice few people need pay much capital transfer tax. The exemption level may remove the 'average' family from the tax net but it also reduces the effective tax rate charged on the larger estates. In real terms the exemption level is much higher now than it was in 1894. Moreover, the effective exemption level can be very much higher than the apparent value of £55,000 every 10 years. This is because each year any individual may give away £3,000 tax free. A married couple can therefore pass on to their children £6,000 each

TABLE 10.2

Rates of Capital transfer tax 1982–83

Value of total estate (£)	Marginal rate (%)	Average rate (%)
55 000	30	0
100 000	40	15
250 000	60	35
1 000 000	65	55

These rates apply to transfers on or within three years before death. Lower rates apply to *inter vivos* gifts.

year without incurring tax at all. This is obviously much easier for the wealthy family which can transfer the ownership of stocks and shares, than for the more typical family whose main assets are in the form of an owner-occupied house the ownership of which is difficult to transfer bit by bit. Over a twenty-year period a couple could pass on more than £230,000 without paying a penny in tax! On top of this there is a tax-free allowance of £5,000 for gifts made in 'consideration of marriage'. There cannot be many married couples who anticipate returning from honeymoon to a cheque for £5,000.

The combination of very high exemption levels at the bottom and high marginal rates at the top has not been very effective in redistributing wealth. Redistribution is about average tax rates and raising revenue, and as we have seen capital taxes in their present form are not major revenue raisers. In 1981–2 the combined revenue from estate duty and capital transfer tax amounted to £498 m., which is about what would be raised by an increase of one-half percentage point on the basic rate of income tax and compares with total income tax receipts of £51 bn. (which of course exclude V.A.T. and other indirect taxes which are collected by the Customs and Excise). It is natural to ask whether this low yield is inevitable, or whether it can be substantially raised. We shall return to this question later.

A wealth tax

It is clear that there are major weaknesses in the existing taxation of capital in Britain. There are two directions, not necessarily incompatible, in which efforts to reform the system can be made. The first would be to overhaul the methods of taxing transfers (gifts and bequests), and the second would be to adopt an annual tax on wealth. We shall discuss the reform of transfer taxation below, and we first examine proposals for an annual wealth tax. The 1974-79 Labour Government considered a wealth tax and published proposals for public discussion in the form of a Green Paper (Cmnd. 5704). These were examined in detail in a report of a Select Committee of the House of Commons (published in 1975: H.C. 696−2). The Committee was, however, unable to agree upon a Report, and the published document contains several minority Reports.

The motive for putting forward the idea of a tax on wealth largely derives from a feeling that the distribution of wealth is too unequal. Table 10.3 shows some of the available evidence on the distribution of

TABLE 10.3

Distribution of personal wealth in Britain, 1979
(%)

	Excluding pension rights	Including pension rights
Top 1%	24	13
Top 5%	45	27
Top 10%	59	37

Source: Social Trends, 1982.

wealth in Britain. These figures have been produced by the Royal Commission on the Distribution of Income and Wealth, although they are subject to both error and difficulties of interpretation. (For a careful analysis of the evidence on wealth distribution see the study of Atkinson and Harrison, 1978.) It is clear from the table that there is substantial inequality in the distribution of wealth, although it is difficult to know what standards of comparison we should use when making value judgements about the distribution of wealth. Another feature is that rich people choose to hold their wealth in very different forms from those of less rich people. Table 10.4 shows how two groups of individuals, those with net wealth in the range £10,000–£20,000 and those with wealth over £200,000, divide their holdings between different assets. The first group holds about one-half in the form of owner-occupied houses and another quarter in savings with life assurance companies and building societies. Holdings of shares and other company securities are negligible. For the richest individuals the picture is very different. Company securities comprise over one-third of the wealth of this group and land 20%.

The figures shown in Table 10.4 do not include wealth held in the form of rights to future pensions. Yet it is clear from Table 10.3 that the estimates of the inequality of wealth-holding depend quite sensitively on whether or not we include the value of pension rights (both occupational and state) in the value of an individual's wealth. An individual cannot sell these rights, and he must live at least to retirement age for them to be of any value. But they have an actuarial value and most people would be very upset if their pension rights were taken away. Estimates by the Government Actuary form the basis of the figures in Table 10.3. To value a pension right to a particular individual we have to estimate his chance of survival until the year when the pension will be paid, the pension which will be paid in future years, the tax rate which will be paid on the pension, and the rate at which the future pension should be discounted. The value of the pension will probably be uncertain, especially if it is 'index-linked', and may therefore depend upon future rates of inflation. The valuation of pension rights involves making forecasts of all these factors over a considerable time period and is a difficult exercise.

TABLE 10.4

Asset composition of Personal Wealth in Britain, 1976

Asset	Range of wealth (£)		Total for all ranges
	10 000–20 000	Over 200 000	
Dwellings[1]	49·1	12·5	34·8
Land	1·0	20·0	3·8
Company securities	2·1	36·1	10·5
Life policies	17·6	2·7	15·1
Building society deposits	9·0	1·2	8·9
Cash and bank deposits	4·9	8·5	6·9
Other[2]	16·3	19·0	20·0
Net wealth	100·0	100·0	100·0

[1] Net of mortgages.
[2] Net of personal debts; principal component is consumer durables.
Source: Royal Commission on the Distribution of Income and Wealth, Report No. 7, Table 4.6 (H.M.S.O., 1979, Cmnd. 7595).

It would not matter so much if the final result was not very sensitive to the assumptions made but, unfortunately, this is not the case. The value to a 40-year-old male of a pension scheme which begins at age 60 and pays the maximum approved benefits is shown in Table 10.5 under various assumptions about the growth of his earnings and the rate of

TABLE 10.5

Value of pension rights of man aged 40
(£)

		With indexation inflation rate			Without indexation inflation rate		
		2½%	7½%	12½%	2½%	7½%	12½%
Real growth	0%	6200	21 000	105 000	4300	11 500	32 000
of earnings	2%	7700	31 500	156 000	6500	17 500	47 500
	5%	14 000	57 500	284 000	11 700	32 000	86 500

Assumptions: (i) Earnings of £5,000 per year at age 40–20 years service in scheme paying maximum I.R. approved benefits based on final salary–retirement at 60;
(ii) no benefit on death before retirement;
(iii) an interest rate of 7½%;
(iv) 'with indexation' assumes pension indexed after retirement; 'without indexation' assumes no subsequent increase.
Source: Own calculations based on English Life Table 12.

inflation. It is easy to see that the value of his pension rights is extremely sensitive to the assumptions made about his earnings prospects, the future rate of inflation, and upon whether or not his pension is indexed. With variations of the magnitude shown in the table it would be impossible to include pension rights in an individual's taxable wealth without provoking bitter dispute about the assumptions made in valuing this right. It would also be impossible to value pension rights in cases where there was no contractual arrangement to provide a pension. For example, a director of a small company may have no formal right to a pension but a very high expectation of a good pension, not least because the directors could decide to award him a pension. In these cases no valuation could reasonably be made and if formal pension rights were taxed informal schemes would proliferate. But if pension rights were not regarded as taxable wealth there would be inequities between those with occupational pension rights and those, such as the self-employed, who had to provide their own pension, and, equally important, inequities between those in generous pension schemes and those in poor schemes. Again this would be unimportant if the numbers were small. But they are not. The total value of occupational and state pension rights is of the same order of magnitude as all the other forms of personal wealth put together, about £200,000 m. each (Royal Commission on the Distribution of Income and Wealth Report No. 4). And, as we have seen, for an individual pension rights can be enormous. Pension rights pose a very serious problem for a wealth tax.

The other form of wealth which it is quite impossible to measure is 'human capital', the value of future earnings, which we discussed in Chapter 5. Since this form of wealth would not be subject to tax, it seems preferable to regard a 'wealth tax' as proposed as an annual assets tax, charged on assets which can be easily identified and valued, which somewhat diminishes its theoretical attractions. In addition to concern with the distribution of wealth, there is the argument that wealth gives rise to 'taxable capacity' in its own right. Thus Kaldor, when discussing tax reform in India, cited the example of a beggar and a man who hoarded gold, both of whom received no current monetary income (1956). But it is clear that in some ill-defined sense the man with great wealth has a greater taxable capacity. If by this is meant that the wealthy man can enjoy a high standard of living then, although this is obviously true, it is an argument for a tax on expenditure rather than a wealth tax as such. Of course, it may be argued that wealth gives power, influence, and security as well as monetary benefits, and this is no doubt true. But it is difficult to relate these non-pecuniary benefits to any monetary valuation of wealth, and power also derives from sources other than wealth. Nevertheless, it suggests the idea that a tax on wealth could be used to tax *all* the benefits of wealth-holding, both pecuniary and non-pecuniary. With this idea a wealth tax would replace all existing taxes on the holding (though not the transfer) of wealth and the income which derives from it. Taxes on unearned income and on capital gains would be replaced by an annual tax on wealth.

Such a proposal has been put forward by Flemming and Little (1974), and we must say that it has evident attractions in principle. But in order to work it would have to be applied to everybody, and this would entail the daunting task of valuing the wealth of each individual every year. Of course, conventions would be adopted, but these would be open to political pressure and in no time concessions and loopholes for the rich would have been opened up, leaving the rest to pay the tax.

Valuation problems have always been considered the biggest obstacle to the introduction of a wealth tax, even for a tax applying only to the top 1% of the wealth distribution. These problems would become enormous if extended to the rest of the population, and in those European countries which use a wealth tax very generous valuations are made, especially for owner-occupiers and no attempt is made to tax pension rights. To exclude the latter from the tax base would be inequitable in the context of a wealth tax which would replace the existing methods of taxing investment income, and to attempt to include them would be impracticable. The idea of a comprehensive wealth tax, although appealing in theory, founders on the problems of what to do about pension rights and of valuation.

An alternative version of a wealth tax is one that applies only to those at the very top of the wealth distribution. This was the basis of the proposals in the Green Paper on Wealth Tax which envisaged a threshold of £100,000 (in 1974). This would mean that the tax applied to only the top 0·6% of wealth-holders. This is such a small proportion of the total distribution that, combined with the concessions proposed for pensions, the 'national heritage', and business assets, the tax would have achieved little by way of real distribution of wealth, and would have been more of an irritant than a comprehensive tax. To adopt a very high threshold for a wealth tax is to throw away one of the attractions of such a tax, namely its relative simplicity as a means of taxing unearned income compared to the current taxation of property income.

In our introduction we discussed what was meant by 'practicable' tax reforms. In these terms, a wealth tax is simply impracticable, although in principle it seems an attractive tax. By this we do not mean that it would be impossible to run something which could be described as a wealth tax, and indeed this is done in other countries though there is none in which it raises substantial revenue. But the simple fact is that the only assets which could be brought fully within the tax would be quoted securities and bank accounts; these amount to a small proportion of all assets and one which would get smaller. The list of those which would or could be dealt with in only a limited or arbitrary way is much longer; private companies, agricultural assets, houses and other durable goods, 'national heritage' items, trusts, life insurance policies, pension rights, and so on. The result is that the base of a wealth tax would be so deficient that it could not, without intolerable administrative strain and complexity, bear the strain of other than very low rates; would inevitably impose extensive anomalies and distortions in operation; and would not raise significant revenue or effect any noticeable redistribution of wealth.

Gifts under a lifetime expenditure tax

There is another way of looking at the distribution of wealth, and that is not to focus on the share of any percentile group, but to look at the continuity of wealth-holding. We ask the question—are the people who are rich today the sons and daughters of those who were rich in the previous generation? This question has been extensively investigated by Harbury and his collaborators who examined the estates of sets of fathers and sons (Harbury and MacMahon, 1973; Harbury and Hitchens, 1976). They found that there was a highly significant correlation between dying rich and having had a rich father. Inherited wealth remains an important determinant of the distribution of wealth at the top of the distribution, although its influence may be declining slightly. Harbury and Hitchens (1979) found that 60% of those who died wealthy had themselves inherited a large amount; so large in fact that had their fathers been a random sample of the male population the figure would have been less than 1%.

In the light of this evidence we are inclined to put more weight on inequalities of wealth caused by inheritance than on inequalities resulting from differences in lifetime accumulations. This leads us away from an annual wealth tax and towards the taxation of gifts and bequests. We shall now consider ways of reforming the taxation of transfers.

The first, and most obvious, change is that gifts *inter vivos* could be taxed at the same rates as apply to estates or gifts made within three years before death. A more important change, however, is to examine closely the rate structure. Too much attention is paid to the high marginal rates at the top end which gives rise to the myth of the terrible burden of death duties. The very high exemption level means that the bulk of wealth which is transferred either on death or by gift pays a very low average rate of tax. We feel that it is important to consider carefully the idea of including all transfers in the tax base. One way of doing this is by a comprehensive income tax which counts as income of an individual all receipts of gifts and bequests during the year. Since an individual may have little control over the timing of receipts of gifts and inheritances, his income defined in this way may fluctuate wildly from year to year. Under a progressive tax system this may mean that he would pay more tax than if he had received the same amount in equal instalments. This possibility has led to an acceptance of the need for averaging provisions under a comprehensive income tax. In Chapter 5 we discussed a better way of measuring an individual's lifetime comprehensive income which we saw was equal to the total use of resources over his lifetime. This can be measured by the sum of his consumption plus gifts and bequests made. So if we wish to impose an annual tax on a measure of the individual's lifetime use of resources, a better way of achieving this objective is to impose an annual tax on consumption plus gifts made during the year, the lifetime expenditure tax. Like the comprehensive income tax it includes transfers in the main personal tax base but the amount included refers to gifts made, not those received, and hence the donor can smooth the timing of gifts if he so wishes which reduces the need for averaging provisions.

There are three main virtues of the lifetime expenditure tax. First, it is genuinely a tax on an individual's lifetime income or uses of resources, and in that sense is superior to a comprehensive income tax. Second, it would widen the tax base quite considerably because all transfers (except for some very small exemption on gifts which had to be included) would come within the tax net. Third, since all transfers would be taxed such a scheme holds out the hope of a reasonably equitable way of taxing owner-occupiers. As we have seen, other attempts to remove the tax subsidy are problematic because the concessions have already been capitalized, and existing home-owners do not have the resources to cope with the removal of the tax concessions to mortgage interest payments. But to tax the value of owner-occupied property transferred by gift or, more usually, on death is a relatively painless way of recouping some of the revenue. This proposal would generate enough revenue to enable a reduction to be made in the tax rate on earned income (or expenditure out of earned income), but it would impose very much heavier taxes on gifts and inherited wealth than currently exist. The extra revenue would arise because the 'typical' estate consisting, say, of a house and little else, would pay tax at full personal tax rates and because a much heavier tax burden would be imposed on medium-sized and large estates resulting from the abolition of the high exemption level. Even with a top marginal tax rate under the lifetime expenditure tax (L.E.T.) of 50% virtually all large estates would pay more tax than at present. Gifts would be included in the annual L.E.T. computation, and the value of the estate resulting from death could be considered as the expenditure of a separate tax year.

The main objection which will be raised to this proposal is that the tax burden on gifts and bequests is far too great. The reply to that is in two parts. First, we have seen that with good advice available to the wealthy, the tax collected from large estates in the past has been small, and our proposal would seek to prevent this occurring in future. Second, we regard it as a merit of the proposal that the average tax-payer who is an owner-occupier will find a large sum of tax collected on his estate. At the moment there are many families who know that at some point they can expect to inherit their parents' house, and we believe many of them would be prepared to trade off part of this wind-fall gain in return for lower tax rates on earned income.

To raise substantial revenue from transfer taxes requires the elimina-tion of the sort of avoidance possibilities which we discussed above, and the extension of the tax net to catch a much larger number of tax-payers. The benefit is that less revenue need be collected from earnings or retirement savings, and tax rates can be reduced. We feel that this is an attractive prospect, and one which reflects the inherent superiority of L.E.T. as a tax on lifetime resources.

Small businesses

The proposals set out above would clearly impose a heavy financial penalty on the transmission of wealth from one generation to the next. This might be thought a severe burden on small businesses because it would not be easy to hand on majority ownership. Although it is evi-dent that small firms would find great difficulty in obtaining cash to meet the transfer tax payments, we believe that the problems of small businesses can best be dealt with by reforms which do not involve special tax concessions which create anomalies and avoidance.

The current tax system already contains a formidable range of con-cessions to small businesses. Small companies pay a lower rate of cor-poration tax; the first £50,000 of capital gains made by the owner or director of a business who is over 65 (and has worked for the firm for ten years) is completely tax-free; and transfers of certain business property can be reduced in value by 50% for the purposes of computing a capital transfer tax liability. In addition, private investors may put up to £20,000 a year into new small businesses (provided they do not work in the business) and deduct the sum so subscribed against their taxable income. This 'business start up scheme' provides tax relief at the individual's marginal tax rate for such savings, and hence is equivalent to an expenditure tax treatment. But since the returns may be received in the form of capital gains, the tax treatment is in fact more favourable than that which would obtain with an expenditure tax because capital gains tax rates are substantially below income tax rates. Despite these concessions there are still complaints that the tax system is biased against individuals trying to build up their own business. The Bolton Committee Report on Small Firms, published in 1971 (Cmnd. 4811), claimed that its basic philosophy on taxation was a 'wish to emphasise again that what is needed is a taxation policy which will restore initiative, encourage entrepreneurial activity and improve the liquidity position of small businesses. We believe that continued reduction in taxation of personal incomes and of estates would be most likely to achieve this result' (p. 200). The Committee's basic recommendations were for further special concessions to small firms, especially for estate duty purposes. Its specific suggestions included lower valuation of business property for estate duty purposes, lower capital gains tax rates for owners of small firms, tax privileges for savings by the self-employed to provide pensions, and changes in the legislation dealing with closely owned companies.

The first of these suggestions affects what happens on the death of the owner of a small business and the second and third relate to what happens when he decides to retire. It is difficult to believe that these are moments at which it is most essential to restore initiative, encourage entrepreneurial activity, and restore the liquidity position of small businesses. We saw in Chapter 4 that the distinctive characteristic of small businesses in the U.K. is not that they die prematurely but that their average age is quite exceptionally high; this does not square with the view that transfer taxes are the major problem and as we have noted estate duty was never a very effective tax anyway. We argued that the real obstacle to the growth of small businesses in Britain was the institutionalization of savings, and it is to that problem that our proposals are directed.

How do these suggestions compare with our proposals for a lifetime expenditure tax and a cash flow corporation tax? Let us leave aside for the moment the taxation of the transfer of the business when the original founder hands on the firm, and consider the treatment of the firm when the founder is creating and building up his firm. Our proposals would mean that any money devoted to investment in the business would escape tax altogether. Tax would be paid only on money which he took out of the business to spend on his personal consumption.

Since in the earliest, and most critical, stages of the firm's life the founder typically works very hard and lives frugally, our proposals would give most encouragement to the creation and expansion of new firms. There would be no capital gains tax and tax would be charged only when the founder took money out of the firm, in which case there would be no liquidity problems in meeting these tax payments. Saving for retirement would be tax-free and the cash flow corporation tax would mean that there would be no need for close company legislation (see Ch. 12), which, as the Bolton Committee pointed out, is costly both to the Inland Revenue and to the small firms concerned. The combination of a lifetime expenditure tax and a cash flow corporation tax offers substantial encouragement to the creation and growth of small businesses, and it does this without any 'special' concessions which can have such undesirable effects.

In return for these incentives to the establishment of small firms our proposals levy a heavy tax on the transfer, whether by gift or on death, of a business to the next generation. This is in sharp contrast to the attitude of the Bolton Committee which viewed estate duty as the major fiscal difficulty facing small firms. Our proposals would distinguish very clearly between those individuals who created firms and those who inherited them.

Would this inability to pass on intact to their heirs ownership of their firms act as a serious disincentive to founders of new firms? The Bolton Committee thought so, but there is very little evidence for such a belief. The most detailed examination of the question is the study by Boswell (1973) of 64 small companies. He found little evidence of the importance of the dynastic motive and even less of its desirability. The firms run by their founders performed better (in terms of profitability) than did those run by inheritors. The founders of business were less interested in handing them on to their children than were those who inherited the business themselves. Family succession can lead to serious management problems, and often occurs through lack of an alternative. Boswell studied 30 inheritors of family firms and found that as far as these were concerned 'positive enthusiasm to enter the firm seems to have been marginal' (p. 125). Moreover, firms run by the original founder who remains in charge well beyond normal retirement age suffer from 'gerontocracy' problems when the founder has lost his verve for business but is unwilling to retire because of problems of management succession. We agree with Boswell that 'it is hard to resist the conclusion that the best point at which to secure necessary changes—humanely as well as effectively—is when small firm bosses reach retirement or die. The method would be a combination of tougher inheritance taxation with public action to deal with transitional problems.' What is needed is *not* concessions on transfer taxation, but public action to develop a market in small businesses to enable ownership and control to be transferred without the destruction of the business. The stock-market achieves this already for larger firms. In return for this tougher inheritance taxation it would, under our proposals, be easier to build up a small firm in the early years than it is at present.

11

PRINCIPLES OF COMPANY TAXATION

IN the U.K. taxes on companies are more recent than personal income taxes. In the U.S. a corporate income tax first appeared in 1909, but the separate taxation of companies began in Britain only in 1947. Before then the taxation of corporate profits was integrated with the personal income tax, and special taxes on profits were used only as wartime measures to raise extra revenue. In 1947 the system was rationalized by raising the rate of profits tax and exempting individuals and partnerships from the tax altogether. In effect, in addition to income tax there was a separate tax on corporate profits. The system of corporation tax has changed at regular intervals, with major changes occurring in 1958, 1965, and 1973. The implications and significance of these changes we discuss below, but it is not surprising that they have produced a widespread feeling that it matters less what the system is than that it should be left alone. Unfortunately this is not possible. The reason is that the system is in total disarray. In 1974, following a crisis of corporate liquidity in which the payments of tax due in 1975 would have led to serious financial difficulties for a number of major firms, a temporary scheme of 'stock relief' was introduced. The effect was to eliminate almost all of the corporation tax liability of UK manufacturing industry, and even for the corporate sector as a whole the real value of tax payments fell throughout the 1970s. Although the scheme was described as temporary, successive Chancellors procrastinated and nothing was done to introduce a permanent reform. It was only when another liquidity crisis threatened industry following the massive rundown of stocks in 1980 that action could no longer be delayed. Stock relief was modified in the 1981 Finance Act, but once again this was simply tacked on to the existing system rather than integrated into a coherent reform of corporate taxation. The prolonged debate over the way in which stock relief should be incorporated into the tax system had demonstrated that a rethink of the basis of corporation tax was necessary. To deal with the underlying problem, a Green Paper on corporation tax (H.M.S.O. 1982) was published early in 1982. This set out both the weaknesses of the present system and a number of options for change, while carefully avoiding a commitment to any specific reform. Corporation tax has ceased to be a major source of revenue for the U.K. exchequer. In Table 11.1 we show recent payments of corporation tax, and their distribution by sectors. The tax burden on manufacturing industry is particularly low, and in real terms has fallen over the last decade.

Since we have come so close to abolishing Corporation Tax, an obvious question to ask is, 'Why tax companies at all?' A common reply, and indeed one that was used in the U.S. to justify the introduction of a corporate income tax, is that corporate status conveys certain privileges, and companies should pay for these privileges. In particular, companies have limited liability status, thus protecting their shareholders in the event of bankruptcy. At first sight this argument has some appeal, but on closer inspection it becomes less attractive. There is no reason to believe that the benefits of incorporation are proportional to profits (indeed the reverse might be the case) and one might as well argue for a licence fee for companies. More fundamentally, although limited liability is a very convenient form of contractual arrangement between shareholders and creditors, it is a voluntary agreement entered into by both sides. Before lending to the company the creditors know full well that the shareholders' liability is limited and can adjust the terms on which they are willing to lend accordingly. There is no reason to tax one party more than the other.

Why then do firms incorporate? For large firms the most important reason is that the existence of shares enables the ownership of the company to be divided among, and transferred between, individuals without affecting the scale of control of the firm. The process of management can continue while the ownership of the company is changing. There are two main tax inducements for small businesses to incorporate. The first is that if money is ploughed back into the business the owner of an incorporated business can avoid paying income tax at the cost of paying corporation tax plus, eventually, also capital gains tax. If his personal income tax rate is high enough, incorporation might be worth while. The second reason is that there are generous tax concessions for contributions to company pension funds, which are not available to a self-employed business man on anything like the same scale. If the latter wanted to save for retirement he might well find it profitable to incorporate simply to take advantage of the tax privileges of a company pension. For large firms, however, taxation

TABLE 11.1

Corporation tax receipts 1976–81 (£ m.)

Sector	1974–5	1975–6	1976–7	1977–8	1978–9	1979–80	1980–1
Manufacturing	600	350	580	800	870	1010	850
Distribution	340	250	350	350	400	440	410
Other home industrial and commercial	430	310	410	580	740	760	860
Financial	320	190	260	360	390	350	360
Overseas	30	20	20	20	40	40	40
North Sea	–	–	–	–	50	170	240
Public corporations	10	–	20	30	70	50	70
All companies	1730	1120	1640	2140	2560	2820	2830

All figures refer to mainstream corporation tax
Source: Cmnd. 8456 (1982) Table 7

is not a significant factor because incorporation is necessary for other reasons.

The mere fact that some firms are incorporated is not a very strong argument for imposing a separate tax on them. Indeed, insistence on treating companies as entities distinct from the individuals who own them has provided a tax shelter for retained earnings. Another argument which has been used is that companies can afford to shoulder an extra burden, and that companies, as well as persons, should pay their fair share of taxes. This argument is completely mistaken. The effect of a tax is to reduce either leisure or consumption (whether this year or in the future via a reduction in savings) or both below the levels which would have been chosen in the absence of the tax. Whether any given tax burden is distributed fairly can only be discussed by reference to the effects on the different individuals in society. Companies are owned by individuals and it is meaningless to talk about the 'welfare' of I.C.I. The fact that a company has a *legal* personality of its own quite distinct from that of its managers, shareholders, and employees cannot change the fact that a tax can only affect the well-being of those who work for or own the company, or consume its products.

The incidence of company taxes

Who then actually pays the corporation tax? Corporation tax is normally levied on company profits, but it is important to distinguish two components which make up the figures which companies report as their profits. One is a return on the capital which companies use in conducting their business—the money they have borrowed to buy fixed assets, stock, etc. In order to attract funds—either from lenders or from those who might wish to buy their shares—companies must offer a return on those funds comparable to that which investors could obtain elsewhere. Companies typically report their gross trading profits—the return they have made before deducting any of these financing costs—and their net profits, which are computed after subtracting the cost of interest payments on the money which they have borrowed, but before deducting the cost of servicing the capital which they have obtained from shareholders (the dividends which they have had to promise in order to secure these funds).

Many companies make a return on capital employed which appears to exceed, often by large amounts, the amount which they need to attract funds from investors. For example, in 1975 Rank Xerox reported a return on capital employed of 41·1%, and Marks & Spencer a return of 36·1% (figures drawn from the *Times 1000*), while the Monopolies Commission (1975) discovered that LRC International had obtained a return on capital employed in the manufacture of contra- ceptive sheaths which exceeded 100% over the period 1969–73. These returns are much greater than these companies would appear to have needed to make, or to promise, to obtain finance for their business. In a competitive economy, it would be difficult for firms to earn such high profit rates, since other people would be attracted into the same line of business by the prospect of these enormous returns: and although many companies seem to earn profits greater than the cost of capital there are few which are as profitable as these. But as these examples suggest, there are at least three reasons why companies might make above-normal profits. Rank Xerox is a company which exists to exploit a highly successful invention, and its profits represent the rewards of being first in the field with a new product (aided by patent protection). Marks & Spencer does not have any single invention which distinguishes it from other companies, but it is an exceptionally successful and efficient firm, which by virtue of effective management and carefully cultivated customer goodwill is able to earn higher profits than other retailers with whom it is competing. We might regard its profits as returns to successful organization. LRC's profits appear to be the rewards of the successful creation and maintenance of a near-monopoly in its products.

Economists describe the amount by which profits such as these exceed the cost of capital as 'pure profits'. Such profits can of course be negative for foolhardy ventures or badly managed firms. At any time some firms will be more successful than the average and others less successful, so that there will be a dispersion of realized rates of return around the cost of capital: lager producers will earn more when the summer is hot and umbrella manufacturers more when it is wet. But the major sources of pure profits are invention, organization, and mono- poly, and we shall broadly describe them as returns to entrepreneurship, noting that in this title we are including activities which we should view with approbation—like successful invention—and others which we would wish to discourage—like the creation of monopolies. Real 'profits taxes' are normally partly a tax on pure profits and partly a tax on capital employed. We shall see that the British corporation tax is a com- bination of a tax on pure profits and a tax on capital. This latter tax ranges from a net *subsidy* to borrowings which are used to buy plant and machinery to a substantial tax on equity finance used to purchase commercial property.

We can therefore identify three main groups who may bear part of the burden of corporation tax. One is the people who supply entrepreneurship—Mr. Marks and Mr. Spencer and others who helped build up their organization, Mr. Carlson who invented the Xerox machine, and the owners of the Xerox Corporation which helped him develop it. A second is the people who supply capital to companies. This group overlaps somewhat with the first—the people who supplied capital to Marks & Spencer or Xerox in the early days of their development did very well out of it, though we might argue that by choosing to support these operations rather than others at a time when their potential was not universally recognized these individuals were themselves supplying entrepreneurship as well as capital. It is clear, however, that the people who own shares in Marks and Spencer now are not entrepreneurs in this or any other sense, and there is no reason to suppose that the return they earn on their investment will be higher than they would expect from any other shares they might buy.

This point is important. The present shareholders in this company are not growing fat on its above-average rate of return on capital. This return has been capitalized: the present owners of Marks & Spencer have bought the right to it from the founders, who were thus able to sell their shares and obtain the proceeds of their entrepreneurial activities. Similarly, the present stockholders in the Xerox Corporation are those who have bought the right to Mr. Carlson's invention from him and his original backers at a price which reflected the expectation of the profits which the company is currently earning.

We have so far only looked at the production side of these activities. The third group of people who may share the burden of corporation tax are those who buy goods and services which are produced by companies. If there is a tax on capital employed in the company sector, and people require a certain rate of return before they will invest in companies (because, for example, they can obtain that return by buying Government bonds or investing overseas), then the tax will have to be paid by those who buy goods which are produced by companies. Part of it may also fall on those who form companies to exploit their entrepreneurial activities.

It should be clear from this that the incidence of corporation tax depends in part on the structure of the tax. If it is a tax on pure profits only, then it falls in the first instance on those who supply entrepreneurship to companies—inventors, successful organizers, would-be monopolists. If, as we might suspect, the supply of such entrepreneurship is not too sensitive to its rewards then these entrepreneurs will pay the tax and that will be the end of the matter: but if they abandon entrepreneurship and enter routine employment instead then consumers will have to bear the burden of the tax, partly in higher prices to induce a little more entrepreneurship and more importantly through the loss of the ideas and efficiency which those people might otherwise have promoted (this is the 'excess burden' of this tax). Moreover, because of capitalization we can tax *past* entrepreneurship at rates as high as we like without the tax being shifted forward to consumers in this way or producing economic inefficiency of any kind. It is possible that if Mr. Marks had known that profits would be taxed at 52% he would not have bothered to think up Marks & Spencer, or that the current shareholders would have been less willing to pay so much to him for his business, but they have made their decisions and there is nothing that they can do about it now.

We should note that similar disincentives apply to entrepreneurship in the unincorporated sector: but there they arise from the effect of the personal income tax rather than the corporation tax. Since the rates of this may well be higher (and certainly will be if the invention is a very successful one), the disincentive brought about by the corporation tax may be less than that which exists in the economy generally from the effects of other taxes: so that although all activities of this kind are penalized the use of the corporate form as a means of exploiting invention reduces the tax burden imposed.

We can therefore see that a tax on pure profits is not without economic attractions—though these depend on the belief that desirable entrepreneurship will be inelastically supplied. (If people are deterred from seeking monopolies by the knowledge that the proceeds will be taxed, that is all to the good.) We shall describe a corporation tax which falls only on pure profits as a neutral tax. If a corporation tax is not neutral, it will fall also on those who supply capital to companies. The incidence of this part of the tax then depends on the response of firms and financiers to this change. If there are profitable investment opportunities elsewhere—and foreign investment is probably available to domestic investors and certainly to overseas investors—then firms will be unable to pass the burden of the tax back to investors. They will then try to substitute other factors of production for the now more expensive capital. To the extent that this raises costs and to the extent that they cannot substitute successfully they will have to share the tax between a reduction in any pure profits they may be making (which may be small or zero for many companies) and a higher price charged to the consumers of their products. If this happens, corporation tax will act as a general sales tax on the goods which companies produce (though at different rates on different goods). We may note that the openness of the economy to capital flows will be an important factor in determining the incidence of corporation tax. The greater this is, the greater the proportion of the tax which is likely to fall on consumers.

We have seen that the analysis of the incidence of corporation tax is a complicated issue—and indeed we have underestimated its complexity because we have examined only the most immediate consequences of the tax. There are likely to be further repercussions from the effects on income distribution of whatever the incidence may turn out to be. Nor have we considered adequately the problems we raised in Chapter 1—what is the alternative tax with which we are implicitly comparing the corporation tax? But in this simple framework it seems that incidence depends on empirical questions which are not easily answered, and it is not surprising that the subject has been in long-standing dispute. What we have suggested—and what has perhaps not received sufficient attention in that dispute—is that incidence is likely to be rather sensitive to the structure of the tax; and that the issue of whether the tax is or is not neutral is critical to this. We therefore turn to analyses of alternative tax structures, focusing on this issue.

But before doing so, we should notice that although corporation taxes do not emerge in a very satisfactory light from this discussion and non-neutral corporation taxes particularly badly, the analysis suggests one argument for such a tax. This is that we have one already. To the extent that the tax falls on pure profits, and stays there, it will be capitalized in share prices; the value of Marks & Spencer is lower than it would be if there were no corporation tax, and this expectation has been reflected in the price at which shares in this company have changed hands in the past. To abolish the tax now would be to confer a windfall gain on these present shareholders. The force of this is weakened by the observation that few British companies are paying much corporation tax; but some (including Marks & Spencer) are, and more expect to in future.

Systems of company taxation

If a separate corporation tax is to be retained, it is important to choose a tax which does not conflict with the objectives of the personal direct tax system. There are two sorts of questions about company taxes we could ask. What are the different types of company tax systems? What are the economic effects of a tax on companies? It is clear that we cannot answer the second question until we know exactly what type of company tax we are talking about, and so we shall describe some of the main corporate tax systems which could be employed. It is useful to classify corporate tax systems in terms of how they tax distributed profits relative to their taxation of undistributed profits. When the corporate tax system in Britain was changed in 1965 and 1973, on both occasions the idea behind the change was to alter the relative tax burden on dividends and retentions. We shall follow this method of classifying company tax systems. An alternative approach is to look at systems in terms of their effects on the investment decisions of firms by asking the question: how does the tax system affect the pre-tax rate of return on an investment project required to induce firms to go ahead with the project? This is a question to which we shall return after having described the different systems of corporation tax.

If there are no taxes the cost of capital is simply the rate of return demanded by the supplier of finance, the rate of interest at which the firm can borrow, for example. In a competitive economy this cost of capital is independent of the particular method of finance which is chosen. While it may appear, for example, that borrowing secured on particular assets is 'cheaper' than other ways of raising new capital, such activities increase the risk, and hence the cost, attached to other financial instruments, such as unsecured loans or equity shares. Since there must be a lender for each borrower, the outcome will be one in which the 'price' of each kind of capital which the firm has will reflect the degree of risk attached to that particular asset, and the over-all cost of capital cannot be reduced by resorting to so-called 'cheap capital'. It follows from this that there is little to choose between alternative methods of financing when there are no tax considerations, and that such decisions will be very sensitive to tax systems which favour one method rather than another. When tax considerations do apply, a firm will use the cheapest source of finance first, though there are practical limits to this, especially when this source is debt or retained earnings.

Between 1947 and 1965 companies in Britain paid tax at the standard rate of income tax plus an additional rate of profits tax which, until 1958, was charged at a different rate on distributed profits than on retained profits. The differential rates were abolished in 1958 and profits tax was imposed at a uniform rate on all profits. In 1965 corporation tax was introduced and the U.K. adopted the *classical system*. This is perhaps the simplest system to understand and is often represented as embodying the principle that the tax liability of the company should be completely independent of that of its shareholders. It is the system employed in the U.S.A. and in Holland amongst other countries, and was in force in Britain until 1973. Under the classical system the company pays a flat rate of corporation tax on its taxable profits, and then the shareholders pay income tax on their dividends and capital gains tax on the gains which arise from corporate retentions. A company wishing to raise a given amount of finance may either retain profits, or distribute the profits as dividends and issue new shares, or borrow the money and pay interest charges on the loan. The classical system discriminates between the first two sources of funds unless capital gains are taxed at the same rate as unearned income, and it favours debt finance if, as is almost always the case, interest payments may be deducted against profits in assessing liability to corporation tax.

It is precisely this discrimination between dividends and retentions which, so it is claimed, constitutes the major objection to the classical system because it involves the 'double taxation of dividends'. The double taxation arises because dividends are subject to both corporation tax and income tax, whereas retentions are liable only to corporation tax. As we have seen, this argument ignores the fact that capital gains tax is payable on gains arising from retentions although of course it is perfectly true that the effective tax rate on capital gains is much less than the rate of income tax. Nevertheless, in 1973 the classical system was replaced by the *imputation system* in order to alleviate part of the 'double' taxation of dividends. The imputation system gives shareholders credit for tax paid by the company, and this credit may be used to offset their income tax liability on dividends. Part of the company's tax liability is 'imputed' to the shareholders and regarded as a prepayment of their income tax on dividends.

The company pays tax on its profits at the rate of corporation tax, and any profits which are subsequently distributed are regarded as having already paid income tax at a certain rate, which we may call the 'rate of imputation'. In Britain the rate of imputation is always set equal to the basic rate of income tax. Shareholders only have to pay additional income tax on their dividends if their marginal rates of income tax exceed the basic rate, while if their marginal rates are less than the basic rate they actually receive a refund from the Revenue. For example, a charity or pension fund will receive a refund of tax deemed to have been paid on their behalf by the company. An alternative method of alleviating the double taxation of dividends is to charge a lower rate of corporation tax on distributed profits than on undistributed profits. This is called the *two-rate* system.

An alternative system is simply to integrate the personal and corporate tax systems, and for tax purposes to regard shareholders as partners in a business. Under the *integrated system*, as it is called, each shareholder is deemed to have earned a fraction of the company's profits equal to the fraction of its shares which he owns. The effect of this is that the company's profits, both distributed *and* undistributed, constitute part of the shareholders' personal taxable income. Once a year each shareholder would receive a piece of paper from the company showing his taxable profits for the last year together with a tax credit for the tax paid by the company on his behalf. The taxable profits would be added to his personal income. A reform along these lines was suggested by the Carter Commission in Canada and was seriously considered in West Germany. In neither country, however, was it adopted, partly on administrative grounds and partly on the irrelevant legal argument that a company is distinct from its shareholders.

Terms and investments

We shall consider first a project financed entirely by borrowing. Imagine a firm contemplating investing in a project which involves buying a piece of machinery and then using it together with labour and raw materials to produce output which is then sold. If the receipts from the sale of output more than cover *all* the costs involved then the project will earn profits for the firm, and the project will be given the go-ahead. What do the costs include? Obviously, they include the payments made for raw materials, fuel, and labour, but they also include the capital costs incurred. These will consist of two parts. The first is the interest payment on the loan taken out to finance the purchase of the machinery, and the second is the deterioration in the value of the machinery itself due to wear and tear caused by use, or to obsolescence caused by the invention of better machinery. This second element is the depreciation charge, and is called 'true economic depreciation'. It is important to note that it consists of the change in the value of the machinery during the firm's accounting period regardless of the way the value has changed. Since firms rarely sell machinery it is extremely difficult to value second-hand plant and so depreciation charges usually follow rather arbitrary rules, such as writing-off the cost of an asset in equal instalments over some assumed average life for assets of that particular type, and only approximate true economic depreciation.

If the receipts from the project exceed all its costs, including capital costs as defined above, then the project will earn a surplus for the shareholders of the firm and will always be a desirable investment, provided the surplus is positive. What matters is not the size of the surplus, but the fact that it is a surplus. A proportional tax on this surplus will still leave a positive surplus for the shareholders, and therefore will not affect investment decisions. In the case we examined investment was financed by borrowing and in that case capital costs consisted of interest payments on the borrowed money and depreciation of the capital equipment. As far as investment financed by borrowing is concerned a corporation tax which allows as deductions both interest payments and true economic depreciation will be neutral.

What happens if the project is not entirely financed by borrowing? The argument remains valid if the costs of different forms of finance can be fully deducted from profits for corporation tax purposes. For financing by new share issues this has never been true, since dividends are not a 'cost' for corporation tax purposes. Under the classical system, no part of dividends can be offset against liability to corporation tax; hence the discrimination against financing projects this way is very heavy and to the extent that such finance is necessary the required rate of return from the project is increased. With the imputation system, dividends are partially deductible for corporation tax purposes; £100 paid out as gross dividends reduces the final corporation tax liability by £30, while £100 paid out in interest or any other cost would reduce it by £52. Thus there is some increase in the required rate of return, but the effect is smaller than under the classical system.

If the investment is undertaken from retained profits, the position is more complex. The cost of internal finance depends on the personal tax rates of the owners of the company because they can avoid paying income tax on their returns by sheltering behind the combined burden of corporation tax and capital gains tax. It is possible that for some wealthy investors this double burden is less than their marginal rate of income tax, which actually lowers the required rate of return on investment projects financed from retained earnings.

We shall now apply these principles to an analysis of how company taxes operate in Britain today.

12

COMPANY TAXATION IN THE U.K.

The present imputation system

SINCE 1973 company taxation in the U.K. has been based on the imputation system. To illustrate how the system works consider a shareholder who has received a cheque for £100 as his annual dividend. With a rate of corporation tax of 52% the company has had to use £208 of pre-tax profits to pay this dividend with the balance of £108 (52% of £208) going to the Revenue in corporation tax. Part of this corporate tax bill is in fact prepayment of income tax at the basic rate on dividends which is deducted at source, and this component is paid to the Revenue when dividends are distributed. Since this is usually before the date when companies are called upon to pay corporation tax on the year's profits, this element of tax is called advance corporation tax (A.C.T.), but in fact it is more properly regarded not as a company tax but as deduction at source of standard rate income tax on dividends. The remaining tax payments to the Revenue are described as 'mainstream' corporation tax. It is these payments which constitute the effective corporate tax burden, since the amounts which are described as A.C.T. would be paid, as income tax, even if corporation tax were completely abolished.

The essence of the imputation system is that when the shareholder receives his dividend cheque for £100 he is deemed to have already paid income tax at the basic rate on the dividend. If all shareholders paid income tax at the basic rate that would be the end of the matter. But some shareholders have higher marginal tax rates and others lower, and this complicates matters somewhat because we have to calculate the amount of extra tax or of refund which is due. To do this we ask the question—what dividend before tax would I need in order to finish up with £100 after payment of basic rate income tax? Suppose the basic rate of income tax is $33\frac{1}{3}\%$. Then to end up with £100 after tax I would need £150 before tax. This is the notional pre-tax dividend which the shareholder receives, the 'grossed-up' dividend, and £50 is the notional tax which he has paid.

If all this seems rather abstract to our shareholder then he should think again, for with his dividend cheque for £100 will come a piece of paper representing a tax credit of £50 exactly equal to the notional tax we have just described. On his tax form the shareholder must enter the notional pre-tax dividend of £150 (which is equivalent to the value of his dividend of £100 plus the tax credit of £50) which will then be added to his other income to calculate his total income tax bill. But since he is deemed to have already paid the notional tax he can use the credit as an offset against his income tax liability. If he pays tax at the basic rate, the credit eliminates his liability and he can forget about the imputation system of corporation tax. If his marginal income tax rate is 60%, then his tax liability on the dividend is £90 minus the tax credit of £50. He will have to send a cheque for the balance of £40 to the Inland Revenue. But if the recipient of the dividend cheque were a charity or pension fund, and hence not liable to tax, the boot would be on the other foot and the Revenue would have to refund the tax credit of £50 to the shareholder. Of the pre-tax profit of £208, a basic rate taxpayer would receive £100, an effective rate of 52%, a charity would receive £150, a tax rate of 28%, and an individual with an income tax rate of 60% would receive £60, an effective tax rate of 71·2%.

We have discussed the example at length so that the reader should understand the principles of the system and not be confused by the terminology used in the actual operation of the imputation system in Britain. It is complex because after they have received their dividends some shareholders owe additional tax and others are owed refunds. The system of tax credits is needed to ensure that the correct amounts are paid.

In the U.K. the rate of imputation is always set equal to the basic rate of income tax because the majority of shareholders pay tax at the basic rate, and hence for a large number of dividend recipients no net payments or refunds are required. Although this may seem appealing on administrative grounds, it is in fact a rather restrictive provision. There is no obvious reason for taking the rate of imputation to be the basic rate of income tax, and there are two objections to it. First, it has the consequence that an increase in the basic rate of income tax increases the tax burden on earned income but has no effect on the tax burden on dividend income of shareholders paying the basic rate, because the tax credit rises in line with the increased income tax liability, and actually benefits exempt shareholders, such as pension funds.

Second, the imputation system was introduced to reduce the fiscal discrimination between dividends and retentions, and hence between the different methods of raising finance. But the basic difficulty with the system is that it can lead to a neutral tax position only for those shareholders paying one particular rate of income tax. If we ignore capital gains tax this neutral position exists only for shareholders paying the basic rate. For other shareholders there will be discrimination in one direction or another. But the neutral tax rate does not coincide with a weighted average of the marginal income tax rates of shareholders, which is somewhat below the basic rate of tax and has been falling rapidly over the last decade or so (see King, 1977 Appendix A and King and Fullerton forthcoming, Chapter 3). The two factors responsible for this fall have been the enormous growth in the shareholdings of tax-exempt institutions, mainly pension funds, and the reduction in personal tax rates on high income individuals in the 1979 Budget.

An additional complexity in the system is advance corporation tax. The Revenue does not wish to pay to shareholders any refunds of tax which it has not received from the company in the first place, and so each company is required to pay A.C.T. before any refunds can be made. A.C.T. is equal to the total of the tax credits received by the company's shareholders. The rate of credit (and hence also A.C.T.) is defined as the ratio of the notional tax paid by the company on behalf of its shareholders to the dividends distributed, and so is always expressed in the rather strange form of 30/70, for example, in the case of a basic rate of income tax of 30%.

A.C.T. may be offset against the company's eventual liability to corporation tax. But there are many companies with small or zero tax liabilities, and for these companies the A.C.T. is unrelieved. This surplus A.C.T. may, however, be offset against the corporation tax of the two previous years or carried forward. In the early 1980s a great deal of concern was expressed about the problem of unrelieved A.C.T. The principle of the imputation system is that part of the company's tax bill is regarded as a credit against the shareholders' income tax liabilities on dividends, but if the company has paid no tax then there is no reason to give the shareholders credit. In practice, it would be too complicated to work out for each holding whether an individual taxpayer was entitled to a credit, and so the principle is enforced by collecting A.C.T. from companies while granting credits to all shareholders. If the company turns out to have no tax liability, then the A.C.T. is simply unrelieved. There are two things to note about this outcome. Firstly, an imputation system rests uneasily with a corporate tax base under which many companies have no tax liability. Secondly, because the imputation system is effectively withdrawn when companies have no mainstream tax liability, the incentives to use different sources of finance vary not only from company to company, but even from year to year for the same company. This is a bizarre outcome which gives firms yet more incentives to devote talented manpower to planing their financial structure rather than to the quality and range of their products.

Tax change in the U.K.

The tax treatment of dividends and retentions has oscillated since the last war, first favouring one and then the other. After the introduction of corporation tax in 1965 debt finance was very attractive, but new equity finance reappeared after the change in 1973. Issues of preference shares (a security with a fixed rate of interest which may if necessary be reduced, thus giving some of the flexibility of equity finance) were virtually killed off in 1965, and yet this sort of finance would have helped some companies with their liquidity problems in 1974.

It is not easy for a company to change its capital structure overnight to take advantage of changes in the tax system, and certain changes might be illegal. But there is one way in which a major change in capital structure can be effected, and that is by merger or take-over. A company with a suitable capital structure may appear an attractive partner for another firm even if the two companies have nothing in common by way of similar products or production methods. Other tax reasons for mergers are unrelieved tax losses or credit for foreign tax which cannot be used because the company has no domestic taxable profit. It is hard to imagine any industrial policy which would encourage mergers of this sort. We do not use the personal tax system to encourage the marriage of otherwise unsuitable partners, so it is hard to see why we would want to do this with companies. Yet we find British American Tobacco operating supermarkets and Consolidated Gold Fields building roads.

The main effect of the many changes in the corporate tax system has been to introduce fiscal considerations into decisions which there is every reason to believe are best left to companies themselves. The capital structure of a company and the method by which it finances its investment are matters which the tax system ought not to try to influence, and if it does it will create difficulties for itself. Divergences from a non-neutral tax system give rise to the need for complex legislation to prevent abuse and avoidance through the conversion of income into whatever legal form happens to be taxed most lightly. The idea of paying shareholders 'scrip dividends' (by giving them shares whose value was taxed as a capital gain) instead of cash dividends taxable as income was outlawed in 1975 when such dividends were deemed to be income for tax purposes. It is very difficult to distinguish clearly between capital and income and yet that is what is required if the present system is to work smoothly. Complaints by companies about the losses they have made on foreign currency loans illustrate how income and changes in capital values are not easy to separate. By repurchasing their own debt at below its nominal value companies can substitute tax-deductible interest payments for repayment of capital, with favourable tax consequences. Even the difference between debt and equity can be blurred, and in the 1960s there was extensive import of the American device of the convertible loan stock, which is debt to the taxman and equity to the holder. The partial indexation of capital gains tax in 1982 increased further the discrepancies between the treatment of debt and equity.

Any deviation from a neutral tax system will provide someone with an opportunity to invent methods of avoiding tax. The authorities then respond with legislation to prevent such abuse, and effort then goes into devising even more ingenious financial operations to save the company and its shareholders tax. £1 in tax saved is worth as much to the company as £1 earned by productive activity. Most of these side-effects of a non-neutral tax system were unintended and, if perhaps not enormously harmful to the economy, nevertheless constitute a diversion of resources of time and skilled manpower to pointless activities. The frequency of the changes in the tax system aggravates the situation.

Investment and the tax system

Applying our previous analysis to the U.K. tax system is complicated by the multiplicity of different ways in which depreciation is treated. For many years depreciation allowances have been becoming more and more generous, and 100% of all investment in plant, machinery, ships, and aircraft, can be depreciated immediately ('free depreciation'). Industrial buildings qualify for a first-year allowance of 75% as well as 4% per annum allowances on the balance of the cost of the asset. In addition there are special cash grants to certain kinds of investment in the assisted regions, and discretionary grants under Sections 7 and 8 of the 1972 Industry Act. No allowances, however, are given for land and commercial buildings (except for hotels which receive an initial allowance of 20% plus further depreciation allowances) because they are expected to retain their value. There is a special form of relief for investment in stocks which we discuss below in the context of inflation accounting. A new scheme of enterprise zones was introduced in the 1980 budget which offered a range of tax concessions in order to encourage businesses (particularly small businesses) to generate activity in derelict areas of the urban conurbations. Within these Enterprise Zones, companies are exempt from rates and receive 100% first-year allowances for investment in buildings as well as on plant and machinery. As yet, the amount of investment in such zones is extremely small.

The net result of the above provisions is that most investment by industrial companies qualifies for 100% first year allowances and the bulk of the remainder for some form of accelerated depreciation. In addition, interest payments are tax deductible, and provided that tax allowances can be claimed, which has not been the case for many companies recently, then the existence of corporation tax at 52% is no disincentive to invest at all. In fact, for investment qualifying for free depreciation and substantially financed by borrowing, the higher the rate of corporation tax the stronger the inducement to undertake the project. Consider the following example. An investment of £200 will yield £30 per annum for sufficiently long that we can simplify matters by neglecting depreciation. Corporation tax is at 50%, so that the yield is 15% before tax and 7½% after tax. However, the company succeeds in borrowing £50 at 12% p.a. to finance the project: so that it must pay £6 in annual interest, leaving £24 return on the £150 supplied by its shareholders. This produces 16% before tax, 8% after tax. Since the cost of the borrowing is less than the yield on the investment, the rate of return on shareholders' funds is increased by this use of external finance.

Free depreciation improves the return dramatically. In the first year of the project the company can deduct the £200 invested from its taxable profit; so that provided it has sufficient profits on its other activities it can reduce its tax bill in that year by £100 (50% of £200). This reduces the amount which the shareholders need contribute from £150 to £50; since the returns and the interest cost remains the same, the net profit after tax is still £12, which is a 24% return on capital. In this example, free depreciation and interest deductibility together imply that the rate of return is higher after tax than it is before: 24% as against the original 16%.

It is easy to see that the *higher* the corporation tax rate, the higher the yield is. Suppose corporation tax went up to 60%. The taxpayer's contribution in the first year is now £120, and the shareholders need only provide £30. In subsequent years the Government takes 60% of the profit after interest of £24, leaving only £9·60 for the shareholders: but this means that the return on capital has actually risen to 32%.

The present system discriminates between investment in different types of asset and between investment in different sectors. Plant and machinery receive favourable treatment whereas commercial buildings do not. Stocks of both raw materials and finished goods received un-favourable treatment until 1974, generous treatment thereafter until the stock relief scheme was modified in 1981, since when stocks have been less highly favoured than plant and machinery. The rationale for these differences is unclear, and we discuss below ways in which they might be remedied.

Stock relief

In 1973 there was a sharp rise in the price of most primary com-modities. The most important and most permanent change was a four-fold increase in the price of oil, but many other raw materials also recorded large price increases. This was associated with a spurt in the general rate of inflation. Many companies recorded large accounting profits on their stocks of commodities. However these book profits—the result of stock appreciation—had to be reinvested immediately in maintaining stocks at the new price levels. This stimulated an extensive debate on the appropriate measure of profit under inflation, which we discuss further in Chapter 13. More immediately, companies were faced with tax bills on these profits and many of them lacked the liquid resources needed to meet them.

It is a surprising idea to many people—including some accountants—that you can make a profit but still be short of cash. But there is nothing contradictory about this. Profitability and liquidity are not the same thing, and this is well understood by owner-occupiers who have found it profitable to purchase a home even if this imposed strains on the liquid resources of the household during the first years of a mortgage. The appropriate conclusion is that profitability is not the only, or necessarily the best, measure of the firm's ability to pay dividends or taxes. As a practical matter, this has long been recognized. Corporation tax has not been even approximately based on profits— however measured—for many years, and there is no likelihood that it ever will be; the actual company tax base is much closer to a measure of corporate cash flow than corporate profits. But discussion of the principles remains confused by the widespread misapprehension that corporation tax is, or should be, a profits based tax.

The need for a clear view as to what should constitute the tax base for companies is illustrated by the experience of stock relief in the 1970s and 1980s. In 1974 companies were facing severe liquidity problems and the Chancellor decided that he could not wait until a permanent method of inflation accounting had been agreed upon before giving some tax concessions to the corporate sectors. With most firms using historic cost accounts it was impossible simply to exempt stock appreciation from tax, and an arbitrary form of relief, stock relief, was introduced in November 1974, retrospective to 1973. Under this scheme companies could deduct for tax purposes the excess of the change in the book value of stocks over 10% of gross trading profits. The increase in the book value of stocks in any year consists of stock appreciation plus the value of physical investment in stocks. The figure of 10% of gross profits was held to be a rough average for the economy of the value of additions to stocks plus 'normal' stock appreciation, from which it was felt exemption from tax was not justified. In 1976 this was changed to 15% of trading profits after depreciation allowances. This was evidently a rough-and-ready justice which took no account of the circumstances of individual companies. Moreover, at the margin the system of stock relief as it operated then allowed purchases of stocks as a tax deduction, thus effectively offering 100% first year allowances to stocks as well as to plant and machinery. But if purchases of stock are allowed as a tax deduction, it is logical that sales of stocks are taxable. Hence when stocks were run down in volume terms in 1980 companies were threatened with large tax payments and again a liquidity crisis prompted further changes in legislation. Concerned about the prospect of relief being 'clawed back', the Government modified the scheme so that relief was restricted to a measure of stock appreciation. But the rate of inflation which is used to compute the increase in the price of stocks is neither the increase in the price of the company's own stocks, nor a measure of inflation in the economy as a whole, but an 'all stocks index' which the Government has devised for the purpose. Stock relief is calculated by multiplying the closing value of stocks at the end of the preceding tax year by the proportionate increase in the index. The reform in 1981 had the effect of increasing the effective marginal tax rate on investment in stocks, and made the tax treatment of stocks more akin to commercial buildings than to plant and machinery. Quite why this should be desirable is hard to see. One lesson of this experience is that it is only too clear that short term considerations have dictated the form in which change has been made. And the development of the system in a series of *ad hoc* changes has led only to the need for subsequent changes. Stability depends upon the adoption of a coherent tax system, and this is yet to be achieved.

As we have seen, the present corporation tax is far removed from a tax on company profits. Before paying tax a company may deduct from its profits interest payments on loans taken out to finance the purchase of some of its capital and also any expenditure on investment on a wide range of assets. On top of this stock relief has eliminated the taxation of stock appreciation. The effect of all these allowances is to reduce the size of taxable profits, thus lowering the burden of corporation tax. For many companies, corporation tax has effectively been abolished. Approximately one third of companies pay corporation tax, another third pay tax in one year but not in the next, and the remaining one third have no immediate prospect of paying tax at all. Large unrelieved tax losses are building up. One of the most disturbing features about this is the fact that companies are treated in so many different ways. The incentives to use different kinds of finance, and to invest in different types of asset, vary from firm to firm. There has been an enormous growth in leasing of assets which enables financial companies, for example, with taxable profits to purchase plant and machinery and lease these assets to manufacturing companies which may not be able to use tax allowances. There is something to be said for the view that it would be better to have a market in tax credits rather than in leases for physical assets.

The fact that many companies pay little or no tax is often not evident from their published company accounts. Some companies show substantial tax charges in their profit and loss accounts when in fact they are paying little or no tax at all. As in earlier editions of this book, we have tried to extract from the published accounts of a number of leading British companies figures on the amounts of mainstream corporation tax paid. But it remains true that many of the largest twenty companies had no liability at all. (Readers who are unfamiliar with company accounts may be surprised that basic information such as how much tax companies pay is not readily available; those who are familiar with them will recognize the difficulty and unreliability of such estimates.)

Not only does corporation tax raise only a small amount of revenue, but there are substantial variations between firms and even greater uncertainty about future tax liabilities. Companies do not face a stable environment in which they can plan, and in the wake of the 1982 Green Paper on corporation tax (Cmnd. 8456) an attempt at permanent reform of the system is to be hoped for. There is a need for a simple and stable tax system, which the current set-up cannot provide, and we turn now to a discussion of possible reforms.

Although it is true that on average companies pay little tax, there are substantial variations between firms, and there is great uncertainty about future tax liabilities. The Chancellor receives little revenue, but comapnies do not face a stable environment in which they can plan. Stock relief is temporary and there is no agreement on how the tax system should embody inflation accounting. There is a need for a simple and stable tax system, but it is clear that the current set-up must be changed, and we turn now to a discussion of possible reforms.

The Future of Corporation Tax

The simplest reform would be to abolish corporation tax altogether. We suggested above that if it did not exist we would not wish to introduce it, and since it contributes little revenue there is something to be said for being rid of it. Attractive though it might seem there are problems with this idea. Earlier we suggested that the reason for retaining the corporation tax is that it exists already. It may be true that the tax does not raise much revenue at the moment but many companies may be expecting to pay taxes in the future. Moreover, although on average the effective tax rate is negligible, some companies are paying a lot of tax and others pay nothing or have unrelieved tax losses. To abolish the tax now would result in windfall gains and losses to individual owners of companies. There is also a desire to extract tax revenue from British subsidiaries of foreign-owned companies and from those shareholders of British companies who are resident overseas. The easiest way of taxing their profits is to have an independent corporation tax.

TABLE 12.1

Payments of mainstream corporation tax, 1976-1982
(£ m.)

Company	1976-7 Profits	1976-7 Tax paid	1981-2 Profits	1981-2 Tax paid
Allied Lyons	63	nil	95	nil
Bass	69	17	126	25
B.A.T.	374	2	684	nil
Bowater	78	nil	107	nil
British Leyland	71	nil	(333)	nil
B.P.	1784	nil	5932	145
Courtaulds	46	nil	5	nil
Distillers	91	7	172	36
Dunlop	74	nil	(3)	nil
Esso	69	nil	805	nil
Ford	122	nil	220	nil
G.E.C.	207	41	476	144
Grand Metropolitan	57	nil	187	nil
G.K.N.	70	nil	46	nil
I.C.I.	540	12	524	nil
Imperial Group	130	9	102	nil
Marks & Spencer	84	29	178	62
P. & O.	31	nil	41	nil
Reed International	37	nil	72	nil
RTZ	279	nil	348	4
	4276	117	9784	416

Notes: Profits are those of the accounting year ending in 1976 or 1981: tax mainstream tax payable in 1977 or 1982.
Source: Own estimates.

We believe that the most desirable reform of the corporate tax system would be to convert the existing mixture of what is, on the one hand, excessively generous relief for investment financed by borrowing and, on the other, only temporary relief for the effects of inflation, into a tax based on cash flows. This is based on the use of free depreciation which allows companies to deduct for tax purposes any investment expenditure as soon as the money is spent. No distinction is made between expenditure on current items (labour, materials, etc.) and the expenditure on capital goods. The tax base is simply the difference between receipts from the sales of goods and services (including the proceeds from selling plant or factories) and the money spent on

acquiring goods and services. For this reason we shall describe such a
tax as a *cash flow corporation tax*. The essence of the tax is that all
receipts and payments, whether they correspond to current or to
capital items, enter into the tax base and therefore there is no need to
worry about how 'true economic depreciation' should be calculated.
Companies would be taxed on their cash flow. However, it is important
to note that our definition of cash flow refers to that of the company,
and does not correspond to an alternative common usage of the term as
cash flow to the shareholders. We do not allow interest payments as a
deduction. Under the cash flow corporation tax expenditure on real
items can be deducted, but the returns to the suppliers of finance,
whether shareholders or creditors, cannot.

What would the effect of such a tax be? Imagine a firm contemplating a specific investment project which would cost £1 m. With a cash
flow tax it would be able to deduct the £1 m. spent on purchasing
equipment against its profits on other projects, thus reducing its total
tax payments. If the tax rate were 50% the reduction in taxes would be
£½ m. The future profits of the project would also be reduced by 50%
by such a tax, and so the net effect is that both the initial outlay and
the subsequent returns are reduced by the same proportion, a proportion equal to the rate of tax. The tax scales down the size of the project
financed by the company, but it does not alter the rate of return on the
money invested in the project by the company. With a 50% tax rate
then what the Government is saying is 'in any project in which you
invest we shall compulsorily acquire a 50% stake, and we shall of course
provide half the finance in return for half the profits'. The reason why
this tax system can raise revenue is that it ensures that if firms are in
a position to earn pure profits then the Government too will get a good
share of the excess profits. It is for this reason that we argue below that
the cash flow tax is well suited for tackling problems such as how to tax
the profits on North Sea oil and gas extraction. We believe that it also
represents the best way of tidying up the present mess into which
corporate taxation has drifted by allowing for inflation in a simple
manner without the need for complicated conventions on how to
account for inflation. It taxes companies on those flows which are most
important to the companies themselves, namely flows of cash.

In the above example it was crucial that the firm had available
profits from other projects against which it could deduct investment
expenditure on new projects. But a new or expanding firm might not
have sufficient profits for this purpose, and such a possibility was an

important element in the decision to replace accelerated depreciation allowances with cash investment grants in 1966. The problem can be partly met by allowing companies to carry forward tax losses, not, as at present, simply at their nominal value, but marked up by an interest factor to allow for the fact that they have to wait to get the benefit of the first-year tax allowances. Alternatively, companies could be allowed to trade unused tax losses so that a company with a tax loss could sell its unused tax credit to a company with positive taxable income.

Because the tax is based on cash flows as and when they occur, there is no need to index for inflation. The distinction between capital and income would be irrelevant, and the effects of inflation would be allowed for automatically without the need for any special adjustment. It is important to stress the simplicity of this system in contrast to the complexity of the alternative methods of calculating taxable profits which have been suggested.

To convert the current tax system to a cash flow corporation tax would necessitate several changes, the net effect of which would probably be to raise the revenue collected from the corporate sector. The first modification would be to extend 100% first-year allowances to all capital expenditure in order to eliminate any distinction between current and capital expenditure. This would be an increase in the allowances currently granted for expenditure on buildings, land, and stocks. But since expenditure on stocks would be tax-deductible there would be no need for any special scheme of 'stock relief' and the existing relief could be abolished. Corporate capital gains would no longer be taxed at concessionary rates, and the proceeds from all sales of assets would be taxed at the full corporate tax rate. The other major set of changes is that no payment to the suppliers of finance would be allowed as a tax deduction. Interest payments would no longer be tax-deductible, and there would be no tax credit for corporate tax paid on dividends. Consequently, we would return to the classical system of corporation tax and abolish the tax deductibility of interest payments.

There are three difficulties with this proposal. The first is that to abandon the imputation system might be seen as a failure to take seriously the E.E.C. Commission's views on harmonization of member countries' tax systems. This is not an objection to which we give much weight because the proposals for harmonization have really been concerned with the cosmetics of the tax system not with any reality. Moreover, at the beginning of 1977 West Germany adopted a corporate tax system which was inconsistent with the Commission's ideas. We discuss the question of harmonization further at the end of the chapter.

The second problem would be the transitional difficulties faced by those companies which had responded to the incentive to use debt which exists under the current regime, and were highly geared. They would face problems if deductibility of interest payments were abolished overnight, and for this reason we suggest a transitional period of several years over which tax deductibility would be gradually phased out.

The final difficulty is the application of the new tax system to financial companies. The logical counterpart to abolishing the tax deductibility of interest payments is the abolition of the taxation of interest income. If this were done then any profit made by lending at higher interest rates money borrowed at lower rates would go untaxed. Yet this is exactly what financial companies do, and often the reason why they pay lower interest rates is because they do not charge market prices for the financial services which they provide. For example, banks do not pay interest on current accounts and in turn do not charge the full price for the banking services they provide. The pure cash flow corporation tax would not work for such cases, and special rules would need to be devised for financial companies. The logical treatment is to regard an interest-free current account as representing a combination of an interest-bearing deposit and a charge for banking services. It has become clear that the tax treatment of these companies, of which the clearing banks are the most important, creates problems for any reform of the corporate tax system which deals with problems posed by inflation. The problems posed by the measurement of bank profits were recognized in 1981 when a special tax on banks related to the size of their deposits was levied.

One remaining point is the treatment of overseas investment. It would be wrong to grant 100% first-year allowances on investment made overseas for reasons to do with the rather complex rules dealing with overseas income and the related credit given against U.K. corporation tax for taxes paid abroad. A company operating abroad pays tax to the foreign government and only pays to the U.K. Revenue the difference between its liability to U.K. corporation tax on the overseas profits and the taxes which have been paid abroad. In other words, it only pays U.K. tax if this is greater than the amount actually paid abroad. It would be anomalous to allow a company which had both domestic and overseas activities to deduct its investment abroad against its domestic profits for tax purposes if the tax on its subsequent overseas profits ended up in the hands of the foreign government, and, because of the existence of credit for foreign tax, no tax was ever paid to the U.K. government. In these circumstances overseas investment can reduce a company's domestic tax liability! Yet in fact this is precisely what British companies can do at the moment by investing in plant and machinery abroad. An overseas investment is actually more attractive to a British company than to a foreign one. We presume this was an unintended side-effect of giving 100% first-year allowances. As long as we are obliged by international agreement to grant credit for foreign tax the easiest way to deal with the problem is to disallow overseas investment as qualifying for 100% allowances.

Harmonization

It is often suggested that one of the constraints on reforming our tax system is the need to keep in line with developments in other E.E.C. countries with whose tax systems we are supposed to be harmonizing. The question of corporate tax systems in member countries has received considerable attention from the E.E.C. Commission which has produced many documents on the subject, and a Draft Directive advocating that member countries aim to harmonize on the imputation system. This proposal is, however, unlikely to have a significant impact on what each member country actually does. One reason for this is that some years ago the E.E.C. appeared to favour the two-rate system before it turned its favours to the classical system. It appears to have been swimming with the tide rather than setting the pace. Consequently, if one or more member countries seem determined to adopt a different system the proposals for harmonization might well be changed. At the beginning of 1977 West Germany adopted a system of corporate taxation which was inconsistent with the recommendations of the Commission. Holland seems determined to retain the classical system with no imputation credit being given at all.

The Commission's concern with harmonization is inspired by a concern about free movement of capital and possible tax barriers to this caused by additional taxes being levied on dividends flowing from one member country to another (although there are rather more serious obstacles to the free movement of capital such as the fact that it is often illegal). In its proposals, therefore, attention is directed entirely at the taxation of distributed profits. Harmonization, it is suggested, should be on the imputation system, with tax credits extended to individuals in other member countries. Any refunds due would be paid by the authorities of the country in which the underlying profits were taxed, not by the authorities of the country of residence of the shareholders. An additional withholding tax would be levied on dividends except where paid to known residents of a member country, or residents of a country which has negotiated an appropriate double tax treaty.

This concern with distributed profits ignores the fact that the effects of a corporate tax are very much bound up with the taxation of undistributed profits and the allowance available for depreciation. Moreover, the corporate tax system cannot be considered in isolation from the personal tax system with which it interacts. Perhaps harmonization, like indexation, is an all-or-nothing business.

The taxation of North Sea oil and gas

The flow of oil from the North Sea brings substantial revenues to the UK exchequer, as well as other economic benefits. These revenues are derived from taxes on the economic rent derived from North Sea activities—the difference between the cost of extracting the oil and its value on world markets. Since the price of oil is several times the cost of obtaining it even from relatively difficult fields this rent, which is equivalent to the value of the right to extract oil from this particular source, is large.

A special tax regime has been constructed for North Sea activities. A royalty is payable of $12\frac{1}{2}\%$ of the value of the oil extracted. Petroleum Revenue Tax, at 75%, is due on the receipts from selling North Sea oil less the costs of finding it, extracting it, and bringing it ashore. The costs are those incurred in the field from which the oil comes—thus P.R.T. is levied on a 'field basis'. Royalties can be treated as a cost in computing P.R.T. An 'uplift' provision allows 135% of initial capital expenditures to be offset against P.R.T. There is an oil allowance of 500,000 tonnes of oil a year which is free of P.R.T., subject to a cumulative total for each field of 5 m. tons. There is also a 'safeguard provision' for rebating P.R.T. if the historic cost profitability of a field becomes too low.

Companies are also liable to Corporation Tax on their profits. A 'ring-fence' is drawn round the North Sea, so that only expenses or allowances relating to North Sea activities can be deducted in computing liabilities. Before North Sea production began, many oil companies had no liability to mainstream corporation tax. They typically had unused relief from capital allowances, stock relief, double tax relief and advance corporation tax from their activities on the U.K. mainland and in the operations in the rest of the world. The ring fence arrangement prevents tax losses and double tax relief derived elsewhere being used against North Sea profits and restricts the capacity of the companies to obtain relief for advance corporation tax.

A fourth tax, supplementary petroleum duty, was introduced in 1980. It is a hybrid between royalties and P.R.T. It is based on 20% of gross revenues less the oil allowance. In 1982 it was renamed advance petroleum revenue tax, and payments of APRT can be offset against future payments of P.R.T. the law provides that any APRT which has not been relieved after five years will be refunded.

One might conclude from the complexity of the system that it was a finely tuned instrument in which each element made a contribution to some carefully conceived overall design. This conclusion would be entirely mistaken. The planning period for investing in offshore oil exploration and development is a very long one and one of the most important objectives of a tax regime for these activities is to provide a stable environment in which such plans can be made. The government has been spectacularly unsuccessful in achieving this objective, and the tax structure and rates have been subject to substantial modifications every year since they were introduced and have often been changed several times in a year.

Worse than that, the interaction of the taxes is riddled with anomalies. On the one hand, there is a North Sea 'poverty trap', in which tax may take more than 100% of additional revenue from a marginal field; on the other, there is the possibility of 'gold-plating', where more than 100% of additional capital expenditure may be deductible against tax. The potential tax charge on the same discovery, or potential deduction for the same expenditure, varies widely across the North Sea according to the company which undertakes it and the field in which it occurs. The combination of the height of the tax rates imposed, uncertainty about their future, and the random relationship of tax to profitability, has now reduced the rate of exploration and development to low levels.

The cash flow principle is particularly well suited to the taxation of this type of activity. The mechanics of applying a progressive tax on cumulative profitability were described by the Part Committee (1982) and the merits of the approach are very clear. Such a tax is relatively simple, robust to changing circumstances, and because it is directly related to the measures which oil companies use in appraising invest-ment—expected cash flow—it secures a substantial share of the revenues of highly successful ventures while minimizing the disincentive to marginal ones.

It is often said that in attempting to reform the tax system we are constrained by history. If we could start from scratch things would be very different. The sorry history of the taxation of North Sea oil demonstrates that this is not true. We had a chance to invent a new tax system in the 1970s, with a clean slate; and we invented something which in its complexity, anomalies, inequities, and disincentives has all the characteristics of the British tax system as a whole. The fault lies, not with our ancestors, but with the ways in which we determine tax policy. Half-baked measures are hastily devised, and then quickly and repeatedly modified to deal with some immediately pressing problem, all without any sense of long term strategy or of how proposals fit into some overall picture. This book describes the consequences.

TABLE 12.2

North Sea Oil Tax Revenues (£ m., 1982 prices)

Year	Royalties	SPD	PRT	APRT	Corp. Tax	Total
1977	400	—	—	—	—	400
1978	450	—	350	—	150	950
1979	750	—	1200	—	450	2400
1980	1150	—	2250	—	600	4000
1981	1500	2000	2750	—	450	6700
1982	1600	2500	3000	—	200	7300
1983	1750	400	3900	2225	350	8625
1984	1900	—	3600	2900	350	8750
1985	2000	—	3700	3000	1300	10 000
1986	1850	—	3800	2900	1700	10 250
1987	1650	—	3700	2500	1350	9200

Source: IFS estimates, assuming average 10% inflation and constant real oil prices.

13

TAXATION AND INFLATION

INFLATION has probably been the most potent influence for change on the structure of the British tax system in the last fifteen years. It raises problems of two distinct kinds. There is the issue of 'bracket indexation' which arises because tax schedules are defined in money terms. Income tax gives a personal allowance of £1,565 for a single person and £2,445 for a married man. Capital transfer tax is imposed on transfers which in total exceed £55,000. It is necessary to register for V.A.T. if your turnover is greater than £17,000. You must pay stamp duty if you buy a house for more than £25,000. There is a tax of 2·1p per cigarette and of 71p per gallon of petrol. With inflation, the meaning of these monetary amounts changes. Fifty years ago, a house costing £25,000 would have been a mansion. Now it is very difficult to find any house in the South of England as cheap as that.

Inflation also poses difficulties for the definition of income itself—the problem of 'capital-income indexation'. When prices are stable, an investor who earns 3% on £100 he deposits in the bank is better off by that amount at the end of the year: £3 is the sum which he can prudently spend while maintaining his capital and his ability to earn a similar sum in future years. When inflation runs at 20% per annum, the man who earns 12 % on his bank deposit is in a very different position. The interest he receives is significantly short of what he needs simply to stay as well off as he was when he deposited the money in the first place. Thus when inflation is taken into account his real income is negative, not positive. He cannot spend this £12 except by making himself worse off in future, and hence it is as much part of his capital as is his basic £100. Nevertheless, the taxman will present a demand for 30% (or up to 75%) of his nominal income of £12, so that the amount by which his receipts after tax fall short of what is required to keep pace with inflation is greater still.

Bracket indexation and fiscal drag

What we have called bracket indexation, following the Meade Committee, was first noticed in relation to income tax and was somewhat inelegantly christened 'fiscal drag'. Inflation means that year by year people earn larger and larger amounts of money even though they are not necessarily better off. But a progressive income tax bases liability on their money income, and so demands each year a higher proportion of their rising money income in tax. With tax brackets fixed in nominal terms, someone with a constant real income will find himself paying higher and higher effective rates of tax. Thus the revenue's take, as a proportion of total personal income, will increase steadily and this is precisely what has happened. Figures 13.1 and 13.2 show why. If we look at the average tax rates shown in Fig. 13.1, the rate schedule appears to have slowly drifted downwards at each level of money income. If, as in Fig. 13.2, one adjusts for the change in average earnings over the period, the picture is dramatically changed. Although tax thresholds have frequently been raised in money terms, they have generally declined in real terms. In 1952–3 a married man had to earn almost £800 per year to be liable for standard rate tax. If his salary kept pace with average earnings between 1952 and 1982, it would have risen to over £10,000 and he would have been on the verge of paying higher rates. At the highest real income levels, however, the burden is now lower than at any time since the war.

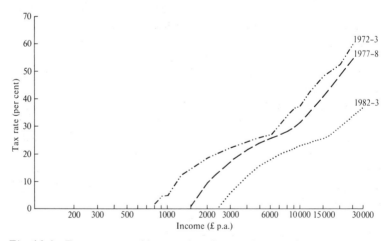

Fig. 13.1. Tax rates payable at various income levels, 1952–83

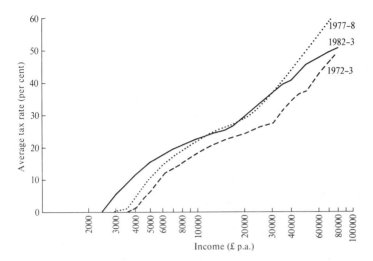

Fig. 13.2. Tax rates payable at various real income levels, 1952–83

Fiscal drag has been a boon for dishonest Chancellors of the Exchequer. Each year they could announce 'reductions' in income tax while each year they would in fact increase the burden of the tax. Until the mid 1970s, this is exactly what happened in most years. In the course of debate on the 1977 Finance Act, back bench pressure secured the passage, against government opposition, of what became known as the Rooker-Wise amendment. This required indexation of the basic single and married (and some other) allowances. Initially the government resisted these measures, but more recently the principle of bracket indexation has been accepted and extended. It now applies to the higher rate bands and to thresholds for capital gains tax, investment income surcharge and capital transfer tax.

Under pressure in 1982 to raise additional revenue, the government introduced a measure to rescind its obligations to increase tax brackets for that year. While widely regarded as a departure from the principle of indexation, this incident was in a sense a reinforcement of it. Indexation is not intended to prevent governments from ever increasing taxes; its purpose is to require them to admit it when they do, and in 1982 this was what the government had to do.

When people talk about fiscal drag they usually refer to income tax, but the same problem is relevant to other taxes with a progressive rate structure. Capital transfer tax also has a series of rate bands, while capital gains tax and the investment income surcharge were progressive in effect because of their high exemption limit. Indexation of CTT poses a special problem. If prices have risen by 50% in the past five years, then a gift of £40,000 made five years ago is equivalent to a gift of £60,000 made now. This change should be reflected in the threshold for C.T.T.; but it should also be reflected in the cumulative total on which C.T.T. is levied. With thoroughgoing indexation, a gift of £40,000 five years ago and of £60,000 now would lead to a cumulative total equivalent to a current transfer of £120,000. Possibly because of the complexity of this procedure, the indexation of capital transfer tax is limited to the threshold and does not apply to the various rate bands.

Proportional taxes are largely unaffected by inflation. The yield from V.A.T. increases in line with rising prices. Revenue from national insurance contributions increases at the same rate as earnings. The yield of car tax moves in line with the price of cars. Some peripheral aspects of these taxes do need regular readjustment, such as the threshold of turnover below which it is unnecessary to register for V.A.T. and the ceiling and floor for national insurance contributions. The V.A.T. threshold has been subject to frequent review and the national insurance limits move in line with changes in the rate of state pension (and hence with prices).

A final group of taxes includes those which are levied as flat monetary amounts. To use a motor vehicle it is necessary to buy an annual licence at a cost of £80, and we described several other taxes of this kind in Chapter 8. When the value of money falls, so does the burden of these taxes. Table 13.1 shows how this has happened. In this table, we show not only the rates of tax levied at the time but also what they would now be if they had been increased in line with prices generally since then. If indirect taxes had kept pace with inflation since 1966, cigarettes would now be dearer by 45p per packet, whisky by £8·50 per bottle, beer by 12p per pint, and petrol by 50p per gallon. Most of the fall occurred in the earlier part of the period. Although there has been and still is no formal indexation of these duties, since the mid-1970s they have in fact been increased in line with inflation on a fairly regular basis.

If the impact of inflation on the tax system is not recognized, then it can have substantial effects on the structure of taxation. Income tax revenue will rise, relatively, while receipts from specific duties will fall. There will be a switch from indirect to direct taxation. Such a move may or may not be desirable, but it should not simply be an

TABLE 13.1

Indirect taxes, 1966–1982

Year	Actual rates				At 1982 prices			
	cigarettes	whisky	beer	petrol	cigarettes	whisky	beer	petrol
1966	16	1·88	4·3	18	114	13·42	31	128
1969	18	2·20	4·7	23	114	13·89	30	145
1972	18	2·20	4·7	23	91	11·13	24	116
1975	29	2·80	7·5	37	93	9·02	24	119
1978	39	3·49	10·0	43	86	7·69	22	94
Tax, 1982					71	4·90	19	82
Retail price, 1982					95	6·30	51	160

Prices and commodities are defined as in Table 8.2, p. 127.
Source: Reports of Customs and Excise, own estimates.

unintended by-product of inflation. Between the mid 1960s and the mid 1970s, this is precisely what did happen. In 1965 income tax (including national insurance contributions) was 45% of total government current receipts; in 1975 it was 53%. At the same time, the share of indirect taxes fell from 29% to 23%. Since then there has been general recognition of the problem. Action has been taken to prevent further unplanned moves in this direction and to restore the proportion of indirect taxes in the total by the 1979 shift from income tax to V.A.T. Although there is considerable tidying up to be done, bracket indexation is now a general feature of the U.K. tax system.

Inflation in the capital market

We have noted that inflation raises problems for the definition of income. When prices are changing, people need to have more money in order simply to maintain the value of their wealth. If I had £100 in the building society last year, and have £110 this year, and prices have risen by 10%, then I am no better off than I was a year ago.

One way of securing protection against inflation would be to lend on terms which were indexed. I would hand over £100 and what I would be repaid would have the same value in the money of the day as £100 has now. If prices had doubled, I would get £200. Obviously I would expect a much lower interest rate on such an investment; however it would be a 'real' interest rate rather than a nominal interest rate and I could go out and spend my annual interest confident that my capital was maintaining its value. I could also quite fairly be taxed on the 'real' interest I received. Notice that there is no logical economic law which says that real interest rates have to be positive. It is possible that I might have to pay someone who offered to keep my capital intact for me, and in fact in most recent years this would have been quite a good deal for most people—better, at least, than other forms of saving and investment offered them.

Several other countries have experimented at various times with indexation of this kind—it has been pursued furthest in Brasil, Finland, Iceland, and Israel.

The possibility that indexed bonds might exist in Britain was first canvassed in the mid 1970s when inflation topped 25%. Merchant banks prepared prospectuses but the Bank of England indicated that it would intervene to prohibit such issues. The reasons for this prohibition, which survived for several years, were obscure. One argument was that indexation involves accepting, or institutionalizing, inflation; but this is a bit like saying that taking an umbrella with you involves accepting, or institutionalizing, bad weather. It was also argued that middle eastern states were so anxious to obtain bonds of this kind that capital would flood into Britain on an unprecedented scale if they were available. This was apparently considered undesirable. It was never clear why the King of Saudi Arabia should wish to link his assets to the price level in Britain and subsequent events have shown that he does not in fact want to do so.

A limited experiment was made in 1975 with 'granny bonds' which allowed pensioners to lend £500 to the government, the sum to be revalued in line with prices before it was repaid with a small bonus in addition. Grannies had to be resident in the U.K. thus cunningly excluding the King of Saudi Arabia. Eventually it was realized that protecting your capital against inflation is more important before you have retired than afterwards and 'granny bonds' were opened to all. Attempts to rechristen them 'people's bonds' were not very successful.

Pressure for wider measures of indexation grew from a variety of sources. Governments which annually ran very large deficits felt under pressure to invent imaginative new ways of borrowing money. Critics of official determination to get inflation down pointed out that a policy of raising money for twenty or thirty years at high fixed interest rates made sense only if the government had no real intention of reducing inflation. Many of the problems of pension funds were attributed to their inability to find assets of known and constant real value. In 1981 the government issued the first index-linked government stock. It was to be repaid in 1996, and the amount of the repayment would be whatever was needed to buy then what £100 would buy in 1982. In the meantime, a real interest rate of 2% was offered; the interest payment would itself be revalued each year in line with the retail price index. Only tax exempt pension funds were allowed to buy the bonds; thus the question of how the interest and capital repayment were to be taxed did not arise.

A world of indexed bonds would need many fewer actuaries and investment managers, and it is perhaps understandable that they did not give the new securities a particularly warm welcome. Since inflation was falling rapidly at the time, they may even have been right. In any event, the bond quickly fell to a discount on its issue price. Partly to stimulate demand, and partly because the predicted disasters from introducing indexation had not materialized, the government in 1982 allowed anyone—even foreigners—to buy index-linked government stock.

Indexation and taxation

This move immediately raised the question of how index-linked securities should be taxed. The longest dated of the index-linked stocks will be repaid in 2011. Even on the most optimistic of views about the future course of inflation, anyone who holds a bond till then will be sitting on a substantial capital gain. With an average inflation rate of only 5%, the maturity value of this stock will be over £400. But every penny of that capital gain will be the result of inflation; none of it will be real gain at all.

The fact that most recent capital gains are of this kind has been recognized for some time. In 1977 the government promised to 'look sympathetically' at the problem. A consultative document was prepared which presented, and demolished, a ridiculous proposal for 'tapering' the tax charge on capital gains according to the length of time for which the asset in question had been held. It is a common administrative tactic to resist suggested change by dissecting, with apparent seriousness of purpose, an impractical version of it. Inexperienced observers of Whitehall may be led to think that the matter has been given careful consideration and that nothing can be done; there is, of course, no reason whatever to suppose that either is true. In the event, the only change was that small gains were exempted from tax. Three years later a further review was undertaken. The outcome was a further increase to £3,000 in the threshold for capital gains tax.

With the arrival of indexed securities, however, the problem could not be evaded any longer. The government announced that it would index capital gains tax. The principle of indexation of capital gains is a reasonably straightforward one. Suppose you buy an asset for £1,000 and sell it some years later for £2,000, by which time prices have risen by 90%. We index your acquisition cost, so that in terms of current purchasing power what you paid for it is not £1,000 but £1,900 and your real gain is £100 not £1,000. If you sell the asset for only £1,500, you have made a real loss of £400, and this is indeed the situation; you would have been able to buy goods worth £400 more, at current prices, if you had spent the money immediately instead of investing it. Although the government announced it was indexing capital gains tax, this is not what they did. Instead they created an 'indexation allowance'. This begins one year after you purchased the asset and runs until you finally dispose of it. Suppose prices increased by 75% during that time. Your indexation allowance is equal to the price rise times the initial acquisition cost, or £750. You can offset this allowance against your nominal gain, so that your gain of £1,000 (if you sold the asset for £2,000) is reduced to £250, and you must then pay tax on £250. If you sold it for £1,500, the indexation allowance eliminates your 'gain' and there is no tax to pay, but you cannot create a real loss or use the rest of your indexation allowance in any other way. If you bought and sold the same assets several times both you and the Inland Revenue will quickly get into a muddle and you will need to hire an accountant to sort it out. On top of all this, the threshold for capital gains tax was further raised to £5,000.

It is vital to understand that the problems of assessing investment income under inflation are not confined to capital gains. Imagine a world with no inflation. People might earn 3% on investment in bonds, 4% on investment in property (to reflect the greater uncertainty about the capital value of property). Now suppose prices rise each year by a general and predictable 10%. The owner of property makes a 10% capital gain each year. What happens in the bond market? For bonds to remain equally attractive, the yield on them will have to rise also. This could happen as a result of a move to indexed loans; these would offer a real yield of 3% and a capital gain of 10% per year, equal to the rate of inflation. If loans remain unindexed, however—and this is the normal situation—then the interest rate on them will have to rise. If they are to maintain the same relationship with property yields, the nominal interest rate will now have to be 13%. In one case, compensation for inflation takes the form of a capital gain; in the other case, there is a rise in the nominal interest rate. Both the capital gain, and the inflationary component in the interest rate, are illusory; an equitable tax base would exclude them both.

But if this is true for lenders then just the same is true for borrowers. If I take out a £10,000 mortgage, pay interest at 13%, and repay my £10,000 either at the end of the mortgage or in instalments over life, then the real value of what I repay is much less than I borrowed. Most of my interest payment is not real interest but repayment of capital. Just as the lender should be taxed only on the real component of the interest he receives, so the borrower should obtain tax relief only on the real component of the interest he pays. The prospect of losing this relief must seem very alarming to companies or to households who think that current interest rates are very high. But the reason they seem so high is precisely because borrowing is undertaken in nominal rather than real terms. A mortgage of 13% fixed in money terms imposes a very serious initial burden which declines steadily as inflation progresses. An indexed mortgage at 3% fixed in real terms would impose a much smaller initial cost, but one which would remain constant over its life. If tax relief were given on real interest only, it would be necessary to reconstruct mortgages in this way, and they would then be no more difficult to afford than at present. It was indexation of the capital market which led us to indexation of the tax system; but it seems that indexation of the tax system leads us back to indexation of the capital market.

The extent of indexation

We described a world in which there was no inflation and where bonds yielded 3% and property 4%. With 10% inflation, the return on bonds might rise to 13%. Property would continue to yield 4% but holders could expect an annual 10% capital gain. If the tax system is fully indexed, then the inflation component of 10% is excluded in computing tax liability on bonds, so that holders pay tax on the real return of 3%. Property owners pay tax only on their real capital gain— the part which exceeds 10%.

Suppose no adjustments whatever are made to the tax system. Then lending is less attractive than before—because the tax burden has increased—and borrowing is more attractive, because the tax burden has declined. Suppose everyone pays tax at 50%. Then the return on bonds would need to rise to 23% before they were equally attractive to lenders. On £100 of loan, tax of £11·50 would be payable on £23 interest. At 10% inflation, the net of tax real return on the loan is £1·50: exactly what it would have been with a 3% yield and no inflation. Moreover, the borrower can afford to pay 23% without being any worse off, because the tax deduction he obtains is now so large.

For a variety of reasons, things do not work as smoothly in practice. Not everyone is subject to tax at the same rate, so that lending becomes very attractive to those who do not pay tax and borrowing is attractive to those who do. Interest rates therefore will not rise as high as 23%. This means that lenders who pay low rates of tax (like pension funds) benefit from inflation; so do borrowers who pay high rates of tax (like people who buy expensive houses). There is therefore redistribution among borrowers and lenders. The interaction of tax and inflation also alters the attractiveness of different kinds of asset. The inflation element of interest payments is taxed as if it were income while the inflation component of the returns from property is treated more favourably as capital gain, so real assets like property become attractive compared to nominal assets like bonds. People may suffer from money illusion, so that they think that 23% is a very high interest rate even if they are told that tax relief and inflation make such borrowing very cheap. And to some extent they are right to think this, since borrowings are structured in such a way that 23% interest is initially very onerous. If the capital market were indexed things might be different but we have not yet reached that stage.

Nevertheless, with no indexation one might reach a sort of equilibrium with a new, much higher level of nominal interest rates. This outcome might not be very different from the position which would be achieved with no inflation. Central to this argument is an element of symmetry in the tax treatment of debt. This means that lenders pay tax on what borrowers are allowed to deduct. If this symmetry exists, and borrowers and lenders are liable to tax at similar rates, then the net effect of inflation on tax receipts and on savings and investment behaviour may be quite small.

Partial indexation—which makes allowance for inflation in some areas, or for certain items, but not for others—presents many difficulties, and that is the position we have now reached. With partial indexation, symmetry disappears. This inevitably means that essentially similar transactions receive different tax treatment; that deductions are available for payments which are not taxable when they are received, or conversely, and that there is endless scope for anomalies and abuse. The present degree of partial indexation is the consequence of the two principal elements so far introduced into the tax system, stock relief (which we discuss further below) and the indexation of capital gains tax.

The present position is one in which relief for inflation is allowed if compensation for it takes the form of a capital gain, but not if it takes the form of an enhanced interest rate. If you own a real asset, and it rises in value because of inflation, you get an indexation allowance. If you hold a bank deposit, and the interest rate rises because of inflation, you pay tax on the full amount of interest received. The distinction between two types of compensation for inflation has nothing to commend it. It has no economic content. It is inequitable; capital gains are already more lightly taxed than income and generally accrue to better off people. It is impractical; as we saw in Chapter 4, income and capital gains can readily be interchanged and this will happen if there is some advantage to the switch. For this last reason, if no other, we do not expect the present position to survive unmodified for long.

Unanticipated inflation as a capital tax

It was an important element in the discussion above that inflation was expected. If everyone anticipates that inflation will run at 10%, then this will be reflected in the terms on which they want to lend or borrow and interest rates will rise correspondingly. If inflation is unanticipated, then many people will find themselves locked into contracts which they made at fixed nominal interest rates. In these circumstances, inflation becomes a tax on capital. Suppose prices have been stable, and are expected to remain so, and many people have lent money at a fixed rate of 3%. If inflation now rises to 10%, they earn a real return of −7%; their capital depreciates in value at 7% per year.

Most of the expenditure undertaken by governments is funded from explicit taxes, like income tax and corporation tax, which we describe in other chapters of this book. However governments do not always match their revenue and expenditure, and meet deficits by printing money or borrowing it. This inflationary finance acquires resources for the government, and divert them from its citizens, in just the same way as other taxes. The form of the tax is a levy on people who hold assets denominated in money terms, such as fixed interest securities or cash itself.

If the tax system is not indexed, then of course the impact of the inflation tax is exaggerated. If your 3% nominal interest is liable to tax at 50%, then the real rate of return which you obtain, after tax, is now −8½%; a net yield of 1½% in money terms, reduced by inflation of 10%. For borrowers, of course, the opposite is true. The burden of their debt has fallen in real terms, and hence unexpected inflation can be seen as a subsidy to debt. It is worth noting that in Britain, as in most modern economies, by far the largest fixed interest borrower is the government itself.

If we regard unanticipated inflation as a tax, then the picture we painted in Chapter 10 of steadily diminishing yields from capital taxation looks very different. Much of the inflation which occurred in the 1970s was unanticipated, and real returns on investment were frequently negative even for non-taxpayers. Inflation acted as a substantial and redistributive capital tax. But as a tax it has little to commend it. It is a tax on assets and a subsidy on liabilities imposed at a rate which has nothing to do with the circumstances of the individual taxpayer, but which depends solely on the rate of inflation, and the extent to which assets are held in money form. This is a very odd state of affairs and does not appear to correspond with the platform of any political party.

Inflation accounting

Concern that company accounts gave a misleading picture of their affairs under inflation rose with the inflation rate itself in the early 1970s. Proposals were produced for a scheme of current purchasing power (C.P.P.) accounting. The government was worried by the wider implications of these ideas—especially for the tax system—and appointed a committee to review them. The Sandilands Committee rejected C.P.P. and put forward a set of proposals of its own, described as C.C.A. (current cost accounting). After lengthy debate a version of C.C.A. has now been adopted as an accounting standard (S.S.A.P. 16) for large companies.

Although the details are complicated, the central difference between C.C.A. and C.P.P. is a simple one. Suppose an oil company holds a large stock of oil, and the oil price rises, while other prices do not. Has the oil company made a profit, or not? Proponents of C.C.A. would argue that it has not, since in order to remain an oil company it is necessary for it to go on holding stocks of oil at the new higher prices and the 'profit' is not something which it can effectively realize. Advocates of

C.P.P. would claim that nevertheless people who held claims to stocks of oil are now better off than people who did not, and that this gain should be reflected in an assessment of profit and loss. C.P.P. measures gains and losses relative to a general price index; C.C.A. relative to one which reflects the structure of the assets held by the business whose affairs are being considered. The issue is one which has no simple answer and it is really not possible to make a judgement on it independently of the particular circumstances in which the profit is obtained.

C.C.A. involves four main adjustments to published accounts. Depreciation charges should no longer be based on the historic cost of the asset but on the current cost of similar items of equipment. A cost of sales adjustment is required to remove from profits the element attributable to increases in the price of goods held in stock. As well as holding stock, many firms find it necessary to extend trade credit to their customers and a monetary working capital adjustment (MWCA) makes allowance for the effect of inflation on the finance necessary to cover outstanding accounts. These three modifications mostly work in the direction of reducing profits. However many firms finance these activities—buying fixed assets, holding stocks, or funding trade credit—from borrowed money. Inflation reduces the value of the amount which needs to be repaid. A gearing adjustment reduces the adjustment to historic cost profits by an amount calculated to reflect the ratio of debt to total assets (or gearing) of the company.

In Chapter 12 we described the pattern of recent modifications to the structure of corporation tax. It is sometimes suggested that corporation tax should be based on current cost profits, and indeed the need to await the agreement of the accountancy profession on an appropriate inflation accounting standard was often cited as a reason for delaying proposals for more fundamental changes to the corporation tax structure. The scheme of stock relief introduced in 1980-1 bears some resemblance to the cost of sales adjustment, but none of the other adjustments required for current cost accounting have counterparts in the tax system. The practical difficulties of introducing C.C.A. into corporation tax would seem considerable. It is not easy to move from a system which allows immediate write-off of expenditure on plant and machinery to one which gives allowances based on replacement cost depreciation. Either you give further allowances on equipment which has already been written off—so that more than the total cost of the item is allowed as a deduction against tax—or you do not, in which case companies receive much reduced allowances on their new equipment purchases, none on their old, and pay greatly increased tax bills. Implementing the gearing adjustment would be difficult for companies with substantial borrowings which might have high current cost profits but no liquid resources to meet their tax bills.

These difficulties could no doubt be overcome if the objective were desirable. But it is not. There are no substantial advantages, and several major disadvantages, to basing tax on current cost profits. Such a tax would not be neutral. If real returns were positive, it would discourage investment of all kinds and discriminate against equity finance (if real returns were not positive, it would not yield any revenue). The use of current cost profits as a tax base would conflict with the development of accounting practice. There is no reason whatever to think that the questions 'what is the most accurate assessment of a company's profits for the year' and 'what should be adopted as the corporate tax base' are ones which have the same answer, and to conflate the two is to make it more difficult to find the right answer to either. The measurement of profit is a subjective matter which depends on the particular circumstances of a particular company, and this conflicts directly with the tax authority's requirement for objectivity and general rules of universal applicability. In Chapter 12 we considered explicitly the question of how companies should be taxed on its own merits. We think this is the right starting-point; and from it we found no reason to choose inflation-adjusted profits as the tax base.

Current cost accounting has come under fire from backwoodsmen of the accountancy profession, who do not see why practices which have served acccountants well for the past century should not suffice equally well for the next hundred years. For this reason many more forward-looking accountants are anxious to see C.C.A. employed for tax purposes 'I need to calculate your current cost profits so that you can pay less tax' will be much more popular with clients than 'I need to calculate your current cost profits in order to comply with the relevant statements of standard accounting practice'. The purpose may be a laudable one, but major distortion of the tax system is not an acceptable means of achieving it.

Inflation and tax policy

In this chapter we have described the adaptation of the British tax system to an era of inflation. The changes we have been describing are substantial, far-reaching, and by no means complete. We do not think that the degree of indexation which has now been achieved can possibly be a final resting place. If inflation falls, substantially and permanently, the issue becomes less important. Otherwise, the government must either retrace its steps—a particularly difficult task for politicians to undertake—or continue down a road which will lead to a very extensive range of indexation provisions. Moreover, we have shown that indexation of the tax system, and indexation of the capital market, are inextricably linked. We are therefore discussing a series of fundamental changes in the British financial system. We would wish to report that such changes had been extensively debated, carefully considered, and skilfully planned. In reality none of these things are true. The argument has been conducted secretively and, we would judge, superficially: each change has occurred as an isolated response to some immediate problem; most have been forced unwillingly on the institution—Bank of England or Inland Revenue—immediately responsible for their implementation.

Concealment is characteristic of much policy formation in Britain. It is, nevertheless, barely credible that announcement of policy decisions as important as the issue of index-linked stock and the indexation of capital gains tax should have come as a surprise even to well-informed observers. It follows that the views of those who would be most involved with the consequences of these decisions cannot have been taken into account, and it is inevitable that there would be serious technical deficiencies in the formulation of the proposals in both cases, as indeed there were. This might matter less if the quality of the strategic thinking behind the decision was high. In fact there is no evidence of any strategic thinking at all. The decision to move to an indexed income tax system rather than to a regime based on cash flows, or not to move at all, is the product of drift rather than decision. The inevitable interim problems of a partially indexed system are to be dealt with, in so far as they are dealt with at all, on a trial and error basis.

In other chapters, we have presented what we believe are strong arguments for moving to a tax base which avoids the use of income concepts—by relating personal taxation to expenditure and company tax to cash flows. But perhaps the most important argument for such a move is that the problems of capital–income indexation we have described in this chapter are entirely avoided. Indexation of income tax is not undesirable—indeed we think it an inescapable part of an efficient and equitable tax system. But it is inevitably rather complicated, poses awkward transitional problems, and has ramifications which extend far beyond the tax system. If any reader needs persuading that there must be a better alternative he should read the clauses and schedules which implement the indexation provisions of the 1982 Finance Act.

14

THE DISTRIBUTION OF THE
TAX BURDEN

OUR concern in this chapter is with the way in which the tax burden is distributed between individuals. We have noted in particular contexts that all taxes are ultimately taxes on individuals, and it is in this connection and only in this connection that considerations of equity enter the analysis of taxation. It simply makes no sense to talk about 'fairness' between sectors of the economy, or industries, or between the personal and corporate sectors. But these aspects of distribution may be very relevant to the effects of the tax system on efficiency and to the way in which the tax burden is distributed between people with different tastes or between wage-earners and the owners of capital.

The theory of public finance has traditionally distinguished between *vertical* and *horizontal* equity in taxation. Vertical equity is concerned with how tax liabilities are arranged among people whose circumstances are acknowledged to be different; with the distributive and redistributive implications of taxation, with the 'rich' and the 'poor'. Horizontal equity is derived from the application of the axiom that similar individuals should be treated similarly. This axiom seems compelling, though it may conflict with other objectives. (Two men are in a lifeboat with only enough water for one. The only horizontally equitable outcome is that both die.)

In practice, horizontal equity is most frequently violated when administrative arrangements are unsatisfactory; when tax impinges heavily on some transactions but can be avoided on others; when tax is paid principally by the honest, or those without effective tax advisers or the readiness to reorganize their affairs so as to minimize their liabilities; when borderlines between activities or commodities cannot be satisfactorily defined. A high proportion of popular complaints about the tax system results from inequities of this kind. We have seen serious difficulties here in the U.K. income tax. They arose to a scandalous extent with the old estate duty and are beginning to do so with capital transfer tax also.

The difficulty of principle in applying horizontal equity is that the identification of 'similar circumstances' raises awkward problems of fact and of values. In general, most people seem to take the view that the tax (and benefit) system should recognize differences where they are involuntary but not where they are a matter of choice. We want to take account of differences in endowments of wealth or skill but would resist more favourable treatment of those who are unlucky enough to have expensive tastes, although the approach is not (and cannot be) pushed very far. The most pressing problem of horizontal equity is to decide how the tax system should take account of household composition and arrangements in defining 'similar circumstances'. This is difficult because these matters involve both choice and necessity. Is having children more akin to losing a leg (which it is agreed should reduce the contribution one is expected to make to national revenue) or to buying a Rolls Royce (which it is agreed should not?). We shall not attempt to answer this question.

In fact the principle of horizontal equity has practical import only in so far as it places constraints on the sorts of taxes which may be used. No two individuals are ever likely to be in exactly similar circumstances, and the real issue is how we should treat people in dissimilar circumstances. For example, should married couples face the same schedule as two single people? Of course, we could postulate hypothetical cases in which there is no difficulty in defining 'similar circumstances'. If in our previous example the two men in the lifeboat had tossed a coin to see who survived some people might claim that horizontal equity had been achieved. But the introduction of the random element in taxation would generally be regarded as unacceptable. More realistically, horizontal equity limits the way in which taxes are determined. Taxes are not a function of race or colour, nor even the football team one supports (though the supporters of more successful teams undoubtedly experience more 'utility' than those of repeatedly unsuccessful teams). In practice, a major practical problem raised by the concept of horizontal equity concerns the definition of the tax unit. We shall therefore examine the relationship between the tax treatment of individuals and that of households. We then look at some empirical evidence on the effects of the tax system on vertical equity, and consider what economic analysis can contribute to the definition and resolution of the issues involved.

The tax unit

The problem of the tax unit is to decide how households should be taxed relative to individuals. This issue arises for all direct personal taxes, but we shall discuss it with primary reference to an income tax. The present British tax and social security system encourages the poor to cohabit, those on average incomes to marry, and the rich to get divorced. It is difficult to imagine any social philosophy which would intend this combination of outcomes. Dissatisfaction with the system has grown to the extent of inducing the government to produce a green paper (Inland Revenue, 1981) outlining alternative proposals.

The British tax system operates on the dependency principle. The income of a married woman is simply treated as if it were her husband's, and in recognition of the burden she imposes on him he receives a specially enhanced married man's allowance. Social pressures have led to two important modifications of this principle. A wife is entitled to a single personal allowance against her own earnings. The household can opt for separate taxation of husband and wife's earnings (but because this involves the loss of the married man's allowance it is rarely advantageous, see p. 25). The underlying principle is self-evidently anachronistic; it dates from a time when Soames Forsyte was the representative taxpayer.

One widely felt objection to it is the elements of sex discrimination which are involved. Many women find it offensive that their husbands are required to prepare, sign and answer for a return of their income. Some men may resent being expected to proffer details of, and be liable for tax on, income to which they may have no legal, and feel no moral, right. It should be noted, however, that a couple can choose to make separate returns and be separately assessed (an option distinct from separate taxation, since separate assessment has no effect on the couple's aggregate tax liability). But if Mrs T earns £30,000 a year as Prime Minister while Mr T stays at home and minds 10 Downing Street, and the couple have no other income, they are liable for tax of £10,300; If Mr T is Prime Minister and Mrs T does the washing up their tax bill rises by £750. There are other instances where liability to tax is a function of the sex of the earner, and it is certainly paradoxical that a Parliament which has outlawed sex discrimination in general should sustain a tax system with these properties.

A more important, if less controversial failing of the present system is that it is far too generous to working couples without dependent children. A couple in this position receive a married man's allowance (MMA) of £2,445 and a personal allowance of £1,565, so that their first £4,010 of joint income is free of tax. Two single people receive joint allowances of £3,130, and a married couple with a dependent child who prevents the wife from working receive tax allowances of £2,445 and child benefit of £304, equivalent to total tax allowances of around £3,500. It is difficult to see any reason why the tax and benefit system should treat the first of these couples so much more favourably than the other two.

A final problem is that aggregation of investment income may lead to a substantial increase in the tax bill on marriage. If Charles with £20,000 of investment income marries Diana who has the same, their joint tax bill will rise by £5,000 p.a. While the plight of this couple will not bring many tears to the eyes, the irrationality of the marriage penalty is evident.

The Green Paper proposed a number of cosmetic changes to reduce the force of these objections but almost all the submissions examined by Kay and Sandler (1982) supported more radical measures which involved the abolition of the married man's allowance. This would yield £3,450 m. in 1982-3 and it is hardly surprising that there are sharp divisions on how this revenue should be used. There are two main possibilities. One is to adopt an *individual* basis, which 'looks through' the household and taxes each member of it as an individual in his or her own right. The other is a *unit* basis, under which husband and wife or perhaps the complete household are taxed together by reference to their joint—or collective—income. The case for the individual basis rests on the view—which many people hold strongly—that they are individuals and their tax position should depend on their own earnings and circumstances and not on the earnings and circumstances of others, even those others with whom they may choose to live. But it is difficult to overlook the fact that in many cases the interdependence of these factors is absolutely fundamental. It is clear that we would wish to discriminate between the millionaire's wife who has no income because she stays at home to oversee the servants and the inebriate woman who sleeps under the arches at Charing Cross, even though on paper their personal financial circumstances may appear to be identical. There is a tension between our desire to respect the rights of an individual to independent treatment, and the desire to relate liabilities and benefits to the whole of that individual's circumstances.

The individual basis has the further disadvantage that the way in which partners choose to arrange their financial affairs within marriage may have important consequences for their joint tax liability. It is easy to reduce tax liabilities by transferring investment income from a high income spouse to a low income spouse. This will cost a lot of tax revenue; nor does it seem desirable that tax avoidance should become a part of everyday family life. It is only necessary to envisage the conversation that runs ' "Why don't you transfer your property to me, darling, and we shall pay less tax" "I love you, darling, but not as much as that" ' to see some of the difficulties. There is a fundamental conflict between the principle that marriage should affect tax payments little, it at all, and the principle that arrangements within marriage should affect tax payments little, if at all.

A unit basis supposes that the living standard of a couple is determined by their joint income, and the quotient is a means of relating that to the level attainable by a single individual. But the underlying premiss is not really valid. A couple in which the husband earns £15,000 per year and the wife nothing is typically much better off than two spouses each earning £7,500 per year. This is partly because there are costs to earning income—not only the cost of bus fares to work and leisure forgone, but also costs attributable to the need to eat convenience foods and to tolerate more dust on the furniture. These are costs which rise quite rapidly if there are dependent children. The unit basis is extremely favourable to households where the wife does not work.

This difference of principle between an individual and a unit basis for taxation is reflected in two main proposals for using the revenue gained from the abolition of the married man's allowance. Supporters of the individual basis would favour an increase in child benefit, leaving in the tax system only a single personal allowance which each individual could use against his or her own income. Supporters of the unit basis favour a scheme of transferable tax allowances, under which each couple would have two allowances available against the income of either. It is interesting that many of those who support transferable allowances begin by saying they favour an individual basis for taxation, a tribute to the fact that the emancipation of women has had more impact on the language people use than on the attitudes which they adopt.

Both proposals would leave two earner couples without children worse off. Transferable allowances would protect the position of women who do not work, but hit working wives with children. Increased child benefit would protect women with children (whether or not they worked), but hit wives who do not have children and do not work.

In our judgement, neither the individual basis or the unit basis can reasonably command unqualified support; and we observe that no country has adopted a purely individual tax system and few have employed a completely unit based structure. Both systems are the expression of objectives which have some merit, and hence we see no alternative to a compromise which involves elements of each, recognising that the nature of the compromise may change as social attitudes do. We have equally little doubt that current social attitudes point towards a largely individual system.

Similar principles seem appropriate for taxing the income of children. Their earnings might be taxed on an individual basis, which means that in practice they would not be taxed; there is no feasible alternative. The tax treatment of the investment income of children has become a political football, kicked from one end of the pitch to the other depending on which party has the ball. Both convenience and common sense suggest that until children are old enough to achieve independent economic status their investment income should be treated as the income of their parents.

If a shift is made in the direction of an expenditure tax, then the individual basis loses some of its appeal, and Kaldor (1955) has argued that a quotient system would then be the most appropriate. After all, a natural way to define a household is as a group of people who incur expenditure on a unit rather than an individual basis, and it is very reasonable to apply the same principle in taxation. And it is even easier for spouses taxed as individuals to arrange their savings and dissavings so as to minimize their joint liability than it is for them to organize their investment income. But the objections to the quotient system apply with equal force under expenditure-based taxation. A couple's standard of living is not related to their joint expenditure alone, but will depend on whether that expenditure is derived from the income of only one of them or equally from both; and the strong discouragement to wives to work which results from the over-generous treatment of non-working wives and which applies under a quotient-based income tax arises equally well with a quotient-based expenditure tax.

Indeed the arguments and conclusions which we have rehearsed in the income tax case are not modified much if expenditure taxes are used instead. Earned income might be taxed on an individual basis, savings and dissavings on a unit principle. It may seem somewhat odd to have an expenditure tax which discriminates between types of income, but if we think of the lifetime expenditure tax as a tax on lifetime receipts (as we know we can) the logic becomes more apparent. It poses no practical problems either; the reader who turns back to the expenditure tax form (Fig. 6.2, p. 88) will see that some items (earnings, pensions) would require that an individual should enter his own receipts, while others (gifts, dividends, sales of securities, etc.) would ask for half the joint total to be entered. The most difficult case is trading receipts, where the distinction between earned and investment income is blurred; this is a familiar difficulty under the present tax system (which is not to say that it is easily or satisfactorily solved).

Any treatment of the tax unit must be related to the social habits of a particular time, and must change as those social habits change. A unit basis supposes that units can be identified and are fairly stable. Adopting marriage as the basis of definition works well in the U.K. at present. If large numbers of couples live together in continuing household units—as is the case in Sweden—or a high proportion of marriages end in divorce—as in the U.S.A.—then a unit basis, of any kind, becomes harder to sustain. Both these trends are increasing in Britain; if this continues an individual basis is likely to be the final outcome and it would then be a desirable outcome.

Taxation and distribution: evidence

There are many difficulties, both practical and conceptual, in assessing the effects of taxes on income distribution. A frequently used method of illustrating the distribution of income, and the effect of factors which alter it, is to draw a Lorenz curve. Such curves are illustrated in Fig. 14.1. They are constructed as follows. We order the entire population in line, starting from the poorest and ending with the richest, and we move along the line, measuring at each stage the proportion of the total population which we have encountered and the proportion of the community's total income which they receive. Thus in Fig. 14.1 we plot on one axis the cumulative percentage of total population, and on the other the cumulative percentage of total income. If income were evenly divided, the poorest 25% of the community would receive 25% of its income, and the Lorenz curve would be the diagonal straight line OA. Since income is not equally divided, the poorest 25% earn less than that and the Lorenz curve lies below the diagonal line of perfect equality. The further away from the diagonal it is, the greater the extent of inequality in distribution.

We show in Fig. 14.1 the Lorenz curve of 'original income', which is basically taxable income excluding state benefits; and of 'final income', which takes account of the effect of all taxes and benefits. The Lorenz curve of final income is at all points closer to the diagonal line of perfect equality than that of original income, so that the combined effect of the tax and benefit system is an unambiguous reduction in inequality.

We should like to consider the ways in which the different elements of the tax system contribute to this over-all result. We shall define a tax as *progressive* if the proportion of an individual's income which is paid in tax increases as his income increases; if the rich pay relatively more than the poor. It is easy to see that progressive taxation leads to an

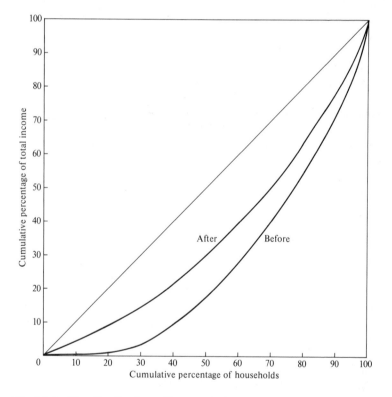

Fig. 14.1. The distribution of income before and after tax and benefits, 1980.

inward shift of Lorenz curves such as those in Fig. 14.1 and so reduces inequality. This definition of progressivity is not universal but it is the most natural and the most common.

If we are to examine how the tax burden is spread over different groups, we need to decide what criteria to use in defining these groups. How do we determine whether a particular household is 'rich' or 'poor' and how much richer or poorer it is than others? We might measure this by income, or expenditure, or wealth, or some combination of these: the same issues arise as those which we raised in our discussion of measures of taxable capacity in Chapter 5 and as we discovered there it is not a question to which there is a simple or single right answer. But we suggested there that expenditure had some advantages as a measure for these purposes, and we think a useful way of measuring the way the tax burden is distributed over rich and poor is to see how tax payments vary at different expenditure levels. We cannot do this with the available data, and instead use 'final income'—income after all taxes and benefits—as the next best measure and our principal criterion.

But this raises another issue. We want to see how taxes are distributed over ranges of income or expenditure. Should the ranges be defined as they are after the tax and benefit system has done its work, or as they would be before the effect of redistributive taxes and social benefits? Do we measure progressivity in relation to final income or to original income? There is a case for looking at both. Imagine a tax system which penalized 'rich capitalists' so severely that they ended up worse off than 'poor workers': there is a sense in which such taxes are progressive and there is a sense in which they are not. It would seem odd to say that a heavy tax on the scrag ends of meat which the impoverished capitalists were forced to eat was a progressive measure though we might not be convinced that this curious tax system was regressive, rather than progressive, in its over-all effect. The ambiguity is a genuine one, and we illustrate both possibilities below by describing progressivity relative to both original and final income.

This discussion relates purely to matters of definition, and the reality of what is going on is not affected by the way in which we choose to present our data. But these issues are not usually spelt out in analyses of tax progressivity, and since statements that certain taxes are progressive or regressive have some persuasive force it is important to be clear what we mean by them. As we see below, the question of whether British indirect taxes are or are not regressive turns on the answer to the problem we have just raised—should we measure regressivity in relation to original or final income?

Empirical information on the effects of taxation on distribution—such as that in Fig. 14.1—is regularly published by the C.S.O. in *Economic Trends*. The figures which underlie it are both much criticized and much used. We should note a number of difficulties. Firstly, the basis of classification is the household unit (so that when we described the construction of the Lorenz curves of Fig. 14.1 it was househouds, or heads of households, who were standing in line). This means that no account is taken of household composition or needs; a single person is categorized with a family of six with the same income, although it is clear that the former is likely to have a higher standard of living. This problem can be avoided by presenting separate analyses for each household type—which the C.S.O. does—or tackled by devising some 'equivalent scale' for comparing different households.

The analysis also makes naive assumptions about tax incidence. Commodity taxes are assumed to fall entirely on the consumers of the goods in question; corporation tax is simply ignored because its incidence is so difficult to establish. Similar American studies have employed a range of assumptions about incidence (Okner and Pechman, 1974) and shown that the results are rather sensitive to such assumptions. To improve on this crude view of incidence it is necessary to use a very fully specified model of the whole economic system. This attempt has been made, though in a very preliminary way, by Whalley and Piggott (1977), who suggest that Fig. 14.1 may slightly understate the redistributive effect of the tax system. The C.S.O. studies also omit death duties and capital gains tax on the argument that they are taxes on capital. This seems to confuse two distinct questions: 'What is the base of the tax?' and 'What measure of economic position should one use in assessing the distributional impact of a tax?' and it would be helpful if the analysis were extended to include these taxes (which presumably fall mainly on high-income groups).

We illustrate in Figs. 14.2 and 14.3 the effects of the three main elements in the U.K. tax and benefit system—cash benefits, direct taxes, and indirect taxes. The basis of construction of these curves is as follows. We saw in Chapter 1 that the analysis of tax incidence requires some counterfactual hypothesis about alternative ways in which public revenue would have been raised or disbursed. In analysing progressivity, we make the counterfactual assumption that each tax (or benefit) is distributed in direct proportion to income, so that relative incomes

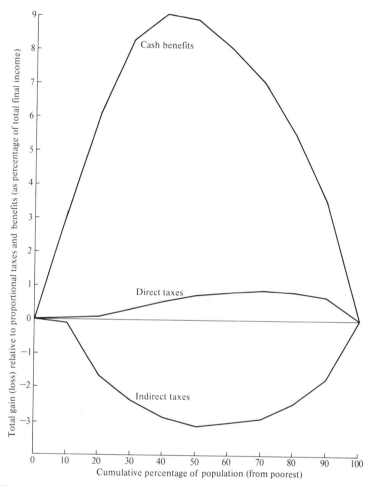

Fig. 14.2. Tax progressivity, relative to original income, 1980
(i.e. income before all taxes and benefits)

before and after the tax (or benefit) are unchanged. We then compare
the actual distribution of the tax gain or loss by the poorest 10%, 20%,
etc. as a proportion of aggregate income. Thus Fig. 14.2 shows that the
poorest 30% of the population were substantially better off as a result
of the allocation of cash benefits than they would have been if these
had been allocated in proportion to income, and that their net gain
amounted to about 8% of the original income of the whole population.

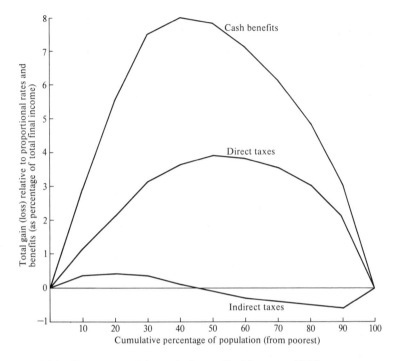

Fig. 14.3. Tax progressivity, relative to final income, 1980
(i.e. income after all taxes and benefits)

Thus if we evaluate the effects of the benefit system on this group, relative to the population as a whole, we observe substantial progressivity. The poorest 30% also gained, in relative terms, from the effect of direct taxes, but this gain was much smaller; the further the curve corresponding to a particular tax (or benefit) is above the horizontal axis (which represents proportional taxation) the greater the degree of progressivity, while a curve lying below that line illustrates a regressive tax. Both cash benefits and direct taxes are unambiguously progressive in incidence.

Indirect taxes are regressive in Fig. 14.2, but this pattern emerges only because that diagram illustrates their incidence in relation to original income. Since many people have very low original incomes—they are wholly dependent on pensions or national insurance benefits—but do have some expenditure, their indirect tax bill forms a very high proportion of their original income (indeed it could quite easily exceed

100% of it). Seen from final income, as in Fig. 14.3, indirect taxes are progressive—they absorb a higher proportion of the income of the rich, although this effect disappears as the highest income ranges are reached. This results mainly from the zero-rating provisions of V.A.T. (see Chapters 8 and 15) , since food and fuel figure more in the budget of poorer families. For similar reasons, direct taxes appear more progressive in Fig. 14.3 than in Fig. 14.2. People with small original incomes may nevertheless pay some income tax on their pensions, while the relative affluence of high-income earners is much reduced if we base our comparison on their income after tax rather than their income before tax.

The net effect of all taxes and benefits, however, is clearly progressive, in relation to both original and final income. How great is the reduction in inequality which results? If we are to answer questions of this type, we need some measure of inequality. A frequently used measure is the area between the Lorenz curve and the diagonal, which is known as the Gini coefficient. While this may seem an attractive idea, the Gini coefficient is a purely statistical artefact with no real underlying economic meaning (Newbery, 1970; Sen, 1974). Some commentators (for example, Nicholson 1974) have sought to make a virtue of necessity by claiming the Gini coefficient is therefore 'objective' in some way that other measures are not, but this is like saying that since we cannot agree on what constitutes beauty we should measure height instead. We prefer an approach suggested by Atkinson (1973a). In effect, Atkinson asks the question: 'Imagine a rich man and a poor man with half his income. How much commission would we pay Robin Hood to transfer £1 from the rich to the poor?' The answer will depend on our view of inequality. But by answering questions of this kind, we can construct a measure of the costs of inequality. For each transfer of income from rich to poor we would be willing to give up some of the transferred as 'commission' in this way. We can envisage a continuing series of such transfers which eventually bring us to a wholly egalitarian outcome, and measure the amount of income which we would be willing to give up in order to bring about this result. This total amount is the 'cost of inequality': the reduction in aggregate income which we would accept in order to achieve complete equality in its distribution.

The size of these costs depends on how much we are offended by inequality. If we were not much worried by it, then the commission we might agree to pay to secure a transfer from rich to poor would be rather low: the efficiency loss we would accept for distributional improvement would be small. By contrast the American philosopher, Rawls, who argues that justice requires that society maximize the welfare of its least advantaged member (Rawls, 1971), would be happy with the arrangement if anything at all reached the hands of the poor. (This is a rather extreme characterization of Rawls's position, though one which is popular with economists.) Because there are different views of equality and its nature and desirability, there can be no unique measure of inequality but a scheme of this kind enables us to express a range of possible views. We consider three possibilities in Table 14.1. A '10% commission rate' implies that we would favour a transfer from a high-income individual to an individual with half that income only if the gain by the latter was at least 90% of the loss of the former, so that we attach equal social value to £1 in the hands of a man earning £10,000 a year, 90p for someone who earns £5,000 and 73p for a man whose income is only £1,250. The radical 90% rate implies that £1 for the £10,000-a-year man and 1p at £2,500 a year are rated equally, so that the range of views covered by the 'commission rates' we use in Table 14.2 is rather wide. (Stern (1977) suggests that the value implicit in the present U.K. tax system is about 75%, but the argument is a somewhat speculative one.)

Table 14.1 shows the 'costs of inequality' and the effect of taxes and benefits in reducing them, under these alternative assumptions. Under the conservative '10% rate' view of inequality, the cost of the inequality of original income is estimated at £377 per household. The actual average household income is £6,353; we shquld be prepared to see this reduced by £377 to £5,976, or by around 5%, if the distribution associated with the lower average income was completely equal, so that each household received an income of £5,976. Correspondingly, we should be prepared to give up egalitarian ambitions and accept the distribution of original income if the result were to raise average income by 5%. The radical approach implicit in the third column demonstrates a very different view; one which would give up over 99% of existing national income if the distribution were equalized. We estimate the (lower) costs of inequality in the distribution of final income in a similar way.

Although the costs differ under different assumptions, the effect of taxes is rather similar in each case. The costs of inequality are greatly reduced by the effects of taxes and benefits; the reduction is between one-half and three-quarters in all cases. Cash benefits are the most

TABLE 14.1

The effects of tax and transfers on inequality, 1977

c (commission rate)	10%	50%	90%
ϵ	0·15	1·0	3·32
Original income			
Actual average	6353	6353	6353
Equivalent, equally distributed	5976	2515	10
'Cost' of inequality	377	3838	6343
Effect on 'cost' of			
Cash benefits	−162	−2434	−3501
Direct taxes	−93	−924	−1349
Indirect taxes less subsidies	+ 8	−49	−2086
Income after tax and transfers			
Actual average	5631	5631	5631
Equivalent, equally distributed	5528	4983	3917
'Cost' of inequality	103	648	1714

Technical note: ϵ is the corresponding 'elasticity of the social marginal valuation of income'; see Atkinson (1975), Stern (1977). Thus for each distribution (y_i) we have computed $\{\Sigma y_i^{1-\epsilon} f_i\}^{1/1-\epsilon}$ where $\epsilon = \dfrac{\log(1-c)}{\log(0\cdot5)}$ and f_i gives proportion of households with income y_i. (When $\epsilon = 1\cdot0$ we have computed the geometric mean of the incomes.)

Source: Own calculations based on data for 1980 F.E.S. sample from *Economic Trends* (Jan. 1982).

important influence on this, with direct taxes next in significance; but indirect taxes operate so as to reduce inequality, though only slightly, under each assumption. The effective reduction in inequality which the tax system brings about is much greater than Fig. 14.1 suggests, because that diagram (and the associated Gini coefficient) does not weight sufficiently what happens at the extremes of poverty and wealth, while our welfare measures do acknowledge that this is of prime importance in analysing inequality.

Taxation and distribution: principles

How should the tax burden be distributed between different individuals and households? We shall discuss this question as if the only tax in the economy was an income tax, but this is simply for expository convenience, an income tax schedule relates tax liability to income received, but as we saw in our discussion of empirical evidence on tax incidence the relevant question is the way in which the burden of all taxes is related to a somewhat broader concept of the individual's resources than his taxable income.[1] But the income tax is for those in work the most important and most flexible influence on the distribution of tax liabilities.

We have defined a progressive tax schedule as one in which the proportion of income which is taken in tax increases with income. This definition implies that the *average* rate of tax should increase with income. It is a common error to think that this means that the *marginal* rate of tax should also increase with income (as it in fact does in the U.K. and most other countries), but this is not the case. A tax system is progressive if, and only if, the marginal rate of tax is higher than the average rate of tax: if you pay a higher rate of tax on any *additional* earnings than you do on your current earnings. Figure 14.4 illustrates one possible relationship between average and marginal rates of tax. On incomes less than A, both marginal and average rates of tax are increasing. At incomes above A, the marginal rate of tax begins to fall, but because it is so high the average rate of tax continues to rise. Only at incomes beyond B, where the marginal tax rate falls below the average rate, does the average rate start to fall: this tax schedule is progressive throughout the range OB.

The schedule shown in Fig. 14.4 is not a very likely one, but the case illustrated in Fig. 14.5 is important. This shows a tax schedule in which a certain amount of income, OX, is exempt from tax, and earnings in excess of that are taxed at a rate of OY. Someone whose income barely exceeds OX pays virtually no tax, and hence his average tax rate is very low (although his marginal rate is OY). As income increases, the fraction of it which is taxed becomes larger and larger, until for those with very substantial incomes the allowance OX is hardly significant and their average rate of tax is nearly equal to OY. If the personal

---

[1] Readers of recent literature on 'optimal income taxes' will realize that the lifetime expenditure tax discussed in Chapters 5 and 6 is much closer to the taxes analysed there than are real-life income taxes.

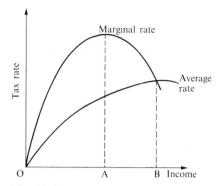

Fig. 14.4

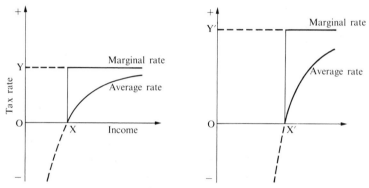

Fig. 14.5. Alternative tax schedules   Fig. 14.6

allowance is paid as a 'tax credit' to those with incomes too low to make full use of it (i.e. those with incomes below OX), then the schedules of average and marginal rates are extended as shown by the dotted lines. This is a *linear tax schedule*, and it is completely described by two parameters; the basic allowance OX (which we shall assume is greater than zero) and the tax rate OY.

A linear tax system is progressive, since the average tax rate increases steadily with income. The slope of the schedule of average rates gives the rate at which the average rate rises, and is an indication of the degree of progressivity of the schedule. If OX and OY are both increased, as to OX' and OY' in Fig. 14.6, then the curve of average rates becomes steeper and the rate structure is more progressive. For most taxpayers the present British tax system with its personal allowance and wide basic rate band is a linear one (if we ignore its interaction with national insurance contributions and means-tested benefits).

The appropriate structure for a tax schedule was extensively discussed in the nineteenth century, in an era when the view was widely held that the utilities enjoyed by different individuals could be measured and compared in much the same way as their heights. Debate raged between the principle of equal sacrifice (by which tax should be computed so as to impose equal utility losses on all), the principle of equiproportional sacrifice (everyone should lose the same fraction of their utility), and the principle of minimum aggregate sacrifice (the total utility loss of the community as a whole should be minimized). The objective of minimum aggregate sacrifice might have won the day, were it not rather easy to show that if one adds the assumptions (i) that everyone has the same capacity to enjoy income; (ii) that utility increases with income but at a decreasing rate; (iii) that the tax schedule does not modify behaviour in ways which would change incomes before tax (there are no disincentive effects), the conclusion is that everyone should have the same income, net of tax: 'the crowning height of the utilitarian principle, from which the steps of a sublime deduction lead to the high tableland of equality' as Edgeworth put it (1897, p. 553).

Since neither the objective nor the assumptions are very plausible, this analysis received as little attention as it deserved; and until recently economists had little constructive to say about tax schedules. But this ignores an important problem. Progressivity requires high marginal tax rates, but as we saw in Chapter 3 it is precisely this aspect of the tax system which generates disincentive effects. Thus there is a basic conflict between equity and efficiency considerations in the design of tax schedules, and it is important to understand the interrelationships and the empirical information which is needed to determine these issues. While few people now happily accept the utilitarian objective or the assumption of identical tastes, it is nevertheless necessary to express some view on the consequences of drawing tax revenue from people at one income level rather than another. We might start by characterizing two extreme positions. In one, the Government is simply indifferent to the source of its tax revenue; a pound is a pound and valued equally whether it is in the wallet of a rich man or a poor man. The other extreme, which we have already attributed to Rawls, only looks at the welfare of the least advantaged; the fate of others matters only in so far as their activities have effects on him (which mainly take the form of generating tax revenue for his benefit). In effect, one position ignores considerations of income distribution altogether; the other thinks of nothing else. It is possible to go beyond either of these extreme viewpoints; to argue that inequality built Versailles and commissioned Beethoven's late string quartets and is desirable for its own sake, or that inequality is so offensive that the rich should be made worse off even if no one else's standard of living rises as a result. But many people might be willing to agree that an appropriate stance was somewhere between these two.

Even the Rawlsian view, however, implies less than perfect egalitarianism. Under it, public policy is concerned with the interests of the rich only in their function as milch cows for the poor, valued only for the tax revenue they provide. But the interests of the poor require that tax revenue from the rich be maximized, and this is not achieved by 100% rates. People who find themselves paying 100% of income, or additional income, in tax are unlikely to trouble to earn much of it; and we would obtain more tax revenue if we retained some incentive by allowing them to keep part of their earnings for themselves. In fact it is possible to go beyond this and show that the marginal tax rate faced by the man with the highest income should, under an optimal rate schedule, be zero. The argument hinges on the point that tax revenue depends on average rates of tax but disincentives on marginal rates. If we lower the *marginal* tax rate on the richest man, we reduce disincentive effects on him without reducing the amount of tax which he (or anyone else) pays. So if these disincentives are of any significance, earnings will increase and so will tax revenue. It does not matter if we attach no value to the welfare of this man, so that we give no weight to the increase in his post-tax income. So long as we do not actually wish to see him made worse off, whether anyone else benefits or not, the increase in tax revenue allows lower average tax rates on everyone else and an unequivocal all-round gain. This argument should not be taken absolutely literally. We cannot have different tax rates for each individual, and it tells us nothing even about the appropriate tax rate on the second-richest man. But it does show that even a firm belief in progressive taxation does not imply that marginal, as distinct from average, rates should increase with income.

A rather similar argument may be applied at the opposite end of the distribution: the marginal tax rate faced by the lowest income group should also be very low. This is not the same as saying that the average tax rate on the lowest income group should be very low—as most people would agree it should—since it is quite possible to have low (or negative) average rates of tax on low incomes but high marginal rates. We saw in Chapter 7 that this is precisely what the 'poverty trap' and a number of proposed social security reforms entail. The case for low marginal rates is different, and derived from efficiency rather than distributional considerations. The problem with reducing marginal tax rates on low incomes, as Chancellors have discovered, is that it reduces the average tax rate faced by absolutely everyone, and so is extremely costly in revenue. The reintroduction of the 'reduced rate band' had to face this difficulty. We can offset the cost by lowering the tax threshold, so that the lower rate is payable from a lower level of income; the problem with this is that while it has desirable effects on incentives and reduces the 'poverty trap' it raises the amount of tax payable by people with low incomes who are now brought into the system as a result of the reduction in the basic allowance. But at the lowest levels of income there is no one 'below' who will be caught up in the tax net; and it is therefore possible to reduce marginal rates of tax without compromising distributional objectives.

These conclusions—that marginal tax rates should be low at both the highest and the lowest levels of income—contrast sharply with what most people have previously believed (ourselves included). They also suggest a pattern different from that observed in the U.K. and most other countries—where, as we saw in Chapter 3, the *highest* marginal rates are found at the top and bottom of the income distribution (because of higher rates in one case and the poverty trap in the other). But the arguments which lie behind them are in fact rather familiar, and we have only focused rather sharply on points which have been widely if indistinctly appreciated. High marginal tax rates on the largest incomes bring in very little revenue, and are not worth pursuing if they have any adverse consequences. Measures of support for low-income families achieve rather less than nothing if their receipts are recouped by high marginal rates of tax. But it is of particular interest that the conclusions reached remain valid over a rather catholic range of views about the ethical importance and empirical significance of distributional factors and tax disincentives—for any, in fact, between the extreme Rawlsian and extreme output maximization positions we have described.

But this is not quite as encouraging as it might appear. A major difficulty with these arguments is that although they tell us about marginal tax rates at the very top and very bottom of the income scale they tell us little about the rates in between, even at income levels rather close to these extremes. In answering this question, the relative weights which are given to disincentives and to distribution are absolutely crucial. But it is important to see that the answer is likely to go in the same direction at both ends of the scale. If we think disincentive effects are probably not too substantial, or that equality of after-tax incomes is very important, then we would want to select rather high *marginal* tax rates throughout the intermediate range. We would be anxious to narrow the gap between the poor and the very poor, the rich and the very rich, and would not be unduly concerned by the disincentive effects which stem from the high marginal tax rates necessary to do it. We would in this way compress the whole distribution of income after tax. If, on the other hand, we attach a lot of emphasis to incentives and are not much worried about the resulting distribution, then we would choose low marginal rates throughout. It does not follow from this that the marginal rate would, in either case, be the same throughout the distribution, and in general the appropriate tax structure is a rather complicated function of the two underlying objectives—distribution and incentives—and the distribution of earning capacities in the population. But since this information is not easily obtained, and a linear tax schedule has obvious administrative advantages, it is worth examining further the properties of such a system.

Linear tax systems

One of the commonest criticisms of the British tax system is that too wide a range of income is taxed at the basic rate. It is often suggested that it is unfair that a married man with an income of £15,000 should pay the same basic rate of tax as one with an income of only £2,500; or that someone who is only just paying tax should be charged at a rate as high as 30%.

Much of this criticism results from a simple confusion between average and marginal rates of tax. It is true that someone who earns £2,500 is liable to tax at the basic rate of 30%, and so is someone who earns £15,000. However the man on £2,500 pays annual tax of £16·50 —equivalent to an average rate of tax of 0·7%. His counterpart on £15,000 has to pay £3,766·50, an average tax rate of 25·7%. The fact that they are both in the basic rate band does not prevent the man with the higher income from paying a much higher proportion of his income in tax.

But isn't the marginal rate too high on those with low incomes? It is clear that equity demands a lower *average* rate of tax on the poor than the rich. It is much less clear that it demands a lower *marginal* rate. Marginal rates are relevant to individuals because they determine their incentive or disincentive to work, and there is no obvious reason why it is either just or efficient to impose a greater disincentive on high income earners than we do on people whose incomes are low. It is possible that disincentives have a greater impact on the work effort of poor households, but we know of no convincing evidence.

The British tax system could certainly be made more progressive if the existing basic rate band were replaced by a more graduated pattern of marginal rates. In Table 14.2 we describe such a schedule, which would raise about the same revenue as the existing income tax. Table 14.3 shows the gain in progressivity which is achieved; the average rate of tax is lower on incomes up to £9,000 and higher on incomes above that level. The price of that greater progressivity is an increase in disincentives. The average of marginal rates faced by households has risen from 31% to 41%.

Very similar results could be achieved, however, by simply increasing the threshold and the basic rate. In Table 14.2 an alternative schedule is described in which the tax allowance rises to £4,250 and the basic rate to 42%. From Table 14.3 it can be seen that the change in the pattern of average rates is very similar to that achieved under the more complicated graduated structure. Low income and high income households do slightly better, middle income households slightly worse, but overall the similarities are more significant that the differences.

Many people continue to find it surprising that there is no inconsistency between a linear tax schedule and substantial progressivity— indeed we can have a completely egalitarian outcome if the basic allowance is equal to average income and the marginal tax rate is 100%, though it is not likely that this is a good idea.

The fact that someone is paying a marginal rate of tax of 75% demonstrates that he is facing a substantial disincentive to work, a strong temptation to convert his income into other forms, and that he is likely to be rather disenchanted with the way the tax system affects him; but it does not necessarily mean that he is paying a lot of tax, because that is a function of his average rather than his marginal rate. The mathematical properties of rate schedules imply that this average rate an individual pays depends not on his own marginal rate, but on the marginal tax rates of everyone below him in the income distribution.

TABLE 14.2

Alternative Tax Schedules, 1982-3

The Current System		
Income (£)	Rate	No. of taxpayers in band (m)
0–2445	0	0
2445–15225	30	21·4
15225+	40+	1·9
Average marginal rate = 30·6%		

Graduated rates		
Income (£)	Rate	No of taxpayers in band (m)
0–2500	0	0·2
2500–3750	10	3·8
3750–5000	20	2·0
5000–6250	30	2·0
6250–8000	40	2·2
8000–10000	50	4·5
10000+	60	7·6
Average marginal rate = 40·7%		

High threshold		
Income (£)	Rate	No of taxpayers in band (m)
0–4250	0	4·6
4250–1500	42	16·8
1500+	42+	0·9
Average marginal rate = 33·3%		

Source: IFS estimates.

This was illustrated most clearly by the tax system as it stood before the reforms of 1979. In 1976-7, a household with net income of around £7,500 faced a marginal tax rate of 50%: to pay an average rate of tax of 50% it was necessary to have an income around £20,000. Over one million households come into the former category; 60,000 households were in the latter group (*Inland Revenue Statistics*, 1978). A system with escalating marginal rates imposes high marginal rates on relatively many and high average rates on relatively few.

TABLE 14.3

Average Tax Rates under various schedules

Income level (£)	Average Tax Rate (%)		
	Current System	Graduated schedule	High threshold
4000	11·7	4·4	0
5000	15·3	7·5	6·3
6000	17·8	11·3	12·3
7000	19·5	15·0	16·5
8000	20·8	18·1	19·7
9000	21·9	21·7	22·2
10000	22·7	24·5	24·2
12000	23·9	30·4	27·1
15000	25·1	36·3	30·1

There are two other important constraints on the progressivity of a tax system. The first of these relates to administrative feasibility. We have shown in Chapters 3 and 4 that the highest rates of tax in the U.K. did not work, and it is very improbable that they could be made to work. This might not be too important if they were uniformly ineffective, but this is not the case; the result of this (and the general result of procedures which are administratively impracticable) is that the outcome is erratically and unfairly effective. But it is difficult to assess what the maximum marginal tax rate that can work reasonably well in practice is likely to be. The top rates in most developed countries lie in the range from 50% to 70%. Britain has historically been outside this range but has now moved within it.

The second constraint is the possibility of migration. The simplest framework for analysing this is the Rawlsian one, in which we attach no weight to the welfare of Rod Stewart (a distinguished pop star and tax exile) or his friends, and regret his going only for the tax revenue which is lost with him. Even this consideration may have a surprisingly substantial effect on a well-designed tax system. Mr. Stewart is presumably influenced by a comparison of his net-of-tax incomes at home and abroad; his incentive to migrate is related to his average tax rate rather than to his marginal rate, which distinguishes this from other incentive effects. The issue then hinges on the sensitivity of migration decisions to after-tax income. There is little systematic evidence on this. Recent trends in migration from the U.K. are shown in Table 14.4.

TABLE 14.4

Emigration from U.K.
('000s)

| Year | Occupational category | | Total |
	Professional and managerial	Manual and clerical	
1966	32·6	64·9	110·9
1971	43·4	55·4	98·9
1977	43·2	37·3	80·5
1980	44·5	32·4	76·9

Source: *Population Trends* (Spring 1982).

'Professional and managerial' emigration might be compared with an annual output of 70,000 university graduates at a cost of £708 m. (in 1976–7; *Annual Abstract of Statistics*, 1979). The trends are rather striking, but are probably as much influenced by the declining significance of emigration to 'old Commonwealth' countries by non-professional groups as by changes in relative incomes; there has also been an increase in the proportion of 'professional and managerial' immigrants. The most relevant study known to us (Psacharopoulos, 1976) suggests that a 10% change in net income might induce a 3% rise in emigration. This figure is very tentative, especially since the international study on which it is based suggests that Britain (as a low-income English-speaking country) is peculiarly vulnerable to migration. But a 10% change in net income (corresponding, say, to a change from 50% to 55% in the average tax rate faced by the affected groups) might lead to an increase of 3,000 in annual emigration; if these emigrants took with them an expected present value of tax revenue (net of associated public expenditures) of £50,000 the resulting loss from emigration would be £150 m. p.a. These back-of-envelope calculations do no more than suggest the difficulty of systematic appraisal; but it does seem possible that the orders of magnitude are such that this consideration ought to be a significant influence on tax policy.

We must now bring out explicitly two assumptions which have been underlying our analysis. We have assumed that all income is earned. At high levels of income this is only the case to a very limited extent, though the discussion of incentives applies equally to earnings which although classed as investment income are in fact the return to business activities. While incentives—of a different kind—also affect investment incomes, it is clear that the factors which should influence the taxation of income or expenditure from inherited wealth are rather different and the reasons for limiting top marginal rates are less compelling. We should note, however, that the arguments on migration and on feasibility apply to unearned incomes also; and that it is probably on employment incomes that the present top rates of tax are less easily avoided and come closest to working as intended.

The second assumption is that the value of people's work is approximated by what they are paid. If they are paid more than their work is worth, there will be losses to everyone else if they are induced to do more such work: if they are paid less, then the argument operates in the reverse direction. At low and medium ranges of income, our assumption is not too bad, but for high-income earners the position is more complicated, and the relationship between the value of work and the way in which it is remunerated becomes much more tenuous. We should also note that the work they do will often be intrinsically attractive and disincentive effects consequently less serious. These groups will include people in the City who occupy sinecures or perform services of no social value, they will also include people in positions where the competent exercise of their functions can generate benefits far greater than anyone would consider paying them. If under Sir Arnold Weinstock the productivity of G.E.C. is ½% higher than it would be under the best alternative manager, then the benefits of this are £20 m. per year and one such individual can compensate for the entire boards of several merchant banks. The direction of bias in this area is therefore unclear.

We conclude that the definition of the tax base—the issue we discussed in Chapter 5—is more important in determining the effective progressivity of taxation, especially at high-income and expenditure levels, than the shape of the rate structure. The difficulty in constructing rate schedules is that substantial progressivity requires that average rates should be much higher at high-income levels than at lower ones; but this requires high *marginal* rates on those in between. If the majority of income-earners are concentrated in a rather narrow range—and about 95% of all units have incomes below £15,000 per year—then these marginal rates may have to be distinctly high and will have to be imposed on people who are not the primary target of redistributive taxation. High marginal rates at the top lead to many of the adverse consequences of progressive taxation without having much real effect on distribution, because the number of people who face correspondingly high *average* rates as a result is very small.

THE TAX SYSTEM AS A WHOLE

Is Britain over-taxed?

WE have devoted a good deal of attention to the structural deficiencies of the British tax system. We have not, however, considered explicitly the view that these structural deficiencies would not be very important if the rates of tax were not so high. This argument has considerable validity. The base of the American income tax, for example, is probably more defective than that of the U.K., but because tax rates are much lower at all income levels the anomalies, loopholes, and distortions which result are less significant. Is the real problem that the British are simply over-taxed?

Since there are few people who do not believe that they personally are over-taxed, we must search for some more objective yardstick. A natural one to use is an international comparison; is the tax system required to raise more revenue in Britain than in similar countries overseas? Table 15.1 sets out what figures we have on this matter. It shows the ratio of total tax revenue to G.N.P. in 1980 for 15 major O.E.C.D. countries. The highest tax ratios are to be found, not surprisingly, in the Scandinavian countries, followed, perhaps more surprisingly, by several of the successful post-war economies, the Netherlands, Belgium, Germany, and France. In this league table Britain comes ninth out of the 15 countries. Nor was 1980 an atypical year. If we examine the U.K.'s position in the league table of tax ratios of the same 15 countries for each year since 1965 we find that the U.K. never came higher than fifth and never lower than ninth.

International comparisons can be misleading, and all we can do is to point to some of the difficulties which arise. The decision as to whether a certain payment is or is not a tax is often an arbitrary one. For example, help to families may take the form either of extra tax allowances, which reduce taxation, or of cash payments, as with child benefits in Britain. The latter are often regarded as Government expenditure rather than negative taxation, thus making it difficult to

TABLE 15.1

Level of taxation in selected countries, 1980
(Tax revenues including social security contributions as % of
G.N.P. at market prices)

	All taxes	Taxes on			
		Spending	Income	Social security contributions	Other
Sweden	49·6	12·1	21·6	14·2	1·7
Norway	47·3	16·7	22·3	7·2	1·1
Netherlands	46·2	11·4	15·2	17·6	2·0
Denmark	45·7	17·0	24·9	0·8	3·0
Belgium	44·7	11·5	18·4	13·7	1·1
France	42·6	12·8	7·7	18·4	3·7
Germany	37·4	10·1	13·2	12·8	1·3
Ireland	36·7	16·0	13·4	5·3	2·0
UNITED KINGDOM	36·1	10·4	13·6	6·1	6·0
Canada	32·9	10·8	15·2	3·4	3·5
Italy	32·4	8·7	10·7	11·6	1·4
Australia	30·9	9·6	17·2	—	3·2
Switzerland	30·8	6·3	12·8	9·5	2·2
U.S.	30·7	5·1	14·4	8·1	3·1
Japan	26·1	4·3	10·8	7·6	3·4

Individual figures may not sum to totals because of rounding errors.
Source: Revenue Statistics of OECD Member Countries Paris, O.E.C.D.,
         Paris.

compare tax ratios in cases when countries adopt different forms of family support. The same argument applies to investment incentives which may be given either as tax allowances or as investment grants. A less obvious, but probably more important, source of difficulty is the treatment of pension contributions. In many Continental countries state pensions are much higher (relative to average earnings) than in Britain, and occupational pensions correspondingly less developed. Contributions to these state schemes are financed by social security contributions and not by payments to private schemes. In Table 15.1 the former are regarded as taxation and the latter not. If social security contributions were excluded the U.K. would move from ninth to sixth place in the league table of tax ratios. On the other hand, there are very good reasons for regarding social security contributions as equivalent to a tax on earned income, as we have argued in Chapter 3. Contributions to health insurance may take the form of voluntary, semi-compulsory, or compulsory contributions to private or state schemes, or may simply be incorporated in general taxation: such payments may sometimes count as taxes and at other times not, but the practical difference is often very slight.

It is possible to quibble endlessly about these problems of definition (in a way which suggests that the underlying question has not been carefully formulated), and some people are willing to do so (Bracewell-Milnes, 1976, and the references therein). But it is difficult to avoid an impression that there are three main groups of developed countries for these purposes: Holland and the Scandinavian countries, other Western European countries, and a somewhat disparate group containing Japan, Switzerland, and the U.S.A. These groupings reflect different attitudes to the value of public services and the role of the state in promoting social welfare, and Britain's placing in the second group seems an appropriate reflection of prevailing ideologies. It is true that if Britain were to move into the first or third of these divisions (and we shall not say which we think is which) the problems confronting the tax system would be rather different; but it is clear that such a decision should be taken on the basis of a much wider assessment of gains and losses than those which result from dissatisfaction with the tax system. Nor do we think it probable that either of these shifts will occur.

Although the U.K. tax ratio can only be described as average, the sources of the revenue it produces are superficially somewhat different. The most striking feature of Table 15.1 is the small dependence of the British system on social security contributions, but if one believes that it is more appropriate to include these with taxes on income then the only difference between Britain and other countries is the slightly smaller reliance in this country on taxes levied on consumption spending. Even this difference was diminished by the increase in V.A.T. in 1979.

A broader tax base?

We have seen that the revenue required from the British tax system is not out of line with that raised in other European countries. We have argued, however, that most of the undesirable effects of taxation are the result of high marginal rates of tax, and we should consider whether it might be possible to effect substantial reductions in *marginal* rates without correspondingly large reductions in average rates and hence in total tax revenue.

We are currently experiencing one of the best opportunities for this which is ever likely to be available. The cause is the growth in oil revenues from the North Sea. In Table 12.2 we showed the size and rate of growth of these receipts and between 1980 and 1985 they are likely to transform the budgetary position of the British government. It is not unrealistic to anticipate a yield equivalent to one third the revenue from income tax or two thirds of the receipts from value added tax. Not only do we have this bonanza, but we derive it from taxes which have very few adverse economic effects; indeed if the inept design of the North Sea regime were not so discouraging to marginal fields there need to be no disincentive effects at all. North Sea oil taxes are principally—and could have been entirely—a tax on economic rent, the difference between the value of oil output and the costs of oil extraction.

So far North Sea oil revenues have been spent on funding increasing levels of unemployment. But if unemployment falls, or even stabilizes, they will become available for making reductions in the levels of existing taxes. This provides a once-and-for all opportunity for effecting tax reform in a context in which there need only be gainers. The lack of imaginative planning for this opportunity, or indeed of any planning for it whatever, is perhaps the single most dispiriting aspect of current British tax policy. This is a transitory opportunity, and almost certainly a wasted one. We should consider, then, whether the tax base might be expanded in some other, more permanent, way. It is often suggested that if only all allowances could be swept away we could be happy with a single low rate of tax on all income. In 1976 the Economist suggested that this would allow a tax rate of 15%. Similar proposals have recently been widely canvassed in the United States. But they do not survive careful scrutiny.

Much the most important allowances are the basic personal allowances. If these were removed, the result would be a very substantial redistribution to those with above-average incomes from those below. We saw above how the degree of progressivity of a tax system could be altered by varying the parameters of a linear tax schedule: the proposal for a single tax rate eliminates all progressivity by abolishing the personal allowances altogether. We therefore look at untaxed components of incomes, of which some are listed in Table 15.2. It is

TABLE 15.2

The Cost of Principal Tax Allowances and Expenditures, 1982–2
(£ m.)

Married man's allowance	8540	Mortgage interest relief	2030
Single person's allowance	4640	Interest on national savings	
Wife's earned income relief	2390	certs	230
Age allowance	390	Exemption for charities	200
Relief for approved pension		Exemption of unemployment	
schemes	1000	benefit	460
Life assurance relief	530	Exemption of sickness	
Self employment retirement		benefit	200
annuities	310		

Source: estimates made available by Inland Revenue.

certainly possible to impose tax on contributions to pension funds and the income which they earn; but the problem of unfunded schemes seems intractable, and these would certainly become more common if funded schemes were taxed; while to the extent that the measure was effective it would simply be likely to lead to an increase in the contributions of both employer and employee, which is not very different in effect from a general increase in taxation.

The most serious possibilities for broadening the income tax base are (i) to modify the present favourable treatment of owner-occupied housing; (ii) to withdraw subsidies from life insurance policies; (iii) to tax capital gains as ordinary income. The first of these is certainly capable of producing substantial revenue; tax relief on mortgage repayments cost £2,030 m. in 1981–2 and to tax the 'imputed income' from owner-occupied property (see p. 57) could easily raise £3,000 m depending on the level at which the notional 'rents' for such property were set. But these figures should be viewed sceptically. We have suggested that, given the capitalization of these tax benefits, the case in equity for withdrawing them has little merit; that considerable hardship would be caused to many people; and that we should hesitate to make such changes except in the context of a general review of housing policy. And if the objective of change is to rearrange the tax burden in a way which is likely to provoke less public hostility, we need spend little time considering this particular alternative.

We can more readily envisage removing the present tax relief on life insurance premiums and taxing more effectively the funds of such companies (see p. 60). We can also tax capital gains more heavily, though this would require that the top rates of tax on investment income be reduced to realistic levels, while to admit a case for indexation of capital gains would turn these revenue gains into revenue losses. There is much to be said for changes in the way life insurance and capital gains are treated, but the likely revenue gains are not very large. A figure of £600 m. for life insurance and of £250 m. for capital gains would be optimistic estimates, and these would allow the basic rate of income tax to be reduced by only 1%.

If we turn to V.A.T., the two most important categories of exemption are housing and food. It would be possible to bring housing within the scope of V.A.T. by imposing it on rents and on new construction. But as we have seen, there is already a very heavy indirect tax on housing (rates), and our usual caveats about piecemeal changes in the housing market apply. There is a long tradition in Britain of slightly hysterical opposition to the taxation of food; the origins of these sentiments lie in controversies over the relative political roles of agriculture and commerce and the desirability and effects of Imperial Preference in tariff policy which have no contemporary relevance. It is now suggested that food is a necessity; but very little of the food which would not be eaten if it were 15% dearer is in the least necessary and other taxed goods such as clothing are 'necessary' in exactly the same (limited) sense. The substantive argument for exempting food is that such exemption is progressive in its distributional effects; the rich spend a smaller proportion of their incomes on food than the poor. (The main category for which this is not true—meals away from home—is subject to V.A.T.).

In Fig. 15.1 the circles and crosses show the cost to households at various income levels of paying standard rate V.A.T. on all currently exempt items (including fuel and light, children's clothing, travel, books and newspapers, but not housing). The two lines show the gains which would accrue to households if the income tax thresholds were raised by £259 for a single person and by £423 for a married couple, while the basic rate of tax was reduced by 0·78%. These changes in income tax have been chosen to provide the best offset to the distributional impact of abolishing zero rating, and as Fig. 15.1 shows they do approximate it very well indeed. This illustrates two points. First, as we noted in Chapter 14, the distributional flexibility of a linear tax schedule is considerable; simply by altering its two parameters we can reproduce the distributional effect of zero rating with some precision. Second, it shows the kind of tax change which would be possible if we aimed to

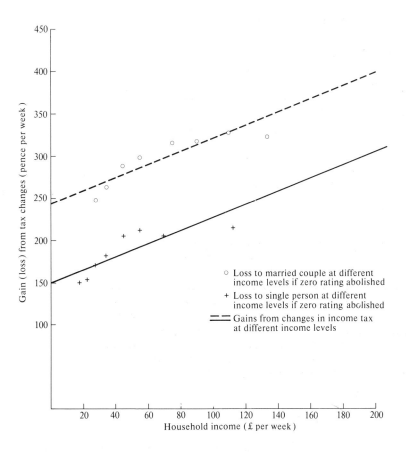

Fig. 15.1. The effects of abolishing zero rating for V.A.T.
  Notes: Based on estimated equation
  V.A.T. = 149·7 + 94·5D + 0·775Y
                    (8·1)   (0·087)
      V.A.T.. = weekly loss from abolition of zero rating by
        household (pence)
      D = ; 0 for one-person household, D = 1 for two-person
        household
      Y = weekly income (£).
Figures are at 1977 prices but based on 1979 V.A.T. rates.
Source: *Family Expenditure Survey* (1977).

reduce marginal rates of tax by broadening the tax base in this way, assuming we are not aiming to change the progressivity of the tax system; the reduction in marginal tax rate of under 1% which can be achieved is small.

The main feasible methods of broadening the tax base might allow the basic rate of income tax to be reduced by, say, 2%, if we taxed food and fuel, and taxed life insurance policies and capital gains more effectively. This reduction may be worth having but is not spectacular. We conclude that major improvements in the U.K. tax system must come from more fundamental structural reforms.

Conclusions

We have tried to ask of each part of the tax system 'What are the underlying principles here?' This may appear to conflict with the typical administrator's motto 'We start from where we are'. It is often believed that this 'practical' approach removes the need to give thought to where, in the long run, we are aiming to go. It is true that the practical man who knows where he is, and has not given any thought to where he is going, may appear more in command of his situation than the academic theorist who knows where he wants to go but is unsure of how to get there; but both of them end up comprehensively lost. It is in this way that we have finished up where we are.

The mess into which the present British tax system has drifted has been documented in earlier chapters. Anyone who came to it for the first time would regard the present system with some incredulity. There is a maze of taxes on different kinds of income, each tax with its own rules for determining taxable income and liability. The interaction between these taxes is difficult to comprehend, and, because of this, is rarely brought out into the open when tax changes are discussed. To take one obvious example of the general problem; in addition to income tax there are distinct and separately administered surcharges on each of employment incomes, investment incomes, and income from self-employment. The first of these is levied non-cumulatively on current earnings of less than a stated amount, the second cumulatively on current earnings of more than a stated amount, and the third cumulatively on preceding year earnings in excess of one amount and less than another amount. No one would design such a system on purpose and nobody did. Only a historical explanation of how it came about can be offered as a justification. That is not a justification, but a demonstration of how seemingly individually rational decisions can have absurd effects in aggregate.

There are more important examples than this one, but it illustrates how pragmatism which is not motivated by an over-all view of the principles and operation of the tax system as a whole is not a principle of good administration, but a recipe for unnecessary complexity and excessive administrative costs. We expect that some readers of this book will think that the objections to the existing British tax system we have made carry some weight, but might be more appropriately met by measures which stop short of any radical reappraisal of the principles of taxation. The idea of a lifetime expenditure tax may seem appealing but perhaps many of the benefits of such a reform might be obtained by some further concessions to savings within the context of the existing income tax. If they think this, they have completely misunderstood our whole argument. It is true that some of the deficiencies we have noted could be ameliorated by further *ad hoc* modifications of the shambles we have portrayed. It is certain, however, that these modifications would lead to still greater complexity in the tax system and to further abuses, anomalies, and loopholes, few of which will be anticipated.

The only prospect for an efficient tax system, whether efficiency refers to its economic effect or to the cost-effectiveness of its administration, is to adopt one which is based on a small set of clear principles, and which departs from them only in a number of limited and clearly recognized ways. The alternative to this course is to devise particular rules for each situation as and when it arises, and since we cannot define or anticipate all possible situations or even fully appreciate the consequences of our last decision, these rules are bound to proliferate indefinitely.

'Income Tax', ruled Lord Macnaghten, 'is a tax on income', and this has been the principle, if one may call it that, underlying direct taxation in the U.K. since the days of Pitt. But, as we saw in Chapter 5, it is not a very useful principle for practical purposes, because income is not an easy concept to define precisely nor to measure objectively. The fact is that in many circumstances there is only a tenuous relationship between monetary transactions and whatever it is that one means by income, and any attempt to pretend otherwise leads either to the kinds of difficulties we have described in earlier chapters, or to the forced adoption of cash flows as the measure of taxable income.

The case against the existing structure of the U.K. tax system and for the kind of reforms we have proposed rest on an accumulation of arguments rather than on a single decisive argument, and we are reluctant to summarize the main points of our thesis. Nevertheless, there are three points to which we would give special emphasis.

First, there has been enormous misdirection of the redistributive elements of the tax system. These have rested mainly on high tax rates on individuals with large incomes from employment. But high earnings are not an important source of wealth inequality in the U.K., so that these taxes fall heavily on those engaged in productive sectors of the economy without achieving much in the way of redistribution. The tax system has been—rightly—criticized on both counts; the conflict between equity and efficiency in tax policy has appeared very acute. Although this trade-off is a real one, preoccupation with rates of tax and with the appearance of the tax system rather than the reality have led to excessive emphasis on it; and to a futile process in which political parties have sought to compensate for deficiencies in the structure of taxation by changes in the rates. The expenditure tax proposal is capable of achieving both greater equity and greater efficiency by imposing lower rates on a tax base which is more closely related to taxable capacity.

The second argument for an expenditure tax rests on the deficiencies of the present methods of taxing savings and investment income. They are not simple, they are not fair, they are not effective, and they have been characterized by rates of tax which are tolerable only because they are not intended seriously. It is difficult to believe that at least some objectives could not be achieved better in other ways. The logic of the income-based approach suggests that a comprehensive income tax, which would remove existing savings concessions and integrate the tax treatment of income and capital gains, is the way forward. We analysed this proposal in Chapter 5, and found it unattractive. It is not an accident that we have the income tax we do, and not a comprehensive income tax; and it is only to a limited extent true that this result is attributable to the frailties of politicians in the face of pressure from particular interest groups. Most of the changes which are required to transform the existing income tax into a comprehensive one either involve acute administrative difficulty (such as the taxation of life insurance and pension fund income) or require the introduction of charges which would be widely perceived as unfair—and not just by those involved in paying them (such as the taxation of imputed income from durable ownership and the consequences of the treatment of investment income is the expenditure tax proposal. Not only does this not suffer from these difficulties but it is probably closer to the reality of what we in fact do.

The third argument for an expenditure tax is administrative. It is only gradually being realized how many of the avoidance opportunities intrinsic in the income tax, and how much of the complexity of income tax codes, is the result of the difficulty of applying an income concept in a modern economy with a sophisticated financial system. Hicks wrote that income and capital 'are bad tools, which break in our hands', and they have broken. It is a common thread of the proposals we have made for reform that they abandon the use of an income concept and adopt a tax base which is closely related to identifiable and measurable flows of cash.

Is it possible that our proposals are in fact more radical than necessary, and that a shift of emphasis towards existing—indirect—taxes on expenditure would achieve the same results as a shift towards a direct expenditure tax more simply and less controversially? We might examine this suggestion in the light of the three principal arguments we have set out above. We suggested that an expenditure tax could achieve desired redistribution with less damage to incentives. Because this argument requires that the *progressive* elements of the tax system should be expenditure based, it is only a direct expenditure tax which can achieve it, and a switch to existing indirect taxes is of no assistance. Our second argument concerned the tax treatment of savings and investment. A broadly based expenditure tax such as V.A.T. does avoid the distortions and anomalies which income tax introduces. But to eliminate these distortions it would be necessary to eliminate income tax, and to reduce them substantially it would be necessary to reduce income tax substantially. Neither of these can be achieved with the existing limited V.A.T. base, although marginal gains are possible.

Our third argument concerned administration. It is only possible to get rid of the administrative costs and complexity of income tax by getting rid of income tax. It is true that some gains can be achieved by reductions in the rates; there are some avoidance schemes which are not worth undertaking when tax rates are lower and some inequities or problems which are more readily tolerable. There are some minor benefits from a shift from the basic rate of income tax to the standard rate of V.A.T., and more substantial benefits from reductions in the top rates of income tax. On balance, there are small advantages to be derived from a shift from income tax to indirect taxes, and we do, in the absence of substantial reform, favour some such shift. The main benefit is some easing of the pressure of capital market distortions. But the central problem remains. Income tax is a deplorable tax, whether one examines its administration or its economic effects. It is highly desirable to be rid of it. Of course, this is not possible next year, or even in five years time. But the long-term transformation of the existing income tax into a direct expenditure tax is the only serious scheme for abolishing income tax which has been proposed.

Our long-run objective is, therefore, a lifetime expenditure tax. To achieve this objective a number of steps ought to be taken now. The first is the abolition of cumulative P.A.Y.E. and a move towards a non-cumulative system with annual returns from all taxpayers. This would enable us to begin the process of rationalizing the tax and social security systems and to sort out the present unsystematic reliefs to savings, and to envisage the wider changes of abolishing capital gains tax and extending the range of registered assets described in Chapter 6. Such a reform would also allow serious consideration to be given to local taxation and the financing of devolution. The second immediate change would be the transformation of the existing corporation tax into a cash flow tax on the lines set out in Chapter 12. This would involve transitional problems, but these would be no more acute than those experienced in the many previous changes of corporation tax.

We should end with a plea for realism in expectations of what can be achieved by tax reform. The changes we have advocated can only be implemented over a long period of time. They will not transform the British tax system into an instrument of economic progress or social change; though we believe that they will make it simpler, fairer, and more efficient, and reduce the number and extent of its unintended ramifications. They will not satisfy those who are looking for measures which can be adopted in the next budget which will revive small business, restore incentives, effect irreversible change in the distribution of wealth and power, or achieve whatever else was featured on last week's 'Money Programme'. The ill-considered expedients which are constructed to meet the demands of those with large ambitions and little time will leave their objectives as far from realization as ever and the tax system a little more complicated than it was before. We see the British tax system as a chronically diseased patient; but one who, obsessed by the last symptom he happened to observe, disregards considered medical advice and insists on being completely cured by next week. There is never any shortage of quacks willing to minister to his needs; and he never gets even slightly better.

FURTHER READING

WE have not given references for the information on tax rates and benefits which we have used frequently in the text. Tax rates can be found in the Reports of the Commissioners of Inland Revenue and Customs and Excise; but these are necessarily somewhat out of date. The most convenient up-to-date source (for direct taxes) is probably the annual *Hambro Tax Guide*, which provides a non-technical survey of the principal features of tax legislation. The Department of Health and Social Security publishes a *Supplementary Benefits Handbook* which gives the rates of and rules for supplementary benefits. A valuable compendium of social security benefits is now provided by Matthewson and Lambert (1982).

Chapter 1

The theoretical issues underlying our analysis of the British tax system are not dealt with in a wholly satisfactory manner by any of the current textbooks on public finance. Much of the material is contained in journal articles and the level of discussion makes them inaccessible to many students and the general reader. A good introduction to the subject will be found in the volume of essays published by the Brookings Institution (1974). The classic textbooks on public finance remain those by Musgrave (1959) and Shoup (1969). A modern, but advanced, textbook on public finance is Atkinson and Stiglitz (1980). A more recent book by Musgrave and Musgrave (1976) is very good although its institutional material is aimed at American students. For a British account see Prest (1975).

Chapter 2

Statistics about the tax system are contained in a volume published annually called *Inland Revenue Statistics* and in the Annual Reports of H.M. Commissioners of the Inland Revenue. There are several commercial guides to the income tax system and each year *Money Which* provides useful advice on how to fill in your tax return. Sabine (1966) is a history of income tax in the U.K., while Johnston (1965) describes the operations of Inland Revenue.

A review of some aspects of U.K. tax administration and proposals for its reform are contained in Barr, James, and Prest (1977). A somewhat complacent appraisal of suggestions for possible changes is in

Inland Revenue (1979). A survey of studies of the black economy is
Tanzi (1982).

Chapter 3

On the incentive effects of taxation there is a helpful introduction
by Break in the Brookings Institution volume (1974). More technical
surveys of the disincentive effect of income tax on work decisions have
been written by Stern (1976) and Godfrey (1975). For a detailed
analysis of the American evidence, including an account of the results
of the New Jersey negative income tax experiment, see the volumes by
Cain and Watts (1973) and Pechman and Timpane (1975). Some econometric results for Britain based on a research project at Stirling University are discussed in Brown, Levin, and Ulph (1976). The redistributive
role of taxation and the determinants of the distributions of income
and wealth are analysed in Atkinson (1975).

Chapter 4

It is difficult to find in one volume a coherent account of the theory
and practice of the taxation of investment incomes and savings. Titmuss
(1962) discusses some of the main issues but this study is now
obviously rather out of date. A formal analysis of the effects of the
British tax system on incentives to save and invest is contained in
Chapter 4 of the Meade Report.

Chapter 5

The best-known and most detailed proposals for a comprehensive
income tax are those put forward in Canada by the Carter Commission
(1966). The concept of income is discussed by Hicks (1939) and
Simons (1938), but the best survey is that by Kaldor (1955, Appendix).
A collection of some of the more important contributions on the
subject has been edited by Parker and Harcourt (1969).

Chapter 6

The two most cogent cases for an expenditure tax are the classic
exposition of Kaldor (1955), arguing from the theoretical viewpoint,
and the case put by Andrews (1974) on practical grounds. Official
reports explaining how an expenditure tax would work have been
produced abroad, in the U.S.A. (U.S. Treasury, 1977) in Sweden
(Lodin, 1978), and in Ireland (Irish Tax Commission, 1982). A recent
survey of the issues is Pechman (1980).

Chapter 7

An excellent introduction to the social security system in Britain
and possible directions for reform is Atkinson (1969). Although it is

somewhat outdated it repays reading. An outline of the system of means-tested benefits is given in National Consumer Council (1977), and statistical information is provided in *Social Security Statistics* and Reports of the *Family Expenditure Survey* (both annual). The most recent study of the causes and characteristics of poverty is that by Beckerman and Clark (1982), and a good general discussion of the problem may be found in Atkinson (1975). On schemes of funda-mental reform (social dividend/tax credits/negative income tax) see Meade (1972) and the Report of the Select Committee on Tax Credit (1973).

Chapter 8

Statistics on the collection of indirect taxes are contained in Customs and Excise Reports. The distinction between direct and in-direct taxes is at best an arbitrary one, and for further reading on the theoretical issues contained in this chapter the reader is referred to the notes on Chapters 3 and 14. An introduction to the theory of optimal indirect taxation is Sandmo (1976).

Chapter 9

The broad issues of the relationship between central and local taxa-tion are discussed in the paper by Netzer in Brookings Institution (1974). In the U.K. context the most helpful sources are the Layfield Committee Report (H.M.S.O., 1976), the 1981 Green Paper, and Travers (1982).

Chapter 10

The best information on the distribution of wealth in Britain is to be found in Atkinson and Harrison (1978); see also the various Reports of the Royal Commission on the Distribution of Income and Wealth. The principles of taxing capital are discussed in Sandford (1971). For the theoretical and practical arguments for and against a wealth tax, see the *Report of the Select Committee of the House of Commons on Wealth Tax* (H.M.S.O., 1975), Flemming and Little (1974), and Sandford, Willis, and Ironside (1975).

Chapters 11 and 12

A detailed analysis of corporate tax systems and their effects on firms' financing and investment decisions may be found in King (1977). The Green Paper on Corporation Tax provides a good survey of the issues involved in reform of the U.K. system.

Chapter 13

An excellent discussion of the impact of inflation in the tax system is contained in Chapter 6 of the Meade Report; a wider discussion is in Liesner and King (1975). A survey of progress towards indexation in other countries is Q.E.C.D. (1976). The issues raised by inflation accounting are discussed by Whittington (1982); one of the few discussions of the general issues raised by indexation is Mukherjee and Orlans (1975).

Chapter 14

Each year *Economic Trends* contains an article examining the impact of the tax system on the distribution of income. The methodology behind these studies is assessed in contributions contained in Atkinson (1976). The theoretical literature on the distribution of the tax burden is extremely technical. The pioneering contribution was that by Mirrlees (1971). A less technical but still demanding paper is Atkinson (1973b); for the theory of the measurement of inequality see Atkinson (1973a) which contains a very useful non-mathematical discussion of the main concepts.

Chapter 15

Discussions of how the tax systems should be changed are not difficult to find. The most comprehensive survey of the British tax system and possibilities for reform is the Meade Report. A rather different view of reform is Field, Meacher, and Pond (1977) which concentrates on the tax system and poverty. A recent report on reforming the U.S. tax system is U.S. Treasury (1977), and another interesting American study is that by Break and Pechman (1975).

REFERENCES

ALLEN REPORT (1965). Committee of Inquiry into the Impact of Rates on Households, Cmnd. 2582, H.M.S.O., London.

ANDREWS, W. D. (1974), 'A Consumption-Type or Cash Flow Personal Income Tax, *Harvard Law Review, 87.*

ATKINSON, A. B. (1969). *Poverty in Britain and the Reform of Social Security*, Cambridge Univ. Press, London.

—— (1972). *Unequal Shares*, Allen Lane, London.

—— (1973a). 'On the Measurement of Inequality', reprinted with non-mathematical summary in A. B. Atkinson (ed.), *Wealth, Income and Inequality*, Penguin, London. (Originally published in *Journal of Economic Theory*, 2, 1970.)

—— (1973b). 'How Progressive Should Income Tax Be?', in M. Parkin (ed.), *Essays on Modern Economics*, Longman, London.

—— (1975). *The Economics of Inequality*, Oxford Univ. Press, London.

—— (ed.) (1976). *The Personal Distribution of Incomes*, Allen & Unwin, London.

—— and HARRISON, A. J. (1978). *The Distribution of Personal Wealth in Britain*, Cambridge Univ. Press, London.

—— and MEADE, T. W. (1974). 'Methods and preliminary findings in assessing the economic and Health Services consequences of smoking, with particular reference to lung cancer', *Journal of the Royal Statistical Society*, Ser. A, 137.

—— and TOWNSEND, J. L. (1977). 'Economic Aspects of Reduced Smoking', *Lancet* 3 Sept. 1977, No. 8036, vol. 2 for 1977.

B.I.M. (1974). British Institute of Management, M.S. Report 18, *Business Cars in the UK*, London.

BARR, N. A., JAMES, S. R., and PREST, A. R. (1977). *Self Assessment for Income Tax*, Heinemann, London.

BAUMOL, W. J. and BRADFORD, D. F. (1970). 'Optimal Departures from Marginal Cost Pricing', *American Economic Review*, 60.

BECKERMAN, W. and CLARK, S. (1982). *Poverty and Social Security in Britain since 1961*, Oxford Univ. Press.

BEVERIDGE, W. (1942). *Social Insurance and Allied Services*, Cmnd. 6404, H.M.S.O., London.

BOLTON COMMITTEE (1971). *Small Firms: Report of the Committee of Inquiry on Small Firms*, Cmnd. 4811, H.M.S.O., London.

BOSKIN, M. J. (1977). 'Taxation, Saving and the Rate of Interest', *Journal of Political Economy*, **86**, No. 2, S3–S28.

BOSWELL, J. (1973). *The Rise and Decline of Small Firms*, Allen & Unwin, London.

BRACEWELL-MILNES, B. (1976). *The Camel's Back*, Centre for Policy Studies, London.

BREAK, G. F. (1957). 'Income Taxes and Incentives to Work: An Empirical Study', *American Economic Review*, **47**.

—— and PECHMAN, J. A. (1975). *Federal Tax Reform: The Impossible Dream?*, Brookings Institution, Washington, D.C.

BROOKINGS INSTITUTION (1974). *The Economics of Public Finance*, Brookings Institution, Washington, D.C.

BROWN, C. V. (1968). 'Misconceptions about Income Tax and Incentives', *Scottish Journal of Political Economy*, **15**.

——, LEVIN, E., and ULPH, D. T. (1976). 'Estimates of Labour Hours Supplied by Married Male Workers in Great Britain', *Scottish Journal of Political Economy*, **23**.

BUREAU OF THE CENSUS (1976). *Historical Statistics of the U.S.*, U.S. Department of Commerce, Washington D.C.

BUSINESS MONITOR M3 (1977). *Company Finance*, Department of Industry, Business Statistics Office, H.M.S.O., London.

CAIN, C. and WATTS, H. (1973). *Income Maintenance and Labour Supply*, Markham, New York.

CARTER COMMISSION (1966). *Report of the Royal Commission on Taxation*, Ottawa.

CHAWLA, O. P. (1972). *Personal Taxation in India*, Somaiya Publications, Bombay.

C.I.P.F.A. (Annual). *Return of Rates*, Chartered Institute of Public Finance and Accountancy, London.

C.I.R. (1979). '121st Report of the Commissioners of Inland Revenue', Cmnd. 7473, H.M.S.O., London.

CRIPPS, T. F. and GODLEY, W. (1976). *Local Government Finance and its Reform*, Department of Applied Economics, Cambridge.

CUSTOMS AND EXCISE (1976). *Report of the Commissioners*, H.M.S.O., London.

DEATON, A. S. (1975). *Models and Projections of Demand in Post-war Britain*, Chapman & Hall, London.

DIAMOND, P. A. and MIRRLEES, J. A. (1971). 'Optimal Taxation and Public Production', *American Economic Review*, **41**.

DIAMOND COMMISSION (1976). Royal Commission on the Distribution of Income and Wealth, Report No. 3, Cmnd. 6383, H.M.S.O., London.

—— (1977). Royal Commission on the Distribution of Income and Wealth, Report No. 4, Cmnd. 6626, H.M.S.O., London.

—— (1979). Royal Commission on the Distribution of Income and Wealth, Report No. 7, Cmnd. 7595, H.M.S.O., London.

DILNOT, A. W. and MORRIS, C. N. (1981). What do we know about the black economy? *Fiscal Studies* Vol. 2, No. 1.

—— and —— (1982). 'The tax system and distribution, 1979–82' in KAY, J. A. (ed.), *The 1982 Budget*, Blackwell, Oxford.

EDGEWORTH, F. Y. (1897). 'The Pure Theory of Taxation (III)', *Economic Journal*, 3.

ERRITT, M. J. and ALEXANDER, J. C. D. (1977). 'Ownership of Company Shares: A New Survey', *Economic Trends*.

F.E.S. REPORT (1975). *Report on the Family Expenditure Survey*, H.M.S.O., London.

FEIGE, E. (1979). How big is the irregular economy? *Challenge* 22.

FIEGEHEN, G. C. and REDDAWAY, W. B. (1981). *Companies, Incentives and Senior Managers*, Oxford Univ. Press.

—— LANSLEY, P. S., and SMITH, A. D. (1977). *Poverty and Progress in Britain 1953–73*, National Institute of Economic and Social Research Occasional Paper xxix, Cambridge Univ. Press, London.

FIELD, F., MEACHER, M., and POND, C. (1977). *To Him Who Hath: A Study of Poverty and Taxation*, Penguin, London.

FIELDS, D. B. and STANBURY, W. T. (1971). 'Income Taxes and Incentives to Work: Some Additional Empirical Evidence', *American Economic Review*, 41.

FLEMMING, J. S. and LITTLE, I. M. D. (1974). *Why We Need a Wealth Tax*, Methuen, London.

GODFREY, L. (1975). *Theoretical and Empirical Aspects of the Effects of Taxation on the Supply of Labour*, O.E.C.D., Paris.

GOLDTHORPE, J., LOCKWOOD, D., BECKHOFER, F., and PLATT, J. (1970). *The Affluent Worker. Industrial Attitudes and Behaviour*, Cambridge Univ. Press, London.

GOODE, R. (1976). *The Individual Income Tax*, Brookings Institution, Washington, D.C.

HANNAH, L. and KAY, J. A. (1977). *Concentration in Modern Industry*, Macmillan, London.

HARBURY, C. D. and HITCHENS, D. M. (1976). 'The Inheritances of Top Wealth Leavers', *Economic Journal*, 86.

—— (1979). *Inheritance and Wealth Inequality in Britain*, Allen & Unwin, London.

HAY-M.S.L. LTD. (1976). 'An Analysis of Managerial Remuneration in the U.K. and Overseas, a Report' (background paper for the Diamond Commission), H.M.S.O., London.

HEMMING, R. and KAY, J. A. (1982). 'The Costs of the State Earnings Related Pension Scheme', *Economics Journal*, **92**.

HICKS, J. R. (1939). *Value and Capital. An Inquiry into some Fundamental Principles of Economic Theory*, Clarendon Press, Oxford.

H.M.S.O. (1942). *The Taxation of Weekly Wage Earners*, Cmnd. 6348, London.

—— (1972). *Taxation of Capital on Death* (Green Paper), Cmnd. 4930, London.

—— (1974). *Wealth Tax* (Green Paper), Cmnd. 5704, London.

—— (1975). *Report of the Select Committee of the House of Commons on Wealth Tax*, H.C. 696-I, London.

—— (1976). *Local Government Finance*, Report of the Committee of Inquiry (Chairman F. Layfield), Cmnd. 6453, London.

—— (1977). *Local Government Finance*, presented to Parliament by the Secretary of State for the Environment and the Secretary of State for Wales, Cmnd. 6813, London.

—— (1980). *The Taxation of Husband and Wife*, Cmnd 8093, London.

—— (1982). *Alternatives to Domestic Rates*, Cmnd 8449, London.

HOBBES, T. (1651). *Leviathan or, the Matter, Forme and Power of A Commonwealth Ecclesiasticall and Civil*, Andrew Crooke, London.

HORSMAN, E. G. (1975). 'The Avoidance of Estate Duty by Gifts *Inter Vivos*', *Economic Journal*, **85**.

HOWREY, E. P. and HYMANS, S. (1978). 'The Measurement and Determination of Loanable Funds Saving', *Brookings Papers on Economic Activity*, No. 3, 655–85.

ILERSIC, A. (1973). 'Grant Determination and Its Distribution' in Institute for Fiscal Studies, *Proceedings of a Conference on Local Government Finance*, I.F.S., London.

INLAND REVENUE (1979). 'P.A.Y.E.–Possible Future Developments', Inland Revenue discussion document, London.

INSTITUTE FOR FISCAL STUDIES (1973). *Proceedings of a Conference on Local Government Finance*, I.F.S., London.

IRS (1979). *Estimates of Income Unreported on Individual Income Tax Returns*, U.S. Internal Revenue Service, Washington.

IRISH COMMISSION ON TAXATION (1982). First Report, *Direct Taxation*, The Stationery Office, Dublin.

JOHNSTON, A. (1965). *The Inland Revenue*, Allen & Unwin, London.

KALDOR, N. (1955). *An Expenditure Tax*, Allen & Unwin, London.

—— (1956). *Indian Tax Reform*, Ministry of Finance, India.

—— (1980). *Reports on Taxation, I*, Duckworth, London.

KAY, J. A. (1977). 'Inflation Accounting—A Review Article', *Economic Journal*, 87, 300–11.

—— (1982). 'The Taxation of Life Insurance in the U.K.', I.F.S. working paper.

KAY, J. A. and KEEN, M. J. (1982). *The Structure of Tobacco Taxes in the European Community*, IFS Report Series No. 1, London.

KAY, J. A. and MORRIS, C. N. (1979). Direct and Indirect Taxes. Fiscal Studies Vol. 1, No. 1.

KAY, J. A. and SANDLER, C. J. (1982). 'The taxation of husband and wife', *Fiscal Studies*, Vol. 3, No. 3.

KING, M. A. (1977). *Public Policy and the Corporation*, Chapman & Hall, London.

KING, M. A. and FULLERTON, D. (eds.), forthcoming, *The Taxation of Income from Capital*, Chicago Univ. Press.

LAYFIELD REPORT, *see* H.M.S.O. (1976).

LEWIS, A. (1978). 'Perceptions of Tax Rates', *British Tax Review*, no. 6.

LIESNER, T. and KING, M. A. (1975). *Indexing for Inflation*, Heinemann Educational Books, London.

LIFE OFFICES ASSOCIATION (1982). *Life Assurance in the United Kingdom*, London.

LODIN, S. O. (1978). *Progressive Expenditure Tax—an Alternative*, Liber Forlag, Stockholm.

MACAFFEE, K. (1980). 'A glimpse of the hidden economy in the national accounts', *Economic Trends*, No. 316.

MATTHEWMAN, J. and LAMBERT, N. (1982). *Social Security and State Benefits*, Tolley's, Croydon.

MEADE, J. E. (1972). 'Poverty in the Welfare State', *Oxford Economic Papers*, 24.

MEADE COMMITTEE (1978). *The Structure and Reform of Direct Taxation*, Allen & Unwin, London.

MERRETT-CYRIAX ASSOCIATES (1971). *Dynamics of Small Firms*, Research Report for the Bolton Committee, H.M.S.O., London.

MILL, J. S. (1865). *Principles of Political Economy* (6th edn.), Longman, London.

MINFORD, A. P. (1982). 'The development of monetary strategy', in KAY (ed.) (1982), *The 1982 Budget*. Blackwell, Oxford.

MIRRLEES, J. A. (1971). 'An Exploration in the Theory of Optimum Income Taxation', *Review of Economic Studies*, 38.

MONOPOLIES COMMISSION (1975). *Contraceptive Sheaths*, H.C. 135, H.M.S.O., London.

MORRIS, C. N. (1982). 'The Structure of Personal Income Taxation and income Support', *Fiscal Studies*, Vol. 3, No. 3.

MORRIS, C. N. and WARREN, N. A. (1982). 'Taxation of the Family', *Fiscal Studies*, Vol. 2, No. 1.

MUKHERJEE, S. and ORLANDS, C. (1975). *Indexation in an inflationary economy*, PEP, London.

MUSGRAVE, R. A. (1959). *The Theory of Public Finance*, McGraw-Hill, New York.

—— and MUSGRAVE, P. B. (1976). *Public Finance in Theory and Practice* (2nd edn.), McGraw-Hill, New York.

NATIONAL CONSUMER COUNCIL (1977). *Means-Tested Benefits: A Discussion Paper*, National Consumer Council Report, London.

NEWBERY, D. (1970). 'A Theorem on the Measurement of Inequality', *Journal of Economic Theory*, 2.

NICHOLSON, J. L. (1974). *The Distribution and Redistribution of Income in the U.K.*, in D. Wedderburn (ed.), *Poverty, Inequality and Class Structure*, Cambridge Univ. Press, London.

NORDHAUS, W. D. (1975). 'The Political Business Cycle', *Review of Economic Studies*, 42.

O.E.C.D. (1976). *The Adjustment of Personal Income Tax Systems for Inflation*, Paris.

OKNER, B. A. and PECHMAN, J. A. (1974). *Who Bears the Tax Burden?*, Brookings Institution, Washington, D.C.

OPINION RESEARCH CENTRE (1977). 'A Survey of the Motivation of British Management', London.

PARKER, R. H. and HARCOURT, G. C. (eds.) (1969). *Readings in the Concept and Measurement of Income*, Cambridge Univ. Press, London.

PARR, M. and DAY, J. (1977). 'Value Added Tax in the United Kingdom', *National Westminster Bank Review*.

PART, A. (1982). *The Taxation of North Sea Oil Report of a Committee*, Institute for Fiscal Studies, London.

PECHMAN, J. A. and TIMPANE, P. M. (eds.) (1975). *Work Incentives and Income Guarantees: The New Jersey Negative Income Tax Experiment*, Brookings Institution, Washington, D.C.

PECHMAN, J. A. (ed.) (1980). *What Should be Taxed: Income or Expenditure?* Brookings Institution, Washington D.C.

PRAIS, S. J. (1976). *The Evolution of Giant Firms in Britain*, Cambridge Univ. Press, London.

PREST, A. R. (1975). *Public Finance in Theory and Practice* (5th edn.), Weidenfeld & Nicholson, London.

PSACHAROPOULOS, G. (1976). 'Estimating some Key Parameters in the Brain Drain Taxation Model', in J. N. Bhagwati (ed.), *The Brain Drain and Taxation*, North Holland, Amsterdam.

PUBLIC ACCOUNTS COMMITTEE (1977–8). Sixth Report of the Public Accounts Committee, H.C. 574, H.M.S.O., London.

RADCLIFFE REPORT (1954). *Report of the Royal Commission on Taxation of Profits and Income*, No. 2, Cmnd. 9105, H.M.S.O., London.

RAMSEY, F. A. (1928). 'A Mathematical Theory of Savings', *Economic Journal, 38*.

RAWLS, J. (1971). *A Theory of Justice*, Clarendon Press, Oxford.

REVELL, J. (1965). 'Changes in the Social Distribution of Property in Britain during the Twentieth Century', paper given to Third International Conference of Economic History, Munich, 1965.

—— (1967). *The Wealth of the Nation; the National Balance Sheet of the United Kingdom, 1957–1961*, Cambridge Univ. Press, London.

RICHARDSON REPORT (1964). *Report of the Committee on Turnover Taxation*, Cmnd. 2300, H.M.S.O., London.

RUBENSTEIN, W. D. (1974). 'Men of Property: Some Aspects of Occupation, Inheritance and Power among Top British Wealth-holders', in P. Stanworth and A. Giddens (eds.), *Elites and Power in British Society*, Cambridge Univ. Press, London.

SABINE, B. E. V. (1966). *A History of Income Tax*, Allen & Unwin, London.

SANDFORD, C. T. (1971). *Taxing Personal Wealth*, Allen & Unwin, London.

—— (1973). *Hidden Costs of Taxation*, I.F.S., London.

——, WILLIS, J. R., and IRONSIDE, D. J. (1975). *An Annual Wealth Tax*, Heinemann Educational Books, London.

SANDFORD, C. T. *et al* (1982). *Costs and Benefits of Vat*, Heinemann, London.

SANDILANDS (1975). *Report of the Inflation Accounting Committee*, Cmnd. 6225, H.M.S.O., London.

SANDMO, A. (1976). 'Optimal Taxation—An Introduction to the Literature', *Journal of Public Economics, 6*.

SELECT COMMITTEE ON TAX CREDIT (1973). *Report and Proceedings of the Committee*, H.M.S.O., London.

SEN, A. K. (1974). 'Informational Bases of Alternative Welfare Approaches; Aggregation and Income Distribution', *Journal of Public Economics, 3*.

SHOUP, C. S. (1969). *Public Finance*, Weidenfeld & Nicolson, London.

SIMONS, H. C. (1938). *Personal Income Taxation*, Univ. of Chicago Press, Chicago.

SSAC (1982). First report of the Social Security Advisory Committee.

STANWORTH, P. and GIDDENS, A. (eds.) (1974). *Elites and Power in British Society*, Cambridge Univ. Press, London.

Statistical Abstract of U.S. (Annual). U.S. Department of Commerce, Washington, D.C.

STERN, N. H. (1976). 'Taxation and Labour Supply—A Partial Survey', in *Proceedings of a Conference on Taxation and Incentives*, I.F.S., London.

—— (1977). 'The Marginal Valuation of Income', in *The Proceedings of the Association of University Teachers of Economics*, Edinburgh, 1976, ed. M. J. Artis and A. R. Nobay, Basil Blackwell, Oxford.

STONEFROST, M. (1982). The GLC reports to its shareholders, *Fiscal Studies*, Vol. 3, No. 1.

TANZI, V. (1982). *The Underground Economy in the United States and Abroad*, D. C. Heath, Lexington, Mass.

TITMUSS, R. M. (1962). *Income Distribution and Social Change*. Allen & Unwin, London.

TOWNSEND, P. (1979). *Poverty in the United Kingdom*, Penguin, London.

TRAVERS, A. (1982). Block grant: origins objects and use, *Fiscal Studies*, Vol. 3, No. 1.

U.S. TREASURY (1977). *Blueprints for Basic Tax Reform*, U.S. Govt. Printing Office, Washington.

Vision (1977), No. 75, Feb.

WHALLEY, J. and PIGGOTT, J. R. (1977). 'General Equilibrium Investigations of U.K. tax subsidy policy', in *The Proceedings of the Association of University Teachers of Economics*, Edinburgh, 1976, ed. M. J. Artis and A. R. Nobay, Basil Blackwell, Oxford.

WHEATCROFT, G. S. A. (1965). 'Proposals for a System of Estate and Gift Taxation', in G. S. A. Wheatcroft (ed.), *Estate and Gift Taxation: A Comparative Study*, Sweet & Maxwell, London.

WHITTINGTON, G. (1983). *The Theory of Inflation Accounting*, Cambridge University Press.

WILSON, P. (1982). *Free School Meals*, OPCS, Occasional Paper 23.

WORSWICK, G. N. D. (1971). 'Fiscal Policy and Stabilization in Britain', in A. Cairncross (ed.), *Britain's Economic Prospects Reconsidered*, Allen & Unwin, London.

ZABALZA, A., PISSARIDES, C., PIACHAUD, D., and BARTON, M. (1979). 'Social Security and the Choice between Full-Time Work, Part-Time Work and Retirement', paper presented to N.B.E.R./ S.S.R.C. Conference on Econometric Studies in Public Finance, Cambridge, mimeo.

INDEX